GLOBALIZATION, SOVEREIGNTY AND CITIZENSHIP IN THE CARIBBEAN

GLOBALIZATION, SOVEREIGNTY AND CITIZENSHIP IN THE CARIBBEAN

Edited by

HILBOURNE A. WATSON

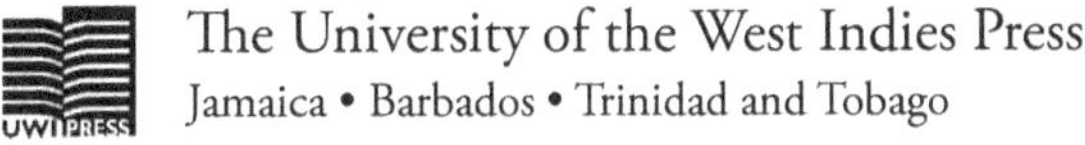
The University of the West Indies Press
Jamaica • Barbados • Trinidad and Tobago

The University of the West Indies Press
7A Gibraltar Hall Road, Mona
Kingston 7, Jamaica
www.uwipress.com

A catalogue record of this book is available from the National Library of Jamaica.

ISBN: 978-976-640-550-2 (print)
978-976-640-559-5 (Kindle)
978-976-640-568-7 (ePub)

Cover design by Robert Harris
Typesetting by The Beget, India
Printed in the United States of America

Contents

Preface

Crisis, which inheres in all spheres of capitalist social relations, is reflected existentially in subtle ways in the organization and cultural expression of everyday life, until devastating eruptions, such as the Great Depression of the 1930s or the most recent economic and financial crisis of 2008, occur. Therefore, when we study the contradictory process of capitalist globalization, with attention to how it conditions and is conditioned by the exercise of state sovereignty and how citizens experience citizenship and national belonging, mediated by gender, ethnicity and other "identities" within the broader dimensions of class relations, it is necessary to consider the role of crises and market anarchy.

In *Seventeen Contradictions and the End of Capitalism* (New York: Oxford University Press, 2014), David Harvey argues that it "is in the course of crises that the instabilities of capitalism are confronted, reshaped and re-engineered to create a new version of what capitalism is about" (ix). He points out that "what is so striking about crises is not so much the wholesale reconfiguration of physical landscapes, but dramatic changes in ways of thought and understanding, of institutions and dominant ideologies, of political allegiances and processes, of political subjectivities, of technologies and organizational forms, of social relations, of the mental conceptions of the world and of our place in it to the very core" (ix). Harvey also emphasizes that "we, as restless participants and inhabitants of this new emerging world, have to adapt, through coercion and consent, to the new state of things . . . by virtue of what we do and how we think and behave, [we] add our two cents' worth to the messy qualities of this world" (x).

The issues raised in the chapters that comprise this volume bear the imprint of crises. All societies are organized around the tools they create to achieve the ends of their social reproduction, which makes culture the medium through which we work to free ourselves from the constraints our biological species-being imposes on us. Our historically determined, open-ended social existence reminds us that globalization, sovereignty, citizenship, belonging, democracy, freedom and justice are not finished projects. They are integral and contradictory expressions of continuous plebiscites – means to higher ends under historical capitalism.

Acting without any deliberate plan or strategy and reflecting the anarchy that anchors social life under capitalism (of which the production of intellectual culture is a part), a number of Caribbean Studies Association (CSA) members began, in 2000, to work on collections based on papers presented at special CSA panels. The first was *Caribbean Charisma: Reflections on Leadership, Legitimacy and Populist Politics*, edited by Anton L. Allahar and published in 2001. The most recent is *Caribbean Sovereignty, Development and Democracy in an Age of Globalization*, edited by Linden Lewis and published in 2013. Dave Ramsaran is editing a volume, "Contradictory Existence: Neoliberalism and Democracy in the Caribbean", and a publication on the sociology of Oliver Cromwell Cox was published in the *Canadian Journal of Latin American and Caribbean Studies* 39, no. 3 (April 2015) from papers presented at the CSA 2014 conference in Merida, Mexico. This volume – *Globalization, Sovereignty and Citizenship in the Caribbean* – joins in similar labour, having resulted from papers that were presented at the CSA's Thirty-Seventh Annual Conference on Unpacking Caribbean Citizenship(s): Rights, Participation and Belonging, held in Pointe-à-Pitre, Guadeloupe, 28 May–1 June 2012.

When the panel and paper proposals were being organized with an edited volume in mind, sincere efforts were made to achieve the broadest representation and coverage of the Caribbean region. Unfortunately, this was not possible but the book reflects a reasonably broad representation of the independent countries and the non-independent territories of the Caribbean. This volume stands out for the range and scope of its emphasis on philosophical, theoretical and empirical issues and problems in historical perspective, with special reference to the critical attention it draws to the dominant academic, intellectual and political-cultural illusions about sovereignty, citizenship and belonging in the Caribbean region. Unlike other studies on related themes that tend to treat the Caribbean in segmented ways, this collection of essays targets the region as a whole and should appeal to a wider audience.

Introduction

Hilbourne A. Watson

This collection addresses issues and problems around state sovereignty and colonial and postcolonial citizenships and belonging in the Caribbean. Neither sovereign autonomy nor citizenship came to Caribbean countries as a uniform linear process, as will be shown in due course. Contemporary Caribbean reality reflects the coexistence of sovereign states and non-independent territories that are heavily conditioned by the continuing presence, role and security strategies of certain European powers – the United Kingdom, France and the Netherlands – and the United States, which dominates the entire region. The Caribbean was created as an integral part of the modern world, helping to shape the contours of modernity in areas that have included the internationalization of commodity production of sugar and other agricultural exports, slavery, capital investment, trade and the organization of modern science and technology to fuel industrial production in Europe. The entire region has served as supplier and destination, consistent with the uneven spatial organization of the capitalist process.

Henry Fraser's recent comments on Barbados could be readily adapted and applied to several other Caribbean colonies:

> When the Reverend Griffith Hughes, parish priest of St. Lucy, published his *Natural History of Barbados* in 1750, he literally launched the Age of Enlightenment in Barbados. Newspapers proliferated, theatre flourished and three secondary schools – Combermere, Harrison, and Lodge – were established. Barbadians were making a name for themselves, in Britain and North America. Eminent physicians such as

> Dr. William Hillary were attracted to Barbados and carried out ground-breaking research in the 1750s. (caribbean360.com, 20 July 2014)

Fraser's point draws attention to the fact that capitalist slavery was not incompatible with modern science and the rise of an increasingly cosmopolitan outlook, which reflected European class-based and racialized conceptions of freedom and liberty on the one hand and servitude, dehumanization and the denial of those very values on the other. This contradictory relationship between capitalism, freedom, liberty and justice permeated both the edicts and processes of emancipation and conditioned the emergence of new forms of struggle for self-determination, independence and gender equality on a rigidly patriarchal landscape that nurtures citizenship and belonging, albeit on a modified terrain.

There exists across the Caribbean an abiding nationalist tendency to imagine that integration into the European international world order and into contemporary capitalist globalization is at variance with the achievement of self-determination, sovereign autonomy and the rights of states to full equality in the community of sovereign states. There is an underlying discomfort with globalization. It is seen as an elaboration of imperialism and an alien force that threatens state sovereignty in an environment where constraints arising from small economic size, limited resources and geopolitical factors, such as the lack of hard power (understood in terms of strategic military capability and the capacity to shape and determine geopolitical outcomes in the region and beyond), continue to be the norm. This way of interpreting Caribbean reality labours under the weight of the "epistemological territorialism", "sovereignty myths" and alienation that pervade the reproduction of intellectual culture in the Caribbean (see chapter 2 for an expansion of these terms). It is difficult to ignore sovereignty myths, which influence the formation of political and ideological consciousness about the place and status of the Caribbean in the modern world, in light of the challenges and uncertainties the region and the bulk of its inhabitants continue to face. Looking at globalization, states, sovereignty and citizenship in historical perspective rather than viewing them as organic forms opens up space for grappling with their contradictory natures and expressions.

This collection explores social phenomena in ways that part with illusions in order to appreciate that it is the capitalist content of globalization rather than the failure to adopt correct public policies or read market signals correctly that holds the achievement of substantive, territorially grounded self-determination at bay. Capital accumulation, which is a global process, requires the globalization of property rights and property income, which in turn require making the entire world available to and safe for capital. Thus property rights, state power and sovereign autonomy transcend the limits of territoriality – which has all manner of implications for how we experience citizenship and our sense of national belonging. Two important questions arise from this contradictory situation: What constitutes the appropriate unit of analysis for studying global politics? And what is the nature of the relationship between the modern state and human subjectivity?

In the chapters that follow, each author helps us see more clearly that sovereignty, citizenship and national belonging in the moment of capitalist globalization exist in a contradictory relationship with the rights of private capital under market-mediated liberal democracy. The foremost right under capitalism is not individual rights; rather, it is the right to transform the means of production into capital, to organize commodity production on the basis of the law of value and to exploit wage labour for the ends of private accumulation on a global scale. National states thus reveal their sovereign power foremost when they register, defend and protect capitalist property rights. The security of the state based on the use of force and coercion is paramount and must be achieved at all costs if capitalism is to survive, which means that the security of the human is always at risk under capitalism. Complex bilateral and multilateral arrangements about diplomacy, investment, trade, military security agreements, the basing of (especially US) military forces in the majority of countries and other provisions and arrangements managed by intergovernmental organizations (for example, the United Nations and NATO) secure the territorial and global geopolitical infrastructures and space that gird the right to exploit. Without these, capitalism will not survive.

Structure and Organization of the Book

In its eight chapters, this volume broadly targets the Caribbean, with representative coverage of the Commonwealth Caribbean.

Alex Dupuy (chapter 3) analyses how the development of capitalist state and class rule and power in Haiti since 1804 affected the working-class, small-farmer and "peasant" experiences of citizenship and belonging, paying close attention to exploitation, repression and other forms of domination. Linden Lewis (chapter 4) explains the contradictory relationship between citizenship and belonging in the Caribbean. Anton L. Allahar (chapter 5) analyses citizenship, identity formation and belonging, with special reference to Trinidad and Tobago and emphasis on West Indian cricket and Trinidad carnival. Allahar also looks at how racialization and alienation affect individual and collective senses of belonging. Aarón Gamaliel Ramos (chapter 6) focuses on the non-independent territories of Puerto Rico and the Netherlands Antilles, with attention to identity politics, citizenship and belonging. Justin Daniel (chapter 7) concentrates on the disillusionment that inhabitants of the French Caribbean territories continue to exhibit as French citizens. Finally, Sean Gill (chapter 8) focuses on the Cayman Islands with attention to the dilemma of citizenship, concentrating on international capital, migrant labour and contradictions arising from Caymanian nationalism in the context of globalization.

In chapter 2 Hilbourne Watson develops a philosophical and theoretical framework to inform his accounts of how the ideology of "Barbadian exceptionalism" helped to shape the constitutional and political development of colonial and postcolonial Barbados, distinctly imprinting the dominant conception of postcolonial sovereignty and citizenship. He discusses how US designs on Cuba from the 1820s to 1840s affected how Cuba interprets and defends its sovereignty and citizenship in the face of ongoing US refusal to recognize post-1959 Cuba on its own terms. Watson argues that a theory of global capitalism is necessary to overcome constraints built into state-centric accounts of globalization, sovereignty and citizenship. Pointing out the territorial trap of "geographical determinism", Watson insists the security and order that the state privileges do not raise the standard for justice and equal rights for all citizens and others living under the class societies organized on the basis of capitalism and claims that that relationship between capitalism and sovereignty makes it impossible to achieve substantive self-determination, freedom and sustainable national economic development.

Watson further elaborates that anti-colonial and anti-imperialist visions of self-determination, freedom, justice, equality and national belonging that are attached to citizenship in the Commonwealth Caribbean do not stand in opposition to patriarchal domination, class exploitation or their unequal gender outcomes, employing the concept of neo-patriarchy to frame his analysis of gender relations. Watson insists that contemporary understanding of sovereign statehood in the Caribbean has not parted with organic (naturalized and neo-religious) notions of the "body politic" (which he treats as a default for patriarchal authority and power). He makes the point that patriarchy operates in subtle ways that cover its forms and consequences in the tracks of liberalism highlighting accounts of order, security and authority at the expense of justice and freedom.

Alex Dupuy argues that the new ruling class in Haiti, which emerged after the defeat of the French in the creation of revolutionary sovereign Haiti in 1804, failed to proletarianize the former slave population in order to maintain the capitalist plantation as the unit of production for export. Dupuy notes that the inability of this class to modernize the productive forces and transform their material and social existence was reflected in the rise and institutionalization of a heterogeneous mass of semi-proletarians, small farmers and self-subsistent "peasants". He argues within a state-centric framework that the ensuing stalemate led the dominant class forces to negotiate away Haiti's sovereignty, leading to Haiti's subordination to "foreign capital", the return of external capital and Haiti's transformation into an exporter of largely working-class citizens as the cheapest labour in the Caribbean. Dupuy contends that this process produces contradictory consequences in the sphere of class relations in terms of citizenship and belonging in Haitian society. Dupuy does not elaborate on the tenuous link between sovereignty and territory in a deterritorializing world. However, he shows through his analysis of the contradictions of citizenship and freedom in Haiti, where class and colour contradictions abound, that sovereignty does not guarantee self-determination, freedom or respect for human rights for the majority of the labouring population, which is compelled to reproduce itself in conditions that are marked by extreme insecurity, deprivation, violence and alienation.

Linden Lewis also addresses issues about citizenship and belonging in the Caribbean, arguing that, in creating a sense of belonging through the medium of citizenship, the state embraces and exploits nationalism as a strategic ideology for nationalizing and socializing the nation. Lewis acknowledges that nations are made through the process of state making. He locates this nationalist goal within a historical framework, noting that different social agents have laid claims to the concept of citizenship for various reasons, and elaborates on the contested nature of citizenship, in the process drawing out often-hidden gender contradictions. He questions the nationalist notion of late-colonial and postcolonial citizenship that represents the highest level of political attainment in the achievement of state sovereignty and deconstructs the notion that citizenship and belonging in the region are settled matters. He explains how national origin, social class and gender mediate the processes through which the inclusion of some in the nation and the exclusion of others from it are understood in relation to the nation's constitution. Lewis is also attentive to how human rights of people who comprise the nation are affected within the context of globalization and the neo-liberal economic policies that complicate citizenship and belonging in the Caribbean.

Anton L. Allahar argues from a state-centric angle that a number of European powers created the modern Caribbean in ways that constructed the basis for capitalist accumulation, imperialism and globalization. He points out that forces of globalization not only uprooted and displaced populations from their "ancestral homes" (Africa, India, Europe) but also conditioned the quest for rootedness and belonging among those diasporic populations. He insists that the "scars of Empire" are still evident in the contemporary Caribbean in ways that fuel the politics of identity in the global age that has witnessed a set of rival, racialized claims for Caribbean authenticity or Caribbean roots and belonging. Allahar concentrates on the English-speaking Caribbean, using as his main empirical foci the West Indies cricket team and the popular culture of Trinidad's carnival, to explain how citizenship differs from belonging under sovereign states. He suggests that citizenship does not necessarily mean that belonging to a nation is a settled matter, especially where the Caribbean ethnic or racial type is concerned, and he stresses that making sense of belonging necessitates looking beyond nationalist ideology to the process and form of social negotiation that involves politics and the societal distribution of power among various groups. The logical conclusion of Allahar's argument is that the racialization of ethnic claims and conflicts and the relations around identity and belonging support the contention that capitalism and sovereignty have not settled the question of self-determination and belonging in the moment of globalization.

Aarón Gamaliel Ramos examines problems of freedom, citizenship and rights in Puerto Rico and the Dutch Caribbean (mainly Aruba and Curaçao) – which he labels "territorial fringes" in relation to their "metropolitan" contexts. He argues that the European powers were reluctant to promote decolonization of the Caribbean territories on security grounds after World War II. He emphasizes that the United States deepened the integration of Puerto Rico into the political economy and geopolitics of the mainland by changing Puerto Rico's status to a commonwealth in 1952, under an "associated statehood" arrangement that was originally presented to the United Nations to regulate decolonization without prejudice to the rights of the colonial powers. He also argues that the modification of the political status of the Dutch Caribbean territories, starting in 1954, resulted in certain adjustments that failed to produce any sustainable qualitative improvement in the treatment meted out to the Caribbean Dutch citizens living at home, in the Netherlands or both. He emphasizes that The Hague continues to interfere in the internal affairs of their self-governing Caribbean territories. On the question of the distribution of power between "the metropolises" – Washington and The Hague – and the Caribbean territories there remains a (metropolitan) scepticism about the capacity of people trapped in a modified colonial relationship for self-determination and full autonomy. In any case, the majority of the people inhabiting the Caribbean territories also remain sceptical of the sovereignty option and what it might entail in terms of access to social goods and the standard of living. There is a sense among the people in those territories that sovereignty has failed to deliver to the majority of the citizens of sovereign Caribbean states what was anticipated during the decolonization struggles.

Justin Daniel contends that Caribbean French citizens inhabiting the overseas departments of Guadeloupe and Martinique (and French Guiana) face serious challenges exercising citizenship rights, a problem he traces to the ways liberal European societies racialize social relations and impose types of exclusion that condition the formation of identity and belonging. Daniel argues that this particular condition has prevailed in various ways since 1804, when slavery was initially abolished, and after 1848, when citizenship was conferred on inhabitants of the French Caribbean territories without abolishing the colonies' colonial status. In exploring the contradictions of citizenship in the French Caribbean, Daniel highlights the disenchantment associated with the ambiguous policy of the French Republic towards its Caribbean citizens. He stresses that the shift to the discourse of formal equality of opportunity and the embrace of multicultural diversity implies a departure from the ambiguous model of republican universalism that came with the territorial civic nation beginning with the French Revolution, without dispelling the feeling of being simultaneously citizens of the French Republic and victims of discrimination within it. Daniel's account, which does not confront state-centric notions of sovereignty, highlights the abiding features of difference, as witnessed through the marginalization and exclusion that plague the Eurocentric liberal concept of rights and belonging and as experienced by Caribbean citizens living in France and in its overseas departments.

In the final chapter, Sean Gill discusses the problematic relationship between migration and economic growth in the Cayman Islands, arguing that the massive economic transformation that took place between the 1970s and 1990s attracted immigrant workers to the Cayman Islands from elsewhere in the Caribbean and businesspeople from the further afield, including the United Kingdom. Gill emphasizes that the Cayman Islands became one of the world's largest financial centres, "its gross national product increased a thousandfold, while its population multiplied five times", thanks to a fortuitous combination of an influx of foreign capital and foreign workers. The Cayman Islands is not a net importer of productive capital, a situation that reflects its status as an offshore financial centre, a money-laundering outpost and a tourist destination. Gill explains that the Caymanian (British) colonial state regulates migrant workers' rights to enter, work and reside permanently. He points out that the 2008 global economic and financial crisis contributed to a dramatic contraction of the migrant population, rising levels of violent crime and unemployment among locals, and staggering levels of government debt that exposed the unstable foundation on which the privileges of (UK-determined) Caymanian citizenship rest. Gill explains how Caribbean working-class migrants, especially from Jamaica, are treated relative to British and other expatriates. His analysis also shows how the British Nationality Act mediates contradictions of class, ethnicity and nationality, with attention to the racialization of identity formation and belonging in the Cayman Islands.

No conscious attempt was made to organize this collection around a single theoretical focus or framework for interpreting concepts and processes concerning globalization, sovereignty, citizenship and belonging. What emerges in the following chapters' discussion of those issues, as they pertain to sovereign states and non-independent territories of the Caribbean, is the suggestion that commensurability weighs more heavily than difference in the framing of the human condition. This reminds us that it is important to understand and appreciate the nature of the ailments before we can advance prescriptions to remedy the social and political problems.

1 Dialectic of Colonial and Postcolonial Citizenships, Belonging and State Sovereignty in the Caribbean

HILBOURNE A. WATSON

A distinct mark of the Western nation state as a site of modern cultural life has been the practice of forcing individuals to become national persons in order to express their subjectivity. Put another way, "becoming national" is the prerequisite for membership in the nation state under sovereign state power. This situation reflects an inherent contradiction in bourgeois modernity, with implications for how people reproduce themselves as agents of history, a process that is further complicated by the fact that we make our history under conditions in which freedom is subsumed under necessity. Capitalist colonialism and imperialism set the terms and conditions under which different social classes and their racialized ethnic and gendered components were reproduced as parts of societies. Struggles for liberation and freedom in the Caribbean have been legendary; however, those struggles were, and still are, conditioned by domination – that is, political and economic forces that reproduce necessity in the guise of freedom, liberation and democracy.

The contemporary moment is characterized by claims and counterclaims about the special case and needs of the Caribbean in the wider world, as when the *Jamaica Observer* took issue with St Lucia's prime minister Kenny Anthony in a 2013 editorial responding to an assertion he made at an International Monetary Fund seminar on Caribbean economic growth. On that occasion Anthony chided Caribbean leaders for not doing enough to convince the "international community of the peculiar circumstances of our region" (*Jamaica Observer*, "Where Dr Kenny Anthony Went Wrong", 24 September 2013). The *Jamaica Observer* reminded Anthony that the international community, including the "multilateral financial institutions . . . [and] the USA, UK, EU and Canada[,] are not convinced that our governments are doing enough to help ourselves to achieve sustainable economic development" and emphasized that regional economists viewed economic size as "an additional but not a binding constraint to economic development" (ibid.). Size remains an inescapable item on the agenda of multilateral organizations such as the Commonwealth Secretariat, the International Monetary Fund, the World Bank, the Inter-American Development Bank, the World Trade Organization and others (see also Jessop 2013).

The *Jamaica Observer* did not emphasize that decision making affecting the Caribbean in critical areas of economic priorities increasingly occurs outside the region, through organizations such as the World Bank, the International Monetary Fund, the Inter-American Development Bank and the World Trade Organization, whose explicit strategy is to build a "single global economy" (DuRand 2013, 3) with which sovereign states and their citizens will have to comply. The multilateral institutions and the dominant states that have the capacity to exercise "effective sovereignty" (Agnew 2009) are acting in ways that enhance the rights of the transnational capitalist class (TCC) forces on whose behalf those multilateral agencies largely operate. Substantively, the multilateral institutions are the core surrogates for an emerging transnational state (TNS), considering that a "single global economy" based on capitalism could hardly operate without an appropriate political organ. The TNS surrogate bodies do not devalue national sovereignty; instead, they and sovereign states are reconfiguring sovereignty to meet challenges and demands that stem from relentless global market integration to strengthen and broaden global capital accumulation: making the world accessible to capital also requires making it safe for capital (Robinson 2004).

The *Jamaica Observer* also failed to consider that it is capital accumulation rather than national economic development and job creation that leads capitalists to invest in profitable ventures in "safe" zones. The relentless pace of global market integration propelled by technological innovation via computerization, artificial intelligence and robotics makes it difficult for most governments (and many businesses) to respond definitively to the contradictions arising from highly disruptive change, which is compounded by capitalist market anarchy. Instability and crisis are inherent in the capitalist process; evidence shows that financial instability in the market destabilizes a state's capital-accumulation strategy, as the current global economic and financial crisis confirms. Economic size matters in terms of scale, scope and complexity of the productive forces, relative to a state's ability to attract and keep capital within its borders. It is necessary to consider the relevance of economic size in neo-liberal times with reference to how liberalization, deregulation, privatization and austerity affect how countries participate in the process of global capital accumulation (Thirlwall 2013). How people reproduce themselves as citizens, female and male workers, and members of ethnic groups is inevitably conditioned by the rhythm of the capital-accumulation process within the multi-scalar – local, national, regional and global – context.

Capitalist globalization, which is a moment in the development of historical capitalism (Robinson 2004), has nothing to do with levelling the global economic playing field for the net benefit of any individual state or its society. Capitalism is based on production for private capital accumulation rather than national economic development; however, politicians will insist that national economic development based on market principles and processes is their priority for meeting the contradictory demands emanating from the various social classes. The most serious forms of tension and conflict between national states and transnational capital revolve around trying to reconcile contradictions between national economic-development priorities and capital-accumulation goals. Broadly speaking, TCC forces consider national borders as temporary obstacles to be demolished, with the aid of sovereign states. It is therefore through TCC integration and TNS formation that the relationship between global capital and national states continues to be refashioned (Robinson 2004).

Without sovereign states globalization as we know it would hardly exist, which implies that the contradiction between capitalism and self-determination cannot be resolved by making ideological claims about defending sovereignty from the predations of globalization, as Caribbean academics are accustomed to assert (see Marshall 2007; Girvan 2008; Joseph 2012). National states make the protection of the rights of capital their first priority. Sovereign states are indispensable for providing the infrastructure of capitalism by levying and collecting taxes; funding or subsidizing research and development activities; building or financing the construction of public projects like ports, roads, highways, and defence and military-security programmes; providing education and supporting the arts and other cultural activities. Making sense of TNS formation requires paying close attention to the fact that "the spread of capitalist markets, values and social relationships around the world, far from being an inevitable outcome of inherently expansionist economic tendencies, has depended on the agency of states" which are historical institutions (Panitch and Gindin 2012, vii).

William Robinson (2004) argues that the TCC and TNS are not final outcomes of history; rather, they are part of a contradictory process in which the ruling strata operates on the basis of hegemony, which rests on consent and domination. TCC integration and TNS formation are neither neutral nor benign, given the disruptive nature of economic crisis, force, violence, domination, dispossession and expulsion associated with state formation and capitalist expansion. Capitalist globalization is not human destiny – the future remains to be made (Agnew 2005). The world has known different types of states and forms of sovereignty (Agnew 2009), with war, terror, subjugation and expropriation prominently featured in mobilizing, organizing and regulating populations in the process of producing forms of the body politic, which retains an underlying, culturally rooted religious character. The production of political space with territorial boundaries has been a violent and disruptive process (Elden 2009, xviii, xix), which prompts Charles Tilly (1985) to label war making and state making via territorialization, deterritorialization and reterritorialization forms of "organized crime".

The ideological claim that sovereignty resides in the citizens is part of the myth making on which the bourgeoisie has relied to nationalize society and strengthen its own class power and hegemonic control. The political equality of citizens of "democratic" societies is deontological (juridical); sovereignty does not level the playing field for the exercise of citizenship (Kantorowicz 1957; Agnew 2009; Elden 2009; Santner 2011). In reality, the achievement of citizenship in the postcolonial states and societies of the Caribbean has been riddled with obstacles to substantive self-determination, given the nature of the contradictory relationship between capitalism, self-determination and state sovereignty.

Plural Citizenships and Belonging in the Modern Caribbean from Abolition to Globalization

When the revolutionary process erupted in the French colony of Saint-Domingue during the 1790s, a heterogeneous mix of social forces (including enslaved majorities and plantation owners) overthrew slavery and declared freedom under the banner of the French Revolution, in the process creating a revolutionary, non-racial form of sovereignty and inclusive citizenship (Blackburn 2008). In 1848 the geopolitical impact of the loss of Haiti left France with little alternative but to abolish slavery in its Caribbean territories and confer citizenship on the inhabitants as colonial subjects. In 1944 France (in a geopolitical move that anticipated the implications of the outcome of World War II for its position as an imperial power) revised the political status of its Caribbean territories to "overseas departments", deepening their integration into the French Republic. This action reinforced forms of difference and exclusion via the racialization of social distinctions and constrained the ability of French Antilleans to exercise French citizenship (see Daniel, chapter 7 in this volume).

The United States granted citizenship to the people of Puerto Rico under the Jones Act in 1917, while denying the newer peoples of Puerto Rico the right to vote for the US president, effectively imposing second-class citizenship on them as colonial subjects (Cabranes 1979). In 1952 the United States adjusted Puerto Rico's political situation by granting the colony commonwealth status – associated statehood. Puerto Ricans were permitted to elect a governor, allowing the colony to send a non-voting delegate to the US House of Representatives. In 1954 the Kingdom of the Netherlands revised the political status of its Caribbean territories through closer association, thereby modifying its relationship with its Caribbean colonies (see Ramos, chapter 6 in this volume). Between 1947 and 1958 the United Kingdom also promoted closer association for a number of its British West Indies territories, based simultaneously on internal territorial self-government and federation – a contradictory approach that contributed immensely to the collapse of the Federation of the West Indies (1958–62). The British anticipated that the Federation of the West Indies might become a sovereign state with all the trappings of autonomy, such as citizenship, and so on.

The initiatives led by France, the United States, the Netherlands and the United Kingdom in the Caribbean reflected the forms of exclusion and alienation that are characteristic of how liberalism – modernity's philosophical anchor – actually works (Losurdo 2011). The United States used its hegemonic Cold War project to force the Caribbean region into compliance with its regional security strategy, as a number of geopolitical developments attest: in British Guiana starting in 1953, Guatemala in 1954, Cuba since 1959, the Dominican Republic in 1965, Grenada in 1983, Panama in 1990 and Haiti in 2004. The post-war hegemonic international order was not a simple extension of imperialism, with the United States becoming simply an exceptional global imperialist state (Agnew 2009); rather, the United States established a global hegemonic project in which allies and client states received certain benefits in return for joining the bloc as formally equal but substantively subordinate members. This post-war arrangement made it virtually impossible for Caribbean states to acquire and exercise what Vaughan Lewis describes as "high political sovereignty" (2003, 519). This outcome imposed certain constraints on the exercise of sovereignty with reference to self-determination and the exercise of citizenship.

The nationalist leaders in the former British West Indies territories associate the achievement of sovereignty with the realization of freedom, justice, equality, individual rights and liberal democracy and with a break with imperialism. In fact, the right to exploit for the ends of private capitalist accumulation is the most fundamental of rights under capitalism, which imposes limits on self-determination and sovereign autonomy and subordinates individual rights, freedom, equality and justice to necessity. Liberal democracy is built on capitalism, which is impossible without the "alienation of power" on which class rule depends (Wood 1995). Capitalism requires a constitutional and juridical framework of the rule of law that is necessarily backed by the coercive power of the state to manage the contradictions between formal political equality and substantive economic inequality. Capitalist commodity production and competition give rise to market anarchy, social fragmentation, individualism and alienation – forms that Marx traced to the "making of abstract labor", which he understood as "the transformation of property-possessing, economically independent, but politically dependent labor into disowned, legally and politically free, but economically dependent wage labor" (Teschke and Heine 2002, 172).

Liberal democracy cannot be sustained without a combination of state political coercion and economic market compulsion, which means that under capitalism we reproduce ourselves as "competition market subjects" who are forced to live under the alienated power of the sovereign state (Reuten and Williams 1989). It is this reality that liberals would have us believe constitutes the high point of individual freedom and democracy under which the capitalist and the worker negotiate the terms and conditions of the actual buying and selling of labour power, as free agents in a market-driven economy. There are problems with this logic: (1) the law of the state is founded on the right to exploit; (2) under capitalism social relations between people assume the form of technical relations between things (commodities) via production and exchange; (3) there exists a fundamental incompatibility between capitalism and national self-determination because capitalism is organized on a transnational basis in which national priorities become secondary to global capital accumulation and (4) freedom is equated to market-mediated priorities where historically determined capitalist competition and private accumulation are misrepresented as a naturally evolved value-free organic process. The ideological expression of this fantastic notion is a society of laws rather than of people – which amounts to romantic fancy.

All historical struggles for individual rights and freedom within frameworks of self-determination throughout the Caribbean were waged on terrains of capitalist economic exploitation and alienated power. This reality posed an irreconcilable contradiction for post-war nationalist leaders who, operating largely in consort with the colonial powers and domestic and international capitalist interests, were at pains to control the struggles waged from below by the largely impoverished rural and urban working class and direct them into political channels that suited the needs of the dominant forces (Mawby 2012). It is therefore disingenuous to cling to the notion that sovereignty is the opposite of colonial status given that the postcolonial moment did not abolish the institutional political architecture of imperialism. On the contrary, its architects skilfully and opportunistically layered independence, representative government, citizenship and national belonging onto the exploitative and repressive foundation of imperialism. The point here is that continuity rather than rupture and discontinuity characterizes the relationship between the colonial and postcolonial moments.

John Agnew highlights the problem with the false logic of an inside-outside dichotomy that informs much postcolonial thinking on the relationship between colonialism and sovereignty. He argues that "the idea that there are natural territorial 'sovereignties' awaiting awakening or liberation from foreign domination is one of the longest-lasting follies of the intellectual influence of the nationalist movements that 'liberated' their peoples from European imperialism in the post–World War II period" (Agnew 2009, 212). There is no justification to assert, as the nationalist leaders and their supporters in the Caribbean do, that individual agency under the sovereign state represents the highest form of human subjectivity and freedom available, bearing in mind that sovereignty is historical and a means to an end rather than organic. More concretely, it is impossible to impose a closure on historical change, which must remain open-ended. Substantively, sovereignty is best theorized as part of the problem of world order rather than its definitive solution. Territorial boundaries are politically, economically and culturally porous, considering that capital accumulation is a global process and the trajectory of contemporary capitalist globalization is in the direction of a deterritorializing world.

The academic habit of objectifying geography has the effect of hiding history and facts (Agnew 2009), a method that relies on reinventing the state of nature and using it as the starting point for theorizing about the nature of the world, human nature, history, culture, politics and change (Jahn 2000). This form of pre-Darwinian naturalistic materialism separates nature from human history in ways that make it difficult to treat human cultural development as the result of conscious human action. Humans and nature share an interdependent – mutually constitutive – relationship; therefore, when we set the two at war with each other, we run the risk of "emptying history" or rendering it "emptiable" (Rosenberg 2000) – a tendency that is widespread in mainstream international relations (Jahn 2000; Van der Pijl 2002, 130–34).

The contemporary moment in world historical development is marked by the intensification of global integration. In 1995 the director-general of the World Trade Organization, Renato Ruggiero, declared, "We are no longer writing the rules of interaction among separate national economies. We are writing the constitution of a single global economy" (quoted in DuRand 2013, 3). In 1997 the World Bank stated that for structural adjustment programmes to be effective they would have to be based on "macroeconomic management by an insulated technocratic elite" (World Bank 1997, 152; see also DuRand 2013, 3). The relationship between state sovereignty and global capital accumulation is reflected partly through legal and policy provisions by states that encourage and permit the top 1 per cent of the global wealthy to engage in reckless behaviour by stashing away between US$23 and US$51 trillion in global tax havens, free from any tax liabilities (Mathiason 2012).[1] The social contradictions arising from this massive concentration of wealth on one hand and of endemic poverty and dehumanization on the other highlight a situation in which approximately one thousand individuals in the world possess more income, wealth and other assets than the entire combined populations of the poorest 145 countries, with only 450 individuals in the United States owning combined income, wealth and assets greater than that of the bottom 150 million in that same country.[2] The majority of humanity endures with massive insecurity, and throngs abide destitution, poor health and ravages wrought by violence that many states execute to protect capitalism.

The modern Caribbean is an integral part of this capitalist process of uneven global – that is, spatial – expansion. The nationalist assertion that the Caribbean is part of a so-called dependent, underdeveloped "periphery" in contrast with a developed, capitalist "centre" is reflective of state-centric thinking and geographical determinism. The centre-periphery dichotomy rests on a false assumption about the relationship between the spatial organization of capitalist production and accumulation on the one hand and the territorial division of the world into national states on the other. Agnew deconstructs the "sovereignty myths" that state-centric thinking fosters, especially the myth that globalization poses an existential threat to territorial sovereignty (2009, 49).

The concept of modern sovereignty rests on the notion of the "body politic", with the state acting on behalf of the "sovereign" people, a claim that fuels "much of the mythic basis on which the claim to state sovereignty now largely rests" (Agnew 2009, 48). In stating that the "myth of sovereignty as a product of peoplehood is invulnerable to much criticism because many of the successes of state-based activities of the recent past – democratization of everyday life, the rule of law, the self-determination of hitherto subjugated social groups, the expansion of social and economic rights, the regulation of economic activities to protect consumers and workers, and so on – have relied on popular sovereignty as both stimulus and justification" (48), Agnew does not conflate sovereignty myths with the misguided notion that sovereignty is a myth. Rather, he argues that myth comes into practice when we treat as natural the social-historical institutions humans create as part of the process of reproducing cultural life. The common belief is that when one "criticizes territorial sovereignty as it is usually invoked, one is thereby criticizing rule 'by the people'. Consequently, the appeal of the idea of sovereignty as resting on popular-territorialized rule should not be underestimated" (48).

Agnew's concept of "effective sovereignty" requires attention to the uneven spatial distribution of power in the global geopolitical and economic context. He explains the difference between "effective sovereignty" and nominal or juridical sovereignty, which all sovereign states have under international law, emphasizing that all sovereign states do not share an equal capacity to exercise "effective sovereignty" (2009, 144–45). One way to grasp the concept of effective sovereignty, he suggests, is to look at how the "migratory propensities of sovereignty" are captured and reflected via the roles that world currencies, such as the US dollar, play. Agnew clarifies that "all currencies today exist increasingly in a global, relational space rather than in the absolute territorial space with which they are symbolically associated". This fact helps us to make sense of the concept of the "migratory aspects of sovereignty" but also the limits to territory and citizenship relative to the operation of the "global sovereignty regime" (144; see also Panitch and Gindin 2012).

Demystifying the State of Nature in Positivist International Relations Scholarship in the Commonwealth Caribbean

Mainstream – that is, realist and liberal – international relations theory is dominated by an intellectual culture that tries to "explain away" the "often paradoxical relationship of . . . theory to reality" (Marx 1981a, 428) through a philosophy of history that makes the fictive state of nature the effective starting point for theorizing about world order. The task of scientific inquiry is "to reduce the visible and merely apparent movement to the actual inner movement" in order to understand and change the world (428). It is necessary to liberate international relations theory and practice from the stranglehold of the grand myth of the state of nature and the theoretical, philosophical and existential constraints that flow therefrom.

The field of international relations that exists in the Commonwealth Caribbean is deeply rooted in this positivist intellectual tradition with its deep European roots. The state of nature serves in lieu of actual political communities for the field's body of literature. In her critique of the state-of-nature logic that dominates mainstream international relations discourse, Beate Jahn makes three central propositions: (1) that European thinkers applied the methods of the natural sciences to the study of what they imagined to be "natural man" – the Indian in the Americas; (2) that on the basis of that unfortunate misrepresentation of historical processes European thinkers redefined history in terms of linear (Rosenberg's "empty" or "emptiable" [2000]) time, using the state of nature as their empirical reference point, while imposing a revelatory schema or "secular telos" upon the actual historical process and (3) that European thinkers used the imagined "natural man" to inform a reconceptualization of their own particular history – imagined to be exceptional – and applied universal laws from the "secular telos" to explain all human historical development as a natural evolution from the state of nature into civil society – a misleading discourse that dominates the entire spectrum of social-contract theory (Jahn 2000, 96).

What Jahn has carefully separated out in her three propositions had been conflated by European thinkers to arrive at a synthesis of the "epistemological, ontological and ethical" dimensions, and they produced a "redefinition of authentic and legitimate political community" that gave us the artifice of a "political community built on natural law" (Jahn 2000, 99). This mischaracterization "inevitably led to the universalist conception of the state of nature" that produced an unrealistic "worldview based on a hierarchy of cultures which serves as the basis for a theory of unequal relations between political communities" (95–96). The liberal and realist outlook is beholden to this ahistorical embrace of the state of nature, Jahn states, which informs the "cultural unity and particularism of European political thought, domestic and international" (97). Not surprisingly, many contemporary scholars rely on a variety of canonical texts produced by European figures, among them "Machiavelli, Hobbes,

Vitoria, Grotius, Pufendorf, Locke, Vattel, Kant, Rousseau", Jahn notes, whose writings connect "domestic and international politics" in self-referential ways that border on narcissistic, which legitimate the "particularism in European thought" and leave undisturbed the cultural contradictions that mark this Eurocentric cultural particularism (99). Jahn's explanatory framework helps us to appreciate the contradictory unity of the domestic and international spheres.

In this section I will focus selectively on scholarship by Jessica Byron and Ivelaw Griffith in international relations and by Keith Nurse, Norman Girvan and Don Marshall in international political economy accounts of the Commonwealth Caribbean. Jessica Byron (2003) traces the origin of academic international relations to the post–World War II period, a problematic perspective that Diana Thorburn (2000) shares, which is contrary to available empirical and theoretical evidence. The elevation of international relations to the status of an academic discipline can be traced to the end of World War I, when an international relations department was created in 1919 at the University College at Aberystwyth, Wales, to study the causes of the Great War and to think of ways to achieve lasting world peace. Prior to World War I international relations concerns were addressed via academic departments, such as history, diplomatic history and politics, and within other social science academic domains (Jackson and Sørensen 2003).

Byron's interpretation of realism and its relevance to international relations theory is inattentive to the fact that realism discovers natural man in the Hobbesian state of nature. Hans Morgenthau objectifies this state of nature when he transfers the imaginary "war genes" of the so-called natural man to man in civil society, the state and the international realm (Morgenthau 1985, 3–17; see also Rosenberg 1994, 1–37 passim) – a move that banishes social relations from international politics. Byron is sympathetic to Barry Buzan's assertion that realism prescribes "timeless wisdom" about world politics (Byron 2003, 67), repeating the fundamental problem with realism's objectification of a condition that lacks historical substance – namely, a fictive state of nature. Byron does not explain how and why such notions, which reduce humans to alienated individualists incapable of participating in any social relations and set theoretical knowledge adrift from any social anchors, could give rise to a so-called timeless wisdom outside the bounds of actual history and any actually existing human societies.

Byron argues that the US global strategy and practice since 11 September 2001 represents a return to a realist paradigm. But this is hardly so. Her review of realism and the relevance of the interventions by John Mearsheimer, Samuel Huntington, Barry Buzan and other contributors (Byron 2003, 67) to mainstream international relations ignores the fact that realism begins with a set of propositions about a fantastic pre-social reality to inform international relations theory. Byron's assertion that the United States is returning to a realist paradigm reflects circular reasoning and discounts the long and varied history of pre-emption, unilateralism and hegemony in US foreign policy. US security strategy has never rested on any single theoretical prescription. Objectively, liberalism and realism have differed by degree rather than kind, and the evidence points to a deepening convergence between these two bodies of largely alienated international relations theory, as can be discerned in the neo-liberal "muscular" offensive that characterizes the US-initiated global war on terror (Burchill 2005). Byron mentions hegemony without paying careful attention to what hegemony represents as the "new shape of global power" (Agnew 2005).

Post–Cold War, the US hegemonic strategy rests on a quest for a unilateral global supremacy and full-spectrum dominance, based on the claim that the post-war international order has been superseded by a new transnational dispensation with fault lines that neoconservatives believe exist within states rather than between states (Zelikow 2003). The United States is exploiting opportunities it helped to create in the post–9/11 moment in order to restructure geopolitical priorities through the global war on terror, with a view to advancing global market integration to enhance the basis of capital accumulation. This is part of what Agnew (2005) calls an unattainable attempt to achieve absolute American control of globalization. The American strategy for ruling simultaneously at home and abroad involves unprecedented coercion and violence (see Harvey 2003; Layne 2006) as witnessed by US wars in Afghanistan and Iraq, the US-led NATO action against Libya, the drone wars under the Obama administration and, in the Caribbean, the violent removal of Jean-Bertrand Aristide from power in Haiti in 2004.

Byron raises salient points in her account of issues of governance and global interdependence; however, she relies on state-centric notions and sovereignty myths that make it very difficult for her to imagine "post-sovereign forms of political life" (Rengger 2000, 152). With the static boundaries of realism and liberalism informing the limits of her conceptual framework, Byron eclectically argues that Caribbean states should forge "a strong multilateral system based on international law, norms of social justice, equity and human well-being" and says it is "in the interest of small societies to protect the multilateral system and to constantly lobby for a focus on human development issues. In this regard Caribbean intellectuals should . . . lead the way in developing an epistemic community on the vulnerabilities as well as developmental possibilities of small size" (Byron 2003, 75). Caribbean states face contradictions arising from disruptive forces shaping our deterritorializing world in which they lack effective sovereignty to protect any part of the multilateral system (see Jessop 2013).

Furthermore the Bush Doctrine declares that sovereign autonomy and territorial borders as recognized under the UN model of sovereign autonomy can no longer protect the juridically delimited territorial integrity of sovereign states, their leaders and citizens (Zelikow 2003). Obama's drone wars and his latest plan for dismembering Syria and intensifying instability and chaos in the Middle East confirm this. The impact on the Caribbean region of the protracted global economic and financial crisis that erupted in 2008 shows that it can be very difficult for even the dominant states whose rulers exercise "effective sovereignty" under the "global sovereignty regime" (Agnew 2009) to control the contradictions of global capitalism. Byron must appreciate that the multilateral system is not fixed; it is being systematically transformed into an integrated single global economy that defies the circular logic that undulates between liberal and realist imaginaries.

The concept of "timeless wisdom" rests on a static conception of history that separates the "theorist from the object of analysis" and assumes "there is an external world out there to study" (Devetak 2005, 157) – an approach that offers only the chimera of "value-free social analysis" based on the notion that "theoretical knowledge is neutral or non-political" (159). Byron seems sympathetic to the view of the "nation state as a normatively desirable mode of political organization" as well as other positivist claims that the "condition of anarchy and the self-regarding actions of states are either natural or immutable" (166–67; see also Bilgin and Morton 2002, 56; Barkawi and Laffey 1999).[3] Buzan also argues that realism is the "natural home of those disposed towards conservative ideology" (quoted in Burchill 2005, 86). To invoke Buzan's notion of "timeless wisdom" is to fail to acknowledge that timeless history is at variance with actual human history and to be seemingly unaware that the "price one has to pay for identifying the 'timeless features' of the political landscape is the sacrifice of understanding the process of change affecting the world" (Rosenberg 1994, 20). Byron falls short of contributing to a critical theory of global capitalism to explain issues of sovereignty and citizenship in the Caribbean in our globalizing world.

Ivelaw Griffith's scholarship is neo-Clausewitzian in orientation, with its linear reading of history and lack of curiosity about any form of rigorous theoretical engagement. In "Understanding Caribbean Security: Back to Basics and Building Blocks" Griffith (2004c) waxes pragmatic about returning to the "basics" and "building blocks", totally inattentive to the dialectic of security problematic of the sovereign state (see Neocleous 2008). Griffith's account cannot help us understand the relationship between theory and knowledge in international relations discourse and practice in the post–9/11 context. In his attempt to scale the mountain of security studies he claims to provide a "holistic schema and not a partial or segmented one in the context of the 21st century realities" (Griffith 2004b, 3); however, he delivers much less than a proverbial mole hill (see Rosenberg 1994, 27–28).

Marx argued that a theory begins to disintegrate when disciples resort to "crass empiricism" and "cunning argument" to reaffirm the relevance of the theory even when reality contradicts their assertions – when "the new theoretical form in which the master had sublimated" the theory is "no longer reality" (Marx 1981b, 428, quoted in Lebowitz 2003, 20, 21). If Griffith were serious about getting "back to basics" or paying attention to terrorism in the Caribbean, he would have to confront the official and unofficial legacies of Western state terrorism, beginning with the Columbus encounter and the ensuing dispossession and systematic genocide that cleared the Caribbean earth for capital, all in the guise of bringing freedom and civilization to savages. He could hardly ignore the deliberate brutalism and terrorism of the Middle Passage in association with procuring labour supplies and the enslavement that ensued. He could hardly ignore European violent responses to slave rebellions and Maroon insurgencies, the disavowal of the Haitian Revolution's actual relationship to bourgeois modernity (Fischer 2004), the terrorism that mediated South Asian indenture in the region, the terror that accompanied US occupation of the Dominican Republic and Haiti, late imperialist responses to working-class rebellions in the Caribbean during the 1930s (see Bolland 2012), and post-war forms of financial terrorism that are part of austerity measures that make the working class pay for capitalist crisis and restructuring.

Griffith reduces the state to its territorial shell, making it impossible for him to appreciate that virtue and terror – in the form of state violence – are mutually constitutive. Stuart Elden reminds us that "terror is disastrous without the state's virtue, and virtue is powerless without terror, which, emanating as it does from the virtue of the state, is nothing but prompt, severe, inflexible justice" (Elden 2009, xxiii; see also Neocleous 2008).

Griffith treats historical events and canonical expressions by certain "great men" as "timeless"; for example, he romanticizes Carl von Clausewitz's assertion that the "greatest and most decisive act which a statesman and commander perform is that of recognizing correctly the kind of war in which they are engaged" (quoted in Griffith 2004a, xxiii). Clausewitz's way of translating political desire into political reality occurred through what Anthony Burke calls a process of "noiseless translation" (Burke 2007, 191).

Much like Byron, Griffith also renders realist theory timeless. He thinks that "positive sovereignty" (see L. Lewis 2013, 4) is a form of domestic sovereignty, indifferent to the fact that concepts such as "effective sovereignty" (Agnew 2009), "high political sovereignty" (V. Lewis 2003) and nominal sovereignty are far more useful concepts to employ for making sense of how those who exercise state power operate under the "global sovereignty regime" (Agnew 2009, 98). Griffith is not alone, as there is ample evidence of the pervasiveness of state-centrism and sovereignty myths in other scholarship on Caribbean international relations – for example, in scholarship produced by Anthony Maingot (1994; 1997; Maingot and Lozano 2005), Jacqueline Braveboy-Wagner (1989) and Clifford Griffin (1997) among others. In order to clarify the role of facts in the analysis of capitalist globalization with the Caribbean in view, it is necessary to appreciate that the spatial organization of capitalism has little in common with state-centric notions of interstate competition. The operation of the global political economy is marked by a complex process of production that integrates rather than separates the units called territorial states. Griffith offers very little that is relevant to the construction of a theory of global capitalism through which to decipher categories such as globalization, sovereignty and citizenship.

When we consider the problem through the lens of international political economy, with reference to contributions by Keith Nurse, Norman Girvan and Don Marshall, it becomes clear that these scholars have not broken with state-centric thinking, and their work does not contribute to a rigorous theory of global capitalism for explaining Caribbean reality. Keith Nurse's analysis of the transatlantic "banana wars" (2005, 1) rests on the state-centric logic that informs Immanuel Wallerstein's world-system theory, which frames Nurse's account of "triadic competition" with reference to the African, Caribbean and Pacific countries that he conveniently assigns to the "periphery" (1). Norman Girvan's (2008) explanation of the Economic Partnership Agreement (EPA) between the European Union and the Forum of the Caribbean Group of African, Caribbean and Pacific States (CARIFORUM) repeats a similar state-centric bias, and Don Marshall's (2007) analysis of offshore financial centres and services and their relevance to the Caribbean is at one with the dominant state-centric paradigm that treats globalization as posing an existential threat to Caribbean sovereignty.

Nurse argues that "the banana case gives an insight into the evolving geopolitical context, especially in terms of core-periphery relations" (2005, 1). He insists that "triadic competition is indicative of the relative decline of US hegemony and the rise of rivalry among the US, the EU and Japan in the global accumulation process" (1). Nurse sees interstate competition everywhere, conflating hegemony with imperialism in the post-imperialism moment, and saying:

> World-systems analysis on leadership or hegemonic cycles argues that the movement from a geopolitical context of hegemony to one of inter-imperialist rivalry is attended by the expansion of colonialism or domination by core countries over the periphery . . . . When power is dispersed over a number of core states competing countries tend to delineate markets and define spheres of influence to defend or expand their share of global value-added. This trend is expressed in the formation of regional blocs and a shift from multilateralism towards bilateralism and/or unilateralism. The sharpening of core-periphery relations . . . raises the resistance quotient, the demands for decolonization and alternative modes of governance. (1)

Nurse's analysis, which assumes the circulation of power as a fixed category between dominant states, with the decline of US hegemony in view, misses several points: global market integration; TCC and TNS formation processes that restructure the environments of capitalist competition; the complex ways in which leading political and business elites from the various countries interact within the multilateral institutions and via the European Union, NAFTA and beyond; and the hegemony the US dollar (a proxy for capitalist financial power) exercises in integrating global financial markets. Nurse's contention that countries – core versus periphery – compete in the global market banishes social relations of production and exploitation from the analysis. He fails to explain why the United States, which was deliberate in deconstructing what remained of the edifices of European imperialism after World War II (having integrated them into its hegemonic project for restructuring the post-war international order), would choose to return to so-called inter-imperialist rivalry. Nurse does not account for the organization of commodity production on a non-linear, multi-scalar spatial basis (see Panitch and Gindin 2012; Agnew 2005; Robinson 2004). In his analysis of a "crisis of hegemony" Stephen Gill examines key changes in world order, theorizing beyond simple notions of the "decline of American state power as was suggested by . . . the Realist and World-Systems traditions", connecting the "crisis of hegemony" with "a transformation in the structures of power . . . dominance and resistance that constitute world order" (2003, 67). Nurse's state-centric world-system framework makes it difficult for him to contribute to a theory of global capitalism for anchoring analysis of globalization, sovereignty, citizenship and other issues in the Caribbean.

Norman Girvan also understands the international economy as an assemblage of competing states and regions, a descriptive state-centric approach that highlights "supranational governance" (2008, 1) while simultaneously putting the economy at the disposal of the state. Girvan says:

> Cariforum-EC Economic Partnership Agreement (EPA) is more than just a trade agreement: its scope embraces many subjects that have [been] . . . mainly within national and regional jurisdiction. . . . As a legally binding international instrument with elaborate implementation and enforcement provisions, it embodies a far higher degree of supranational governance than the corresponding arrangements in the Caribbean Community. It will . . . condition the scope and content of future agreements made between Caricom [Caribbean Community and Common Market] and other major trading partners and the region's stance in WTO [World Trade Organization] negotiations. There is a sense . . . in which the EPA sets up a framework for the future evolution of the economic, social and environmental policies of Caricom states, both separately and collectively, and for the terms on which the region engages with the global community. (1)

Girvan equates the form of the CARIFORUM-EPA arrangement with its actual social content, reducing to technical aspects of interstate relations several important issues around globalization and arguing that certain features of the EPA "appear to have significant implications for national and regional development, for the region's autonomy in policy-making and for its ability to fashion a CSME [Caribbean Single Market and Economy] that responds to its own choices and priorities" (2008, 3). From the perspective of TCC forces that connect Asia, North America and the European Union through their complex web of spatially organized activities, forging transnational alliances to bolster their competitive edge, the notion of "fortress

Europe" reflects fanciful state-centric thinking. The integration of North American and European TCC forces within fields of competition and the TNS strategy via the World Bank and the World Trade Organization (DuRand 2013) points to a radically changing global scenario. Girvan treats supranational and global processes as evidence of quantitative interactions by discrete sovereign states and economies, inattentive to the fact that only those ruling-class forces operating through states with a capacity to exercise "effective sovereignty" can achieve what he romanticizes for Caribbean states that lack the capacity to exercise "high political sovereignty" (V. Lewis 2003).

Girvan ignores Havelock Brewster's observation that after forty years of CARICOM, there is little evidence of measurable economic integration. Brewster points to the unattainable goal of CARICOM leaders to "create a Single Market and Economy with each member retaining maximum national sovereignty. [They intend] to do so apparently through a mode of discretionary inter-governmental cooperation. These objectives are clearly contradictory" (Brewster 2003, 505). Sovereignty, which expresses a relation between and among states, is not restricted or delimited to any single CARICOM country, yet Girvan foregrounds it. States make protecting the rights of capital their main priority. Girvan does not contribute to a theory of global capitalism to make sense of issues of globalization, sovereignty, citizenship and human security in the Caribbean.

Don Marshall examines "two debates on the historical rise of financial globalisation and regulatory challenges . . . and seeks to establish the constitutive role of offshore financial centres (OFCs) in shaping the cultural habitus of late-modern financialisation" (2007, 1). He acknowledges that OFCs are not the proper starting point to discuss the regulation of the international financial framework, and he recognizes that the "nation-state" faces certain limitations in dealing with the pressures from "capital mobility worldwide" (1). However, the problem is that Marshall believes that the so-called nation state is the "primary political unit" of analysis for dealing with "arrangements for global governance structures" while transnational capital lacks "political legitimacy and accountability" (1). He equates the technical division of labour between the state and capital to a substantive separation, highlighting the subjective tendencies that underscore his state-centric way of looking at international political economy processes.

Marshall does not seem to appreciate that the processes the TCC and TNS forces set in motion demand the reconfiguring of the role of the sovereign state under global capitalism, as the World Bank (1997) and especially the World Trade Organization make clear in their insistence on the imperative of building a single global economy (see DuRand 2013). Marshall tends to discount the facts that the state and money are expressions of social relations and money is abstract capital. He juxtaposes the state against the economy in favour of the state, missing the vital point that states assert sovereignty – foremost when they facilitate the global mobility of capital and foster global market integration. Failure to appreciate that the division of labour between the state (politics) and economy (capital) is a technical division leads Marshall to discount the fact that states and markets are integral parts of capitalist social relations that anchor the capital-state relationship in what Agnew calls the "new geography of global power" (Agnew 2005, 32).

Transnational financial capital (TFC) and TNS institutions collaborate to deepen the separation of the state from civil society and of politics from economics, in order to limit the ability of working-class forces to make major claims upon the state for the provision of social goods. This neo-liberal policy initiative depoliticizes and renders working-class political activism suspicious, making it easier to criminalize political activism and restrict the political options of non-capitalist sectors engaging in class struggle. It is also the aim of TFC, which is part of the TCC, to restrict the ability of national states to regulate OFCs to free capital accumulation from "unnecessary" state restrictions. TFC swarms when there is a lack of profitable opportunities in brick-and-mortar production; this is the central point to address with respect to how information and communications technology facilitates the rise and circulation of electronic money. Marshall argues that the Caribbean became an important OFC zone (2007, 25–26); however, he asserts rather curiously that "financial stability discourses set upon Pacific and Caribbean OFCs as despised collectivities" (5). Substantively, the priority of the TCC is to deepen the processes of global capital accumulation; therefore, his fanciful notion of "despised collectivities" reinforces his state-centric notions that incongruously juxtapose centre against periphery, without enriching our understanding of the deepening processes of global capital accumulation and deterritorialization.

American financial dominance lubricates the wheels of hegemony, which Panitch and Gindin (2012) view as the American empire. OFCs were created to expand the circuits of TFC with TNS forces, strengthening the juridical basis of the relationship between states and TFC. Marshall argues that "finance-capital" is "undermining national sovereignty and scope for domestic policy intervention" (2007, 5). It is due to the role of the sovereign state, which is an expression of class power and relations, that the building of the "single global economy" continues apace, given that those states with a capacity to exercise "effective sovereignty" under the "global sovereignty regime" are most deliberate about narrowing the scope for any state to subordinate financial capital to domestic policy dictates (Agnew 2009).

Conclusion

The reality is that TCC forces, regardless of their specializations, are already deeply integrated into TFC, and people as workers, homeowners, pensioners, consumers and borrowers are closely tied to and dependent on the capitalist financial process

(Albo, Gindin and Panitch 2010). Marshall suggests that capitalism and sovereignty are essential for guaranteeing self-determination, which he conflates with democracy, a claim that is theoretically and empirically unsound, given that capitalism limits the field for the exercise of sovereign autonomy, and capitalism and state sovereignty collectively undermine the pursuit of effective self-determination (Holloway 2002; Agnew 2009; Gullì 2010). Marshall's contribution, which fixates on the logic of nation building, does little to clarify how we think about sovereignty, citizenship and national belonging in a globalizing, deterritorializing world.

There is hardly anything that is neutral or innocent about the scientific and technological revolution, as all areas of knowledge production are subject to the norms and imperatives of the market and profitability. Politics, the political process and elections, how political parties and labour organizations reproduce themselves, education, information production and circulation, research and development, banking, finance, credit, food production and consumption, tax policy, trade and trade agreements, the production of scientific and technological knowledge – practically everything under capitalism is subject to the rules of commoditization and profitability. The power of capital, which includes the power of money and how money's ability to render social relations opaque, determines and controls what is produced, what is made public and what is considered public or private. The commoditization of everything extends to the human body and is subject to capitalist determination, given the primacy of production for private accumulation and the inevitability of alienation where private interests trounce social needs. Productive labour dominates creative labour: this is the real meaning of the subsumption of labour and humanity under capital.

Notes

1. Agence France-Presse reported that the International Monetary Fund "set off shockwaves . . . in Washington by suggesting countries fight deficits by raising taxes" ("Tax the Rich? The IMF Sparks a Mini Revolution", 13 October 2013). The International Monetary Fund calls for taxing the rich and better targeting the multinationals. However, it maintains the neo-liberal strategy of cutting public (social) spending, slashing taxes and keeping the value-added tax that affects the broad mass of working-class people disproportionately.
2. Alan Pyke states that of "companies listed on the S&P 500 almost one in nine paid an effective tax rate of zero per cent – or even lower – over the past year" – in other words, "57 separate companies" that include the likes of "Verizon and News Corp and lesser-known corporate giants like the data storage manufacturer Seagate (market value $15.9 billion) and Public Storage (market value $29.5 billion)" (2013, 1).
3. See Jahn 1998 for a critique of "critical theory" of international relations.

References

Agnew, John. 2005. *Hegemony: The New Shape of Global Power*. Philadelphia: Temple University Press.

———. 2009. *Globalization and Sovereignty*. Lanham, MD: Rowman and Littlefield.

Albo, Greg, Sam Gindin and Leo Panitch. 2010. *In and Out of Crisis: Global Financial Meltdown and Left Alternatives*. Oakland, CA: PM Press.

Barkawi, Tarak, and Mark Laffey. 1999. "The Imperial Peace: Democracy, Force and Globalization". *European Journal of International Relations* 5 (4): 403–34.

Bilgin, Pinar, and Adam Morton. 2002. "Historicizing Representations of 'Failed States': Beyond the Cold-War Annexation of the Social Sciences?" *Third World Quarterly* 23 (1): 55–80.

Blackburn, Robin. 2008. *The Overthrow of Colonial Slavery, 1776–1848*. London: Verso.

Bolland, Nigel. 2012. "The Barbados Labour Rebellion, 1937, in a Comparative, Caribbean Perspective". Elsa Goveia Memorial Lecture presented at the University of the West Indies, Cave Hill. 25 April.

Braveboy-Wagner, Jacqueline. 1989. *The Caribbean in World Affairs: The Foreign Policies of the English-Speaking States*. Boulder: Westview.

Brewster, Havelock. 2003. "CARICOM: From Community to Single Market and Economy". In *Governance in the Age of Globalization: Caribbean Perspectives*, edited by Kenneth Hall and Denis Benn, 499–508. Kingston: Ian Randle.

Burchill, Scott. 2005. "Liberalism". In *Theories of International Relations*, Scott Burchill, Andrew Linklater, Richard Devetak, Jack Donnelly, Matthew Paterson, Christian Reus-Smit and Jacqui True, 55–83. New York: Palgrave Macmillan.

Burke, Anthony. 2007. *Beyond Security, Ethics and Violence: War against the Other*. New York: Routledge.

Byron, Jessica. 2003. "Rethinking International Relations: Changing Paradigms or More of the Same? A Caribbean Small State Perspective". In *Governance in the Age of Globalisation: Caribbean Perspectives*, edited by Denis Benn and Kenneth Hall, 63–82. Kingston: Ian Randle.

Cabranes, José A. 1979. *Citizenship and the American Empire: Notes on the Legislative History of the United States Citizenship of Puerto Ricans*. New Haven: Yale University Press.

Devetak, Richard. 2005. "Critical Theory". In *Theories of International Relations*, Scott Burchill, Andrew Linklater, Richard Devetak, Jack Donnelly, Matthew Paterson, Christian Reus-Smit and Jacqui True, 137–60. New York: Palgrave Macmillan.

DuRand, Cliff. 2013. "NAFTA on Steroids: The TransPacific Partnership and Global Neoliberalism". *Truthout*. 19 August, 1–6.

Elden, Stuart. 2009. *Terror and Territory: The Spatial Extent of Sovereignty*. Minneapolis: University of Minnesota Press.

Fischer, Sybille. 2004. *Modernity Disavowed: Haiti and the Cultures of Slavery in the Age of Revolution*. Durham: Duke University Press.

Gill, Stephen. 2003. *Power and Resistance in the New World Order*. New York: Palgrave Macmillan.

Girvan, Norman. 2008. "Implications of the Cariforum-EC EPA". *Norman Girvan* (blog), 26 January. http://www.normangirvan.info/implications-of-cariforum-ec-epa-norman-girvan/.

Griffin, Clifford. 1997. *Democracy and Neoliberalism in the Developing World: Lessons from the Anglophone Caribbean*. Aldershot, UK: Ashgate.

Griffith, Ivelaw, ed. 2004a. *Caribbean Security in the Age of Terror: Challenge and Change*. Kingston: Ian Randle.

———. 2004b. "Introduction: Understanding Reality, Interpreting Change". In *Caribbean Security in the Age of Terror: Challenge and Change*, edited by Ivelaw Griffith, 1–6. Kingston: Ian Randle.

———. 2004c. "Understanding Caribbean Security: Back to Basics and Building Blocks". *Social and Economic Studies* 53 (1): 1–33.

Gullì, Bruno. 2010. *Earthly Plenitudes: A Study on Sovereignty and Labor*. Philadelphia: Temple University Press.

Harvey, David. 2003. *The New Imperialism*. New York: Oxford University Press.

Holloway, John. 2002. *Change the World without Taking Power: The Meaning of Revolution Today*. London: Polity.

Jackson, Robert, and Georg Sørensen. 2003. *Introduction to International Relations: Theories and Approaches*. New York: Oxford University Press.

Jahn, Beate. 1998. "One Step Forward, Two Steps Back: Critical Theory as the Latest Edition of Liberal Idealism". *Millennium Journal of International Studies* 27 (3): 613–41.

———. 2000. *The Cultural Construction of International Relations: The Invention of the State of Nature*. New York: Palgrave Macmillan.

Jessop, David. 2013. "Many Nations Are Lost, Leaderless and Haemorrhaging Their Brightest Young People". *Stabroek News*, 29 September. http://www.stabroeknews.com/2013/features/09/29/many-nations-are-lost-leaderless-and-haemorrhaging-their-brightest-young-people/.

Joseph, Tennyson. 2012. "Towards a New Democracy and a New Independence: A Program for a Second Independence Revolution". Paper presented to a Common Sense Convois at the Lloyd Best Institute of the West Indies, Scarborough, Tobago, 24 March.

Kantorowicz, Ernst. 1957. *The King's Two Bodies: A Study in Medieval Political Theology*. Princeton: Princeton University Press.

Layne, Christopher. 2006. *American Grand Strategy from 1940 to the Present*. Ithaca: Cornell University Press.

Lebowitz, Michael. 2003. *Beyond Capital: Marx's Political Economy of the Working Class*. 2nd ed. New York: Palgrave Macmillan.

Lewis, Linden. 2013. "Introduction". In *Caribbean Sovereignty, Development and Democracy in an Age of Globalization*, edited by Linden Lewis, 1–16. New York: Routledge.

Lewis, Vaughan. 2003. "Regional Integration Institutional Arrangements: Underlying Assumptions and Contemporary Appropriateness". In *Governance in the Age of Globalization: Caribbean Perspectives*, edited by Denis Benn and Kenneth Hall, 508–26. Kingston: Ian Randle.

Losurdo, Domenico. 2011. *Liberalism: A Counter History*. London: Verso.

Maingot, Anthony. 1994. *The United States and the Caribbean: Challenges of an Asymmetrical Relationship*. Boulder: Westview.

———. 1997. "Sovereignty versus the Security Paradox in the Caribbean." In *Cuba and the Caribbean: Regional Issues and Trends in the Post–Cold War Era*, 89–107. Wilmington, DE: SR Books.

Maingot, Anthony, and Wilfredo Lozano. 2005. *The United States and the Caribbean: Transforming Hegemony and Sovereignty*. New York: Routledge.

Marshall, Don D. 2007. "An Elephant in the Room: Reviewing Debates on Financial Globalization and the Missing Offshore Financial Centre Phenomenon". Sir Arthur Institute of Social and Economic Research, University of the West Indies, Cave Hill.

Marx, Karl. 1981a. *Capital*. Vol. 3. New York: Vintage.

———. 1981b. *Theories of Surplus Value*. Part 1. Moscow: Foreign Languages Publishing House.

Mathiason, Nick. 2012. "The World's Super-Rich Have Stashed $21 Trillion in Offshore Accounts". http://www.juancole.com/2012/07/the-worlds-super-rich-have-stashed-21-trillion-in-offshore-accounts-mathiason.html. 26 July.

Mawby, Spencer. 2012. *Ordering Independence: The End of Empire in the Anglophone Caribbean, 1947–1969*. Basingstoke, UK: Palgrave Macmillan.

Morgenthau, Hans. 1985. *Politics among Nations*. 6th ed. New York: Alfred Knopf.

Neocleous, Mark. 2008. *Critique of Security*. Montreal: McGill-Queen's University Press.

Nurse, Keith. 2005. "Triadic Competition and the Periphery: The Case of the Transatlantic 'Banana Wars'". In *Allies as Rivals: The US, Europe, and Japan in a Changing World-System*, edited by Faruk Tabak, 165–86. New York: Paradigm.

Panitch, Leo, and Sam Gindin. 2012. *The Making of Global Capitalism: The Political Economy of American Empire*. London: Verso.

Pyke, Alan. 2013. "Over 10 Percent of America's Largest Companies Pay Zero Percent Tax Rates". www.thinkprogress.org, 27 October.

Rengger, N.J. 2000. *International Relations, Political Theory and the Problem of Order*. London: Routledge.

Reuten, Geert, and Michael Williams. 1989. *Value-Form and the State: The Tendencies of Accumulation and the Determination of Economic Policy in Capitalist Society*. London: Routledge.

Robinson, William I. 2004. *A Theory of Global Capitalism*. Baltimore: Johns Hopkins University Press.

Rosenberg, Justin. 1994. *The Empire of Civil Society: A Critique of the Realist Theory of International Relations*. London: Verso.

———. 2000. *The Follies of Globalisation Theory: Polemical Essays*. London: Verso.

Santner, Eric. 2011. *The Royal Remains: The People's Two Bodies and the Endgame of Sovereignty*. Chicago: University of Chicago Press.

Teschke, Benno, and Christian Heine. 2002. "The Dialectic of Globalization: A Critique of Social Constructivism". In *Historical Materialism and Globalization*, edited by Mark Rupert and Hazel Smith, 165–88. London: Routledge.

Thirlwall, A.P. 2013. *Economic Growth in an Open Developing Economy: The Role of Structure and Demand*. Cheltenham: Edward Elgar.

Thorburn, Diana. 2000. "Feminism Meets International Relations". *SAIS Review* 20 (2): 1–10.

Tilly, Charles. 1985. "War Making and State Making as Organized Crime". In *Bringing the State Back In*, edited by Peter B. Evans, Dietrich Rueschemeyer and Theda Skocpol, 169–91. New York: Cambridge University Press.

Van der Pijl, Kees. 2002. "Historical Materialism and the Emancipation of Labour". In *Historical Materialism and Globalization*, edited by Mark Rupert and Hazel Smith, 129–46. London: Routledge.

Wood, Ellen Meiksins. 1995. *Capitalism against Democracy.* Cambridge: Cambridge University Press.

World Bank. 1997. *World Development Report: The State in a Changing World.* Washington, DC: World Bank.

Zelikow, Philip. 2003. "The Transformation of National Security". *The National Interest* (Spring): 17–28.

2 State Sovereignty, Body Politic, Neo-Patriarchy and Citizenship in the Caribbean

Beyond Epistemological Territorialism and Sovereignty Myths

Hilbourne A. Watson

In this chapter I discuss state sovereignty, forms assumed by the body politic in historical perspective, patriarchy and neo-patriarchy, and citizenship with reference to the Commonwealth Caribbean in the context of capitalist globalization. My aim is to contribute to a theory of global capitalism with a critique of mainstream (by which I mean state-centric) international relations theory, which I view as part of the problem arising from what John Agnew labels "epistemological territorialism" based on "geographical determinism" (Agnew 2009). I argue that modern patriarchy and neo-patriarchy are best theorized within the context of capitalist social relations, and that patriarchy is very important in reproducing male supremacy and shaping the contours of gender relations via the state and civil society. I emphasize that patriarchy operates subtly in and through the body politic, private property, the labour and production process of the capitalist economy, education, the media and family and household units in ways that cause exploitation and oppression to seem natural. I argue further that the anti-colonial struggles that were waged for self-determination and sovereign autonomy in the British West Indies (BWI) were substantively neither anti-British nor anti-capitalist given the weight of liberal notions of freedom, liberty, democracy, statehood, rights and citizenship in the process and outcomes of those struggles. The mainstream discourse of self-determination and sovereignty that prevails in the Commonwealth Caribbean introduces and perpetuates a false dichotomy between the colonial order and the resultant sovereign states (Mawby 2012).

I focus on the two cases of Barbados and Cuba. For Barbados, I discuss colonialism, decolonization and sovereignty, accounting for the sources and development of the idea of Barbadian exceptionalism in order to explain the context in which the social forces that exercise state power, along with civil society, respond to immigration from other Caribbean countries. I examine how the formation of the Barbadian self-image during colonialism and after independence was nurtured by the myth of an intellectual and cultural superiority that Barbadians assign to themselves over other Caribbean people. I emphasize that the self-image of Barbadian exceptionalism survives in modified form in Barbados as a sovereign constitutional monarchy, with Her Majesty Queen Elizabeth II as head of state. I argue that the ideology of Barbadian exceptionalism conditions the popular outlook on sovereignty and functions as a part of the "capitalist social control formation" (Perry 2010) that resonates with the ideology of British racial Anglo-Saxonism, which operates in subterranean ways in Barbadian cultural life, reinforcing populist illusions – sovereignty myths, freedom, democracy and equality – through which loyalty to the postcolonial state is mediated.

My second case deals with US designs for controlling and "harvesting" Cuba, beginning in the early nineteenth century.[1] The Cuban case highlights the historically contingent nature of, and limits to, US sovereignty and hegemony, as reflected through the costly anti-imperialist resistance mounted by the Cuban Revolution since 1959. In their diplomatic relations with Cuba since the early 1970s, Commonwealth Caribbean states did not violate the norms of the US-led Cold War project. Rather, they exploited opportunities that surfaced in the world, in exercising juridical sovereignty when the United States sought rapprochement with the People's Republic of China, as an integral part of restructuring the geopolitical foundation of the post-war international order. I argue that it is not the existence of juridical sovereignty that is at issue; rather it is the nature of the social relations of which sovereignty is an integral part and sovereignty's relationship with capitalism, territory and power that must be re-examined to comprehend the nature and limits of sovereign autonomy in a deterritorializing world.

I stress that forms of domination, inequality, insecurity, fear and alienation are inevitable where production is organized for private capital accumulation, which is a global process. Sovereign states institutionalize the right to exploit, which involves forcing labour to produce capital, which is its opposite, as the precondition for labour's social reproduction. Exploitation is covered over in the tracks of laws of capitalist private property in ways that make it seem natural given that rights, freedom, justice, equality and democracy in capitalist societies are largely abstract or deontological. Under liberal democracy economic exploitation assumes the fantastic appearance of a process through which workers naturally alienate their labour energy – their labour power – in producing commodities. Specifically, under capitalism social relations between humans assume the form of technical relations between things given the role money plays in mediating production, exchange and accumulation. Liberal thought and capitalism fragment historical forms and practices, engendering the separation of economics from politics, the individual from society, the state from the market and civil society, and the alienation of power from its social mooring. In the process, most social phenomena are equated to naturally evolved processes, such that any struggle for popular power tends to be viewed as violating the laws of nature and the absolute limits of the possible. The effect is to render history empty or emptiable (Rosenberg 2000; Jahn 2000).

I also question the commonly held notion that sovereign statehood rests substantively in "the people" as the body politic or fount of popular power. I draw attention to contradictions between sovereignty and self-determination on the grounds that sovereignty resides in the state, which is separated from the people and superimposed on society like an alien power, and capitalism and capital accumulation are integral parts of a global process. I also contest the claim that the state and people form a harmonious, unitary democratic structure – a claim that masks oppression, exploitation and the alienation of the state from civil society. In class societies the state-society relationship is necessarily mediated by force and domination. I therefore insist that the sovereign state is best theorized as part of the problem of world order rather than its definitive solution.

Demystifying the Body Politic: From the State of Nature to Modern Sovereignty

In his explanation of the historical forms assumed by the body politic and state sovereignty John Agnew exposes a pervasive common sense that popularizes certain myths about sovereignty and citizenship, including the belief that sovereignty underwrites "popular self-rule" without which "democratic politics . . . is impossible" (Agnew 2009, 48). One strongly subscribed-to myth about the state, power, sovereignty and citizenship is that political power is a fixed quantity over which states are forced to compete in the arena of interstate relations. John Holloway (2002) identifies two dimensions of power: on the one hand, negative power – "potestas" – referring to control, co-optation, exploitation and domination; on the other, a positive power – "potentia" – which refers to the ability and capacity to resist, act, cooperate and give voluntary assent in the direction of emancipation from exploitation and oppression. States are built on potestas, which Agnew calls "rigid territorial conception[s] of the spatial extent in which power operates", and involve a "dyadic (person-person, person-state, and state-state) definition of the nature of power relationships" (2005, 40). Potestas refers to "power as solely a quantitative capacity of self-evident and pre-existing entities: the ability of a person or a state to direct others or expand its range of influence despite resistance" (40). Potestas privileges a territorial solution to supposedly primordial motives or needs that Hobbesian social-contract theorists trace to a fictive state of nature (see Jahn 2000; Williams 2006).

Proponents of potestas introduce a "homology . . . between individual persons and states" in which "states are treated as if they are the ontological and moral equivalents to individual persons" (Agnew 2005, 40). The positivist or mainstream realist and liberal discourse of sovereignty and citizenship found in the scholarship produced by academics in the Commonwealth Caribbean objectifies the state, equates it to territory and assumes that sovereign states possess fixed borders that necessitate arming themselves to counteract anarchy and chaos that threaten from the outside, given the absence of global sovereign power to maintain world order (Jahn 2000; Osiander 2001). The habit of fixing sovereignty within territorial borders rests on the assumption of an irreconcilable contradiction between sovereignty and anarchy, its other. Sovereignty fails the test of self-recognition, due to a rejection or alienation of part of itself. The so-called sovereign self is forced to abide in the shadow of the fear and insecurity it creates, which makes sovereignty part of the problem of world order. The challenge is to look beyond the sovereign state for solutions to problems and challenges humans face, with a view to pursuing human emancipation as a desirable and realistic goal.

Making autonomy, security, self-determination and freedom from external domination dependent on a sovereign power renders neo-Hobbesian solutions to the state-of-nature myth plausible and fosters the belief that the sovereign state represents the highest form of subjectivity with reference to citizenship, national belonging, loyalty and security (Neocleous 2008; Gullì 2010). When we foreground self-determination in communitarian or nationalist ideology, we privilege difference in ways that help to set the world at variance with itself. It is this romantic liberal notion that treats difference as the decisive and unalterable determinant of our individual subjectivity and rejects the sociality of our human subjectivity (Stepan 1982) to our disadvantage.

Drawing attention to contradictions associated with the nationalization of society, Adrian Oldfield insightfully argues that living as a citizen might make it difficult to "treat everyone like a human being" (1990, 8), and William Connolly notes that the "territorial/security state forms the space of democratic liberation and imprisonment" (1991, 476). With modernity and the national state, we are forced to become national persons and citizens and to choose one form of exclusion that constrains the quest for our universal humanity – a valid concept that rests on the idea that "humanity . . . is the source of durable political legitimacy" (Battersby and Siracusa 2009, 147). For the idea of "personhood" as "a morally objective fact" (Mills 2010) to matter, it must take us beyond the nationalist exclusions based on communitarian prejudices and insecurities as ends in themselves. Secular sovereign statehood conjures up images of an organic – antecedent and unencumbered – body politic in the form of an all-seeing, hyper-patriarchal God who is invented and made to represent the ultimate and eternal source of truth, order, security, authority and justice – the "sovereign exception" – the absolute ideological product of alienation.

Beate Jahn persuasively argues that the state of nature and cultural difference are built into the "fundamental theoretical fabric of mainstream International Relations theory" (2000, 29) – further evidence of alienation that makes the full and complete maturation and development of biological man the prerequisite for human cultural progress. This notion ignores the fact that the development of nature and culture is a dialectically given, mutually constitutive process. To embrace the false nature-culture dichotomy requires that we naturalize human culture and historicize nature, make culture a problem for nature to solve and equate with organic forces sovereignty, the state, power, war and other human inventions. The reality is that "culture . . . is not the cause of politics but its framework and meaning" (15, 147).

Ernst Kantorowicz (1957, 7) hints at this problem when he connects the study of sovereignty to the political theology of the body politic. He says:

> For the king in him has two bodies . . . a Body natural, and a Body politic. His body natural . . . is a body mortal, subject to all infirmaries that come by Nature or Accident, to the imbecility of infancy or old age. . . . But his body politic is a body that cannot be seen or handled, consisting of a policy and government, and constituted for the Director of the People . . . and this body is utterly devoid of Infancy, and old Age, and other natural Defects and Imbecilities, which the body natural is subject to.

The expression "The King is dead. Long live the King!" resonates with Kantorowicz's two concepts of the body politic. Kantorowicz is aware that the objectification of the body politic appears in the mystical sovereign that is miraculously "constituted for the Director of the People" (ibid.) who builds human submissiveness into the process of mediation.

Mikhail Bakhtin points out that the "material bodily principle is contained not in the biological individual, not in the bourgeois ego, but in the people . . . who are continually growing and renewed" (1965, 19) as an abstract (deontological) category. Agnew draws attention to the power of ideology in warning us against underestimating "the appeal of the idea of sovereignty as resting on popular-territorialized rule" (2009, 48), and Eric Santner emphasizes that sovereignty was invented and assigned a mystical form and quality that allows the body politic to acquire the "properties if not exactly of eternal life, then those of the undead . . . representing eternity in the space of secular, political life" (2011, 41; see also Maritain 1951, 11).

The political directorates in Caribbean class societies perpetuate the myth that sovereignty resides in the people, against evidence that it is a defining property of the state, which is the dominant form of the body politic. It has become more difficult for greater numbers of people in Caribbean societies – where the concentration of wealth, property and economic power in few hands continues unabated – to obtain social goods and experience "citizen security" (UNDP 2012, v). Caribbean political leaders invoke the neo-theological body politic (to which Kantorowicz alludes) when they appeal to romantic notions of an irreducible, non-negotiable sovereignty in order to shift attention away from their failed capital accumulation strategies and programmes (Watson 2007).

Jahn argues that we are bound to "always fail" when we "attempt to . . . determine practical goals by . . . inventing a timeless and spaceless 'idea of freedom as a purely interior reality, which is . . . typical of the idealist mentality'" (1998, 623). Etienne Balibar insists that no "nation possesses an ethnic base naturally, but as social formations are nationalized, the populations included within them, divided up among them or dominated by them, are ethnicized – that is, represented in the past or in the future as if they formed a natural community" (quoted in Sand 2009, 23). Eric Hobsbawm exposes the ideological basis for this reasoning when he reiterates that reading history backwards through what Balibar calls "retrospective illusions of the national personality" (Balibar 1991) fuels the romantic nationalist preoccupation that each nation is a distinct, self-contained people with a unique ancestral history of lineage, geography, linguistic univocality and other bearers of symbolic values that frame "the primordial foundations of national culture and the matrices of the national mind" (Hobsbawm 1992, 54).

The state and nation share the same grand founding myths in domination and blood sacrifice, with those exercising state power asserting the "right" to speak in the name of the nation – the people. The "right to kill" is a tenet of the state and ruling class that is draped in nationalist ideology (Koenigsberg 2009).

Cultural differences are manufactured as part of communitarian projects in contrast with commensurabilities, which are more important in highlighting the dialectical relationship between place and space that locates the "geography of political power – and thus sovereignty" beyond the "state territory as the singular unit of political account" (Agnew 2009, 39). Agnew says:

> Rather than emerging in response to absolute antagonism between primordial or essentialized groups, antagonism, like the groups to which it refers . . . had to be made. Beyond the Platonic ideal of the body politic, . . . sovereignty . . . relies for its apparent veracity on the commonsense notion that in the modern world there is a clear "inside" and "outside" to society . . . defined by the territorial nation to which every state has become conjoined. . . . This is the myth of the nation-hyphen-state. (60)

Myth thus helps to render domination, exclusion and marginalization plausible, in effect reinforcing order based on domination.

Hannah Arendt argues that "no political system which is based on parliamentary democracy can really be democratic and produce 'proper' citizens" (quoted in Yuval-Davis 2011, 46; see Oldfield 1990, 8). Arendt recognizes that parliamentary democracy as representative government operates like a canal through which to regulate the flow of the political energies and social demands arising from the heterogeneous working class. This is where the effect of liberal ideology appears as the separation of politics from economics, the state from civil society, and individuals from society and from themselves, resulting in the fragmentation and alienation of the subject and giving rise to alienated forms of identity politics. The bourgeois liberal democratic strategy is organized to prevent the "disalienation of power" (Wood 1995) from becoming a reality. The separation of politics from economics that is reflected in and through market anarchy and economic compulsion requires state coercion to maintain the capitalist organization of society, which makes a farce of individual autonomy and social self-determination (Holloway 2005).

Carl Schmitt says, "It is the sovereign who rules when the standard operation of the law must be suspended" (quoted in Elden 2009, 56). Giorgio Agamben provides an insight into Schmitt's notion of the "state of exception" (Agamben 2005, 14), arguing that it pertains to "an unprecedented generalization of the paradigm of security as the normal technique of government" (14; see Prozorov 2010, 125). Stuart Elden says that Agamben finds Western democracies exploit the "state of exception" by expanding and deepening the paradigm of security "as the normal technique of government" (Elden 2009, 55, 56). Schmitt builds his "key definition of sovereignty" on the "state of exception" (55, 56; see Agamben 2005, 14; Santner 2011, 151–52, 160–61 passim; Schmitt [1932] 1996, 1; Neocleous 2008). Schmitt's political theory foregrounds state sovereignty in the "enmity that humanity inherited from the Fall" of man according to the biblical ideology, emphasizing sovereignty in a pre-social, mystical, theology-based body politic – essentially a form of "politics beyond the political" (quoted in Agnew 2009, 54, 55). Slavoj Žižek contradicts Schmitt's logic, positing that substantive freedom is impossible without "a ground floor" that counts as its "zero". Žižek insists that freedom requires a social content, which means that "before . . . decisions or choices are made – there has to be a ground of tradition . . . [that] cannot be counted". He further argues – correctly – against beginning "directly with self-legislated freedom" that erases the history of struggles through which the zero floor of freedom was built (Žižek 2012, 2).

Santner states: "Because for human beings the enjoyment of life and good is always enjoined with processes and procedures of symbolic entitlement or investiture, the very value of human life . . . is subject to enormous fluctuations." Santner discusses how "early modern and modern societies have attempted to organize, manage and administer such fluctuations by means of the logic of sovereignty, according to which . . . a master 'signifier' comes to represent the subject for all other signifiers, all other bearers of symbolic value" (2011, xx). Santner adds that because

> this logic of representation can never absolve itself of its own ultimate groundlessness – its lack of an anchoring point in the real – the normative pressures it generates for its

> members . . . are always in excess of what could ever be satisfied. Among the crucial tasks of the . . . sovereign is to take up not the slack but rather this excess of the pressure produced by the very logic of sovereignty. (xx–xxi)

The fact that sovereignty fails to offer ways to resolve the contradictions that it was invented to fix necessitates abandoning organic notions of sovereignty that leave unresolved those problems of the body politic that are beholden to patriarchy and class rule.

From Classical Patriarchy to Neo-Patriarchy

Patriarchy, a male-dominated human invention, operates in and through the sovereign state and civil society, connecting religion, power, statehood, nationalism, domination and other areas of the "capitalist social control formation" (Perry 2010), encouraging and sanctioning patriotic loyalty to the state and nation through the religious veils of obfuscation, mysticism and obscurantism. Loyalty to the modern state and nation necessitates the production of malleable and predictable subjects – citizens, whose bodies are sources of labour supplies for capital to facilitate commodity production for the ends of capital accumulation. Loyalty to the state thus plays a role in forging national identity and a sense of belonging to a collectivity in ways that blur the state's internal contradictions. Such loyalty cannot produce substantive equality among citizens, given the ways class exploitation, gender and ethnic oppression, political domination and discrimination and alienation are built into the political economy based on production for private accumulation.

David Richards argues that "patriarchy exercises a controlling power . . . over our conceptions of authority both in religion and in law" and "describes an order of living that elevates fathers, separating fathers from sons . . . and men from women . . . placing both children and women under a father's authority" (2010, 4). Richards elaborates that "patriarchy . . . in placing fathers in this role . . . [also] divides . . . women from women and girls. Patriarchy . . . is an unjust burden on men as well as on women. It divides both from their common humanity and proscribes a structure of authority that expresses their common humanity" (4, 5). Richards traces patriarchy's "later influence in the religion, art, psychology and politics of Western culture including its distortion of democratic constitutionalism" back to a "traumatic loss in intimate life that Christianity absorbed from Roman patriarchal and related practices" (5, 6). Modern patriarchy typically resists, silences and marginalizes the voices and experiences of women ("half of humanity", as Richards points out) who "resist its demands", while flouting the very principle of a "democratic ethics and politics, equal respect for all" (8). Richards emphasizes that when fundamentalism pervades religion and law, the "contradiction between patriarchy and democracy is . . . dismissed – because our religion has so uncritically structured its authority in terms of a patriarchal priesthood and a supporting patriarchal psychology that we . . . regard patriarchy as natural, indeed as God's law" (8).

Gerda Lerner contends that patriarchy does not serve "the needs of men or women and in its inextricable linkage to militarism, hierarchy, and racism it threatens the very existence of life on earth" (1986, 228–29). Cornelius Castoriadis points out that with "the capitalist technique and . . . organization of production, the patriarchal family and the modern bureaucracy have, each in their turn, appeared as the incarnation of an unquestionable 'instrumental' or substantive rationality" (1991, 69). Mark Neocleous notes that patriarchy and patriotism shape our sense of "national identity: its origins, construction, myths and practices", and he asks, "if national identity is integrally linked with the imagination and . . . one of the things about the imagination is that it plays around with fears, dangers and insecurities, then what if the nation is imagined as insecure . . . [and] then what does this tell us about the links between security and identity – between an imagined national identity and an imagined national (in)security?" (2008, 107, 108) The business of fabricating "national security goes hand in hand with the fabrication of national identity, and vice versa" (108). Loyalty to the state operates as a "key political technology for simultaneously gauging identity and reaffirming security" and submissiveness to authority (107, 108; see Agnew 2009, 53; Elden 2009, 33–61 passim).

Gerda Lerner observes that the "sexuality of women consisting of their sexual and . . . reproductive capacities and services, was commodified even prior to the creation of Western civilization. . . . Men as a group had rights in women that women did not have in men" (1986, 212). The "commodification of women – bride price, sale price and children – was appropriated by men. It may very well represent the first accumulation of private property" (213). The "sexual exploitation of lower-class women by upper-class men can be shown in antiquity, feudalism, in the bourgeois households in nineteenth- and twentieth-century Europe, in the complex sex/race relations between women of the colonized countries and their male colonizers – it is ubiquitous and pervasive. For women, sexual exploitation is the very mark of class exploitation" (214–15). Lerner rejects the claim that women are victims of a natural male aggression, repudiates patriarchy and calls for a revolutionary break with tradition, aware that "revolutionary thought has always been based on upgrading the experience of the oppressed" (26–27, 220, 226, 227, 299). Domenico Losurdo (2011) reminds us that democratic struggles have consistently begun from below.

Framing Neo-Patriarchy

The concept of neo-patriarchy is relevant. Patriarchy is historical and has shifted according to the form of the body politic. It is dynamic and necessarily flexible and adaptable as a ruling-class ideology and strategy for social control that helps to regulate gender relations generally and especially for the production of bodies for capital. A history of religious modernization and secularization in especially the West, where the modern Caribbean is grounded, has been important in shaping the dialectic of patriarchy. Transitions in the forms assumed by the body politic, with "the people" moving to the centre of bourgeois (liberal) democracy without social content, are important also in the restructuring of patriarchy. The feminization of areas of capitalist production, which involves the proletarianization of countless female labourers around the world, signals the contradictory ways the process of global capitalist integration is unfolding. The increasing visibility and participation of growing numbers of women in the labour force, politics, trade union politics, activist community politics, the state, education, business and the larger arena of struggles for change in diverse areas of social and political life, as well as women's involvement in transnational political processes, demand a rethinking of conventional notions of patriarchy. This process of change does not in any way limit the exploitation of female labour, even where provisions have been institutionalized to recognize and protect formal rights. The reality, however, is that rights reflect the contradictions in social reality. Large numbers of women continue to feel the brunt of the violence, insecurity and dehumanization associated with capitalist globalization.

Capitalist neo-patriarchy is not benevolent, as can be seen from the intensification of structural (state) and non-state violence in the moment of globalization. Accumulation by dispossession in the form of land grabbing and outright war, such as the US war on Iraq, make more of the world available to capital and strengthen transnational capitalist power. The US global war on terror and its drone wars make structural violence seem normal, with neo-patriarchy playing a central ideological role on behalf of hegemony. As refugees, women and girls become easy targets for rape, sex slavery and human trafficking, and the modern global slave trade contributes innumerable female bodies that help to bolster primitive accumulation and capitalist expansion. When the bodies of a "racially subordinate and oppressed sector within the exploited class [that] occupies the lowest rungs of the particular economy and society within a racially or ethnically stratified working class" (W.I. Robinson 2014, 8) become expendable, because their labour power or productive capacity is made superfluous by a combination of capitalist technological change and state policy, the spectre of ethnic or racial cleansing and genocide begins to loom large. This was the case for Native Americans and is now the situation facing "indigenous groups in Amazonia" (9), Palestinians and growing segments of the African American population today, with lessons coming from Ferguson, Missouri. Increasingly, females bear a disproportionate share of the violence and dehumanization associated with capitalist political economy, which reinforces neo-patriarchy and expands the cycle of global capital accumulation. Neo-patriarchy is a key ideological strut for anchoring property rights and class inequality in bourgeois property relations. Equal rights for females under the law are built into this foundation of exploitation and gender oppression. Any attempt to demystify neo-patriarchy must take into consideration the indisputable fact that where production and exchange are organized on the basis of the law of value – labour exploitation (necessity) across the gender spectrum – for the ends of private capital accumulation, alienation is inevitable and inescapable. More specifically, where this situation is coordinated by the domination and repression that are integral to the making and reproduction of the modern sovereign state, nation and capital for which the law is the key rationalizing support, it is impossible for the law to negate inequality and gender violence, given the inescapable opposition between capital and labour: it is not accidental that most rights under capitalism are largely deontological.

Writing with the Middle East in mind, Hisham Sharabi says, "Neopatriarchy simultaneously involves the disintegration of patriarchal relations and the emergence of modern relations, and the contradictions inherent in neopatriarchy are similar to those present in capitalism with both systems forming a final phase in an historical continuum" (1988, 159). Capitalism provides the material and economic base of neo-patriarchy, and sovereignty and self-determination under capitalism render substantive self-determination illusory. Sharabi imagines solving the problem of neo-patriarchy through the "struggle for human rights, political freedom, and change in the social structure" (159); however, the rights and freedoms Sharabi refers to presuppose the right to exploit and have to be understood in relation to the fundamental capitalist process with contradictions in the form of of overproduction, social polarization, legitimation and sustainability (W.I. Robinson 2004). It is a sign of romantic thinking to suggest that it could be possible to overcome neo-patriarchy and the constraints from nationalism, sovereignty and territorial citizenship without transcending capitalism – the material base for the sovereign state, which is founded on domination and exclusion.

Sharabi's concept of neo-patriarchy is also hampered by the state-centric terms he employs – such as "core-periphery", "an underdeveloped bourgeoisie", and "a dependent capitalist mode of production" (1988, 5–6) – that resonate with dependency analysis. Neo-patriarchy helps to regulate the conditions in which male and female workers are compelled to produce commodities in spatially uneven global production sites, a process that rests on economic compulsion and political coercion.

As the process of global capitalist integration advances, large numbers of females across the world are forced to endure human degradation that mirrors contradictions between the socialization of production and the deepening of the private character of appropriation. Millions of female workers are forced to labour in global market factories for below-subsistence wages in a world where around 3 billion individuals – roughly 45 per cent of humanity – are compelled to subsist on less than the World Bank's estimated poverty line of two US dollars a day, with at least 18 per cent living on less than one dollar a day. Around 955 million people living in affluent societies account for 81 per cent of aggregate global income, while 2,735 million receive 1.2 per cent of aggregate global income. This all stands in dramatic contrast with approximately one thousand billionaires who own more wealth and assets than all the inhabitants of the poorest 145 countries combined. This undeniable face of bourgeois democracy necessitates state repression in the form of the global war on terror and the brutalization of untold numbers whose labour is now rendered superfluous.

David Harvey argues that the "migration of capital to alternative labor sources, and the coerced competitive struggle between different bodily practices and modes of valuation achieved under different historical and cultural conditions, contribute to the uneven geographical valuation of laborers as persons. The manifest effects upon the bodies of laborers who live lives embedded in the circulation of variable capital are powerful indeed" (2005, 109–10). The crisis which inheres in the social relations of production under capitalism intensifies competition between female and male workers for scarce jobs; increasingly all workers are also forced to compete with machines that are designed to reduce the cost of reproducing labour power. Sexual and gender differences are not the cause of differential rates of compensation paid to male and female workers under capitalism; rather, it is the capitalist organization of society that sets the conditions that lead to differential wage rates and compensation between the sexes.

It is necessary to replace ideological gender-based identity politics with a materialist gender politics informed by a "dialectic of totality" and a "pedagogy of totality" (Zavarzadeh 2003, 6) with an awareness of how exploitation conditions forms of social consciousness. Mas'ud Zavarzadeh argues that to change "reality in a sustained way, requires knowing it historically and objectively . . . as a totality in structure and not simply reacting to it as a galaxy of signifiers (as textualists have done); as the working of power in networks of discourses (Foucault), or as a spontaneous reality that is available to us in its full immediacy (as activists have done with eclecticism and sentimentality)" (9). Žižek argues that the "postmodern deconstructionist Left" employs an "anti-materialist" schema as its "critical philosophical response to liberal hegemonism", yielding in the process the "deconstructionist political doxa" for which "the social is the field of structural undecidability . . . forever condemned to non-identity with itself; and 'totalitarianism' is . . . the closure of this undecidability" (2001, 7, 6).

The anti-materialist outlook rests on liberal philosophical individualism that is mired in alienation and dissipates the "fundamental material contradiction of capitalism (the appropriation of products from . . . producers) and . . . becomes preoccupied with the political economy of desire in which socially disembodied conceptions of race, sexuality, gender, money, finance, patriarchy, the state, and the environment . . . surreptitiously banish wage labor as the source of labor and class as the marker of relations of property and exploitation". Class relations express and reflect "the relation of the subject of labor to ownership of the means of production; it is the objective social relations of property, not a story of desire, affect or power" (Zavarzadeh 2003, 8, 9; see Chibber 2013, 283). Stephen Gill argues that one of the structural weaknesses in Michel Foucault's analysis of "epistemological revolution is any sustained analysis of the rise of capital as a social formation, and indeed any attempt to speak of its power either specifically or in general. Missing also is a discussion of historical struggle over the modalities of power and knowledge" (2003, 121). Gill suggests that Foucault's followers talk about the link between power and knowledge through a poststructural theory of power and knowledge, while they largely ignore the "overwhelming evidence of tremendous growth of inequality" (122). The Foucauldian notion of power appeals "mainly to some members of the 'culture of contentment'" (126). In contrast, Gill says, "historical materialism goes much further in an attempt to theorize and to promote collective action to create an alternative form of society. . . . This is why it is necessary to theorize the problem of change in local and global dimensions and to look beyond the currently fragmented forms of opposition to neo-liberal supremacy" (123). Immanuel Wallerstein et al. argue that the "cultural-philosophical critics of various postmodernist persuasions . . . share the same positivist assumptions of capitalism's permanence although not without a big dose of existential despair. Consequently, the cultural postmodernists left themselves with a dislocation of the will to look structural realities in the face" (2013, 6; see Holloway 2005, 179).

Neo-Patriarchy in a Caribbean Context

The United Nations Development Programme (UNDP) publication *Caribbean Human Development Report 2012: Human Development and the Shift to Better Citizen Security* addresses globalization, development and "citizen security" in Latin America and the Caribbean, from the angle of law, order and security.

Violence, crime and other problems and challenges have "social, economic and cultural costs" (UNDP 2012, v) in Latin America and the Caribbean region. This combined area is "home to 8.5 percent of the world's population, yet it concentrates some 27 percent of the world's homicides" (v). These contradictions are indicative of how global capitalism reproduces the reserve army of labour and increases insecurity for the global majority – a salient issue the UNDP report hardly mentions. The fact that the state in Latin American and Caribbean societies employs "short-sighted, mano dura (iron fist)" (v) policies for managing crime, drugs and associated problems – a strategy the UNDP report considers to be largely ineffective and detrimental to the rule of law, democracy, human rights and justice (v) – confirms that one of the state's priorities is to make the world available to and safe for capital by strengthening the state's security apparatuses at the expense of "citizen security".

The "iron fist" model, which is a very violent way to mediate contradictions for mediating capitalism's contradictions, is necessary to protect the right to exploit, which subsumes citizen security under state security in capitalist societies.

Drug production, distribution and trafficking, as well as the growth in use of small arms and light weapons, in human trafficking, in forms of state and non-state violence against persons and property, in challenges to state authority and in the incidence of corruption within the state and civil society compound the myriad problems that are routinely experienced in a growing number of Caribbean societies (Watson 2013). What the UNDP refers to as "citizen security" under the cultural institution of the nation state and the coercive territorial state on which the United Nations was founded compounds the problem of achieving our universal humanity, given also that the United Nations operates in keeping with transnational capitalist class and transnational state priorities, where the United States still holds sway in financial and military terms.

The UNDP understands poverty as a problem to be managed and alleviated but never abolished; however, there is nothing inherent in poverty that makes it a permanent feature of human existence. It is the capitalist economic organization of society based on the right to exploit that necessitates the classification of poverty as "natural". The UNDP report concludes as follows: "For the people of this region, crime, violence and insecurity are profoundly linked in various ways to key development issues such as freedom of choice, equality of opportunity, increased life chances, especially for the most vulnerable, and the greater responsiveness of state institutions to the needs of people. The solution to the problem of insecurity is tied to a process of change and enhanced social justice" (UNDP 2012, 173).

The attention the UNDP devotes to security and insecurity, inequality and poverty, crime and victimization, forms of violence including domestic violence and gang violence, risks factors affecting the youth, corruption, gender issues and other matters of concern (UNDP 2012, 173–85) reflects priorities established around the economic organization of the societies the report targets. The conclusions in the UNDP report rest on the misconception that multilateral institutions and international businesses make the economic development of countries, job creation and rising wages their priority – but private capital accumulation is the vocation of capitalists on the whole. The UNDP report is silent on the reality and necessity of a reserve army of labour without which capitalism cannot operate and which gives rise to the gangs, violence, insecurity and other contradictions that are associated with citizen insecurity in the Caribbean. The problems are bound to intensify among the mass of white-collar and blue-collar working-class people who struggle to reproduce themselves in a world where the innovation-driven scientific and technological changes brought about by computers, robotics and artificial intelligence are rendering droves of professional and skilled workers redundant, if not unemployable, in conjunction with rapidly rising global labour productivity.

One response to the contradictions of capitalism in everyday life is to attribute the growing vulnerability among certain sections of the male population to contradictions between the sexes. Assertions of this type begin from unstated patriarchal assumptions that separate the causes of vulnerability from the contradictory social relations of capitalism, a sentiment that is part of a growing neo-patriarchal discourse. Linden Lewis argues that the impact on Caribbean societies of "the shifting economic terrain, occasioned by . . . globalization, economic restructuring and the . . . neo-liberal agenda in . . . the region" has resulted in "a profound dislocation of traditional gender roles" (2004a, 237) that is discernable in the savaging of male and female labouring subjects. Lewis says that it is

> through culture that patriarchy could be defended and legitimated by appeals to authority, religion, custom and popular practice. . . . It is also through appeals to cultural practice that patriarchal domination in the region tends to dismiss women's claims of sexual and public harassment. The culture of the region . . . plays an invaluable role in the reproduction and integration of the infrastructure of patriarchal domination and should never be overlooked in our discussions of gender. (2004a, 258)

Tracy Robinson analyses gender issues with attention to law and citizenship in Commonwealth Caribbean societies, acknowledging that state power in those societies is not designed to protect women from violence or other violations and abuses like rape.[2] In addressing "violence against women", Robinson discusses the extent of "feminist engagement with the state" (T. Robinson 2000, 1) and its reformist patriarchal practices that hide inequality in the crevices of deontological equal rights. Robinson refuses to "privilege constitutions, statutes and written legal judgments as law and . . . embodiment of truth" (1, 3). In her analysis of citizenship and the law she connects violence with state making and links domination, alienation and violence to sovereignty, citizenship and the law. She criticizes "gender-blind" notions of equality in Caribbean societies that normalize patriarchal oppression, which is built into the material and social relations that are founded on private-property rights. Making sense of individual and social alienation requires paying careful attention to contradictions from religion, the state and capital. Law in Caribbean and other class societies provides the effective juridical cover for economic exploitation and gender oppression that operate on combinations of the state's political coercive power and economic compulsion. Anthony McGrew notes that "violence which occurs within countries is . . . a globalizing dynamic in its own right" (2007, 22). Wherever state security overrides citizen security the outcome is gender oppression and tendencies towards the normalization of violence against women: insecurity and domination mediated by neo-patriarchy are basic to the very founding nature of the state.

Robinson notes that the "law constructs and reconstructs masculinity and femininity and maleness and femaleness and contributes to a common-sense perception of difference that sustains social and sexual practices" (T. Robinson 2000, 9). She concludes that the "challenge for feminist engagement is to . . . contest the meanings of citizen that circumscribe the power of activism. . . . In the same way . . . we must equally acknowledge that legal texts do not operate in isolation and above life, and therefore on their own they may not be capable of effecting the kind of change to women's material existence" (27; see L. Lewis 2004b, 263). Gerda Lerner reminds us that patriarchy (and neo-patriarchy) produce contradictory outcomes with nominal advantage for women in privileged class positions in their dealings with working-class women and men. It is indisputable that patriarchy and male supremacy are built into the capitalist "social control formation" (Perry 2010, 3).

Largely, institutions of civil society in the Caribbean – family, church, political parties, labour unions, the media, education, business entities and others – function in tandem with state power, which limits the extent to which those civil society institutions can operate as sites of protection from the predations of the state or from market forces. It is important to carefully consider how the embrace by postcolonial states and their societies of global white supremacy as the hegemonic mode of world order plays into a passive embrace by white-supremacist hierarchical conceptions of femininity that encourages disrespect towards and abuse of black females. Agnew points out that the "geographical boundaries of the state define the boundaries of the social contract on which modern citizenship rests. . . . Yet the trend toward the globalization of markets and finance opens up the territories of the state to substantially increased international competition" (2005, 221). It is in those "areas of greatest democratic achievement, such as welfare rights, unemployment benefits, public health, etc." that we find state power being exercised increasingly to benefit transnational capitalist class interests (221; see Harvey 2005, 8). The fact that the "state under capitalism cannot be defined except by reference to the wage-relation" (Aumeeruddy, Lautier and Tortajada 1978, 61) also means that citizen insecurity is foundational to all capitalist societies including the Caribbean.

Hannah Arendt's observation that the "secret conflict between state and nation" (1973, 231) is preserved in private-property rights helps to clarify the claim that national self-determination and capitalism are incompatible. Arendt notes that the "very birth of the nation-state" and the strategy under the French revolution to combine "the declaration of the Rights of Man with the demand for national sovereignty" required that those "essential rights" that were "at once claimed as the inalienable heritage of all human beings" had to be subsumed under the "power of capital and the state" (231). The universal rights of man could only be guaranteed abstractly under the bourgeois state where capital's right to exploit is paramount and covered over by the tracks of the market. With globalization and its signature of growing deterritorialization, the "accelerating unbundling of state territorial sovereignty . . . provides the most direct evidence for the reshaping of hegemony away from the more state-centered practices of a previous epoch" (Agnew 2009, 83–84) – which is not an argument for the declining relevance of territory or the functions of state power on a territorial basis (see Elden 2009, 1–32 passim). The point here is that the inheritors of the colonial and postcolonial states could hardly make or keep realistic promises to the working-class forces about transforming the social conditions of their existence, hence their abiding ambivalence, vacillation, opportunism and authoritarianism that typified the populist politics they employed to blunt the class struggle and fight against gender oppression. They found it expedient, therefore, to exploit patriarchal authoritarianism in the state, in party politics and in civil society at large to engineer national consensus and working-class submissiveness (see Bolland 2001; Chibber 2013).

Formation of the Ideological Consciousness of Barbadian Exceptionalism

The hegemonic self-image that was cultivated in Barbados reflects sensibilities with historical roots in the disciplinary, authoritarian British colonial order, features of which survive in the Barbadian state and civil society, helping to regulate the society and fostering a sense of superiority over other Caribbean postcolonial societies. Pedro Welch provides an insight into the origin and formation of the Barbadian self-image and cultural identity during the colonial period in his account of the "contributions of non-plantation social elements to the development of creole identity and culture" (1992, 37), where he discusses the types of societies that emerged during the early slaved-based colonial order over the "non-society" myth (38). Welch argues that there emerged in the early colonial society in Barbados a sense of "community" and "colonial life" and "Barbadianness" among the descendants of English settlers and enslaved Africans and their descendants. He quotes Dr George Pinkard, a late eighteenth-century British visitor to Barbados, who said that by the end of the eighteenth century Barbadian "great planters" lacked any "precise knowledge of the period when their ancestors first arrived. . . . They regard it as their native and only abode, and do not look to England as another and better home" (quoted in Welch 1992). Pinkard claimed that slaves in Barbados "proudly arrogate a superiority above the negroes of other islands" (38), and that they insisted, like descendants of English settlers did, on their authentic Barbadian identity. Pinkard overheard slaves responding to whites as follows: "Me neder Chrab [Carib]; nor Creole, Massa! – me troo Barbadian born" (Welch 1992, 38, 39).[3] Pinkard suggested that the descendants of enslaved Africans had begun to internalize a Barbadian self-image and a feeling of superiority over their counterparts in other Caribbean slave-based colonies.

During the 1870s, when Britain proposed to federate its eastern Caribbean colonies to rationalize colonial administration, Barbadian agro-commercial and political interests opposed the proposal, claiming that Barbados had a superior, independent constitution and would suffer political retardation by federating with the constitutionally less developed colonies. The Barbadian ruling strata invoked the idea of Barbadian constitutional exceptionalism and cultural superiority in a colony that consistently and necessarily depended on exporting large numbers of its relatively surplus population to other BWI colonies to control against absolute material destitution and reduce working-class dependence on the state for relief. Dependence on emigration was evident: the Barbadian population declined by 15,982 from 171,982 to 156,000 between 1911 and 1936, due mainly to net emigration (SOG 1952a, 168). Not long after, remittances increased by $1,120,770 over ten years, from $210,355 in 1940 to $1,331,125 in 1950 (OG 1952, 168; SOG 1950, 21), which had a short-lived salutary effect on panic among the colonial leadership and general population. Low economic growth and chronic unemployment and poverty in Barbados, in conjunction with the restrictive immigration policies of a number of countries, helped to stoke the fires of an anti-immigration sentiment among the colony's political leaders.

During the 1950s the Barbados House of Assembly was divided on how to combat high levels of immigration. The views expressed by certain parliamentarians – the Honourable Messrs Garner, Mapp and Allder contrasted with those of Honourable Messrs Adams, Crawford and Barrow. Garner, Mapp and Allder favoured restricting immigration by especially "Itinerant Peddlers" (CO 32/127, 240) from the Near East and South Asia who typically entered Barbados to sell low-grade merchandise at exorbitant prices, especially to members of the rural working class. Garner argued that Hindus and "Mohammedans" should be excluded because they did not provide employment or other benefits to black Barbadians (240). Crawford, Barrow and Adams objected to preventing people entering Barbados from conducting legitimate business, and Crawford welcomed foreign merchants who could compete with the Bridgetown establishment; however, he proposed enacting legislation to prevent them from robbing the "people of their hard earned wages" (242). Adams and Barrow decried labelling peddlers and other immigrants by nationality or ethnic origin and defended their right to do business in Barbados, provided they entered legally and contributed to economic growth, stressing that it was not a good socialist practice to label, target or exclude foreign minority groups (240–43).

Mapp and Garner favoured "reserving Barbados for Barbadians" (OG 1951a, 49; OG 1951b, 774–75). Garner argued that British Guiana could absorb some of Barbados's surplus population and lamented that the colonial Guianese government opposed Barbadian immigration on racial grounds. He also counted Australia and Latin American countries among those that excluded black West Indians and other coloured people and insisted that a small and overpopulated island like Barbados had a right to export labourers to other countries. However, he saw no contradiction in preventing foreigners from migrating to Barbados. Allder argued that Barbadians were entitled to immigrate to other countries because they always took with them skills and an intellectual and cultural superiority to contribute to other countries' development – contributing to the myth of Barbadian exceptionalism, partly by discounting the factors that made mass emigration from Barbados an absolute necessity.

In the decades after emancipation Barbadians migrated to British Guiana and other BWI colonies where they worked as businessmen, lawyers, magistrates, teachers, policemen, religious ministers and in masses as unskilled agricultural labourers (Alleyne 2012). Barbadians also migrated to Liberia where several of them achieved high political visibility (Newton 2008). Hilary Beckles (2004) argues that the creation of an island-wide public education system in Barbados in the post-emancipation era provided Barbadians with a level of basic functional literacy. It is this totally fortuitous by-product of deliberate British colonial policy that Barbadians consistently exploit to feed the myth of innate intellectual superiority. British investment in public education in Barbados was carefully designed to create loyal colonial subjects who could be exported to serve the needs of the British Empire. Largely, Barbadians exploit an accident of British imperialist practice to project an unwarranted self-image of exceptional intellectual superiority that draws on the lingering moral epistemology of British imperialism, according to which the British Empire epitomized the moral idea of freedom and culture in the world (Thompson 1997).

In reflecting on factors that shaped the nationalist ideology Barbadians project against other West Indians, I argue that the English ideology of "racial Anglo-Saxonism" that anchors global white supremacy has had a lasting influence on the formation of the Barbadian self-image. I do not claim that Barbadians lack agency in developing an ideological (national) self-image; rather, I stress that the formation of a Barbadian nationalist consciousness results from the interplay of complex processes that originated long before independence in 1966.

Reginald Horsman's account of how the English promoted the myth of themselves as an original Anglo-Saxon (Teutonic) people, first encountered in Tacitus's Germania, is instructive.[4] Tacitus romantically depicts the image of a people that reproduced and preserved themselves from contamination by others, standing above other population groups. Horsman argues that Tacitus's depiction in Germania helped to sow the seeds from which sprung an ideological "jumble of race, nation, and language" that resulted in "a hodgepodge of rampant racial nationalism" and "virulent racial theories" (Horsman 1981, 26). English racial Anglo-Saxon ideology drew from Germania and rationalized the power relations that helped to anchor British imperialism. It was projected onto the colonies and beyond with significant consequences.

In the following sections, I argue that Grantley Adams and Errol Barrow traced Barbados's constitutional autochthony to English political institutions, which claimed a palingenetic source, without acknowledging the racialized white-supremacist dimension of that world view. Adams and Barrow contributed immensely to the construction of the self-image that Barbadians developed during decolonization.

Grantley Adams, Errol Barrow and the Myth of Barbadian Exceptionalism

Grantley Adams was rewarded with a British knighthood in 1952 for unstinting loyal service to the British Empire. In his response in the House of Assembly on the significance for Barbados of the honorific title the British bestowed upon him, Adams attributed practically everything to Barbadian superiority and exceptionalism among the BWI and all other British colonies. He said:

> I feel sure that whether a man chooses the political course rather than the legal course, any honour that comes to him comes . . . not as an appreciation of his personal service but because he is a member of an organization and a member of a Parliament which has done or tried to do some good for its country. . . . I know these things because I have been told them and I say them at first hand – I know the . . . unique position which Barbados holds among the Caribbean colonies in the eyes of the Colonial Office and the British Government of whatever political complexion. I hope that our friends in the West Indian colonies will not feel offended if I say that. It is true that the average Barbadian is always conscious of his superiority to other people of the world; but it is a fact that 300 years of representative institutions have created for us a responsibility and a desire objectively to approach political problems that are . . . inevitably lacking in communities which have not had the advantage of three centuries of unbroken representative government. . . . I know that this honour or any other honour which may be bestowed on me by the British Government at any time, or by any international organization, has been due . . . to the fact that Barbados is absolutely unique among the non-self-governing territories in its unbroken parliamentary traditions and in the way we have made use of them . . . I say that if anything has happened to me on the Trade Union side, it is due to the fact that there is a similar recognition in the outside world that Barbados shows as great a success in economic matters as in political matters, and a greater success than in other colonies. (SOG 1952b, 778–99)

Here Adams, an indomitable Anglophile and a monarchist, outlined the case for Barbadian exceptionalism and identified the Barbadian sense of cultural superiority that was heavily influenced by the internalization and adaptation of the English ideology of "racial Anglo-Saxonism" that fostered the grand myth of English exceptionalism. Adams attributed Barbadian political achievements to three hundred years of unbroken colonial domination, self-consciously discounting the role that enslaved labour played in building the material infrastructures of the "representative government" that the largely British-descended agro-commercial capitalists dominated and from which they excluded the enslaved. In 1937, the Barbadian working class rebelled against the tightly managed racialized capitalist class order and forced Britain to introduce reforms which included the introduction of universal adult suffrage under the Representation of the People's Act (1950). In his 1952 speech Adams masked an array of racialized class, gender, ethnic and other contradictions, while emphasizing his condescension towards other colonized subjects.

Adams spoke about Barbadians by drawing liberally on the "old Anglo-Saxon myth" the English created that was "ultimately to appear innocuous alongside an overpowering Aryan myth which helped to transform respect for Anglo-Saxon institutions into a new racial interpretation of English . . . success" (Horsman 1981, 24). The United Nations adopted the Universal Declaration of Human Rights in 1948, the same year in which Alexander Bustamante spoke flatteringly about the need to maintain the British Empire to protect democracy in the world (see Mawby 2012, 46). In 1948, Adams was selected by the Colonial Office as a member of the official British delegation at a special session of the United Nations General Assembly held in Paris at which he unapologetically defended the decaying British Empire. He openly attacked the anti-imperialist labour and working-class struggles around the world as well as socialism and implored Whitehall to proceed with great caution in granting self-government to colonial subjects, on the grounds that they had to be supervised to assume the burden of responsible self-government. Lord Longford commended Adams for his unstinting loyalty during the debate over the constitutional conference on independence for Barbados at Lancaster House in 1966 (CO 1031/5219, 1966).

Horsman reminds us that the English "were never content to accept a theory which submerged the Saxons into a greater European mass. The English . . . continued to elevate the Saxons above all those other groups that supposedly shared a common German . . . heritage. The Saxons became the 'elite of an elite', the . . . 'separate, superior people within a larger Germanic race'" (Horsman 1981, 38). Barbadian leaders and the general population in Barbados see themselves in a similar light in relation to other Caribbean societies. Commenting on the contradictions of colonial and postcolonial subjectivity in the British Caribbean, George Lamming connects the story of the "fall from grace" and the banishment of "fallen angels" from the metaphorical Garden of Eden to the relationship between England (as Garden) and her colonial subjects (as the fallen ones). Lamming says the "fallen ones" imagined imperial Britain as the closest thing to God on earth. In the imagination of colonial subjects, the king and the empire became "bigger than the garden. . . . and nothing else mattered but the empire. . . . The empire and the garden. . . . both belong to God" (Lamming 1953, 67). Since God had "saved the king", the colonial subjects too could expect to "see the garden again" and realize "a sort of salvation . . . through grace" (67, 68). Barbadians identify as West Indians; however, they labour under the grand myth that they possess an innate intellectual and cultural edge over other West Indians.

Errol Barrow, the Fabrication of Barbadian Constitutional Autochthony and the Making of the Sovereign Monarchy of Barbados

In 1966 Errol Barrow, then premier of Barbados, delivered a speech – "No Loitering on Colonial Premises"[5] – at the Barbados Constitutional Conference at Lancaster House, in defence of his government's proposal for independence for Barbados. Here I discuss the philosophical and political content of Barrow's speech, in order to explain his concept of Barbados's "autochthonous" colonial constitution, which he traced to seventeenth-century English constitutional principles. I aim to show how Barrow contributed to the myth of Barbadian exceptionalism. Barrow discusses Barbados's "unique" status among West Indian colonies, asserting that Barbados's constitutional uniqueness – his idea of constitutional autochthony – derived from the colony's 327 years of unbroken "association with the Crown of England" (quoted in Holder 2007, 65). He claimed that the English created Barbados as a colony of "settlement" rather than "conquest or . . . purchase . . . at the time when English political institutions experienced their severest strain" (65). He credited English settlers in Barbados with producing an enduring political culture that laid the foundation for independence. Barrow did not mention that the security of the colonial state that was built on English white supremacy–based agro-commercial capitalism denied justice to the bonded white labourers and African slaves and their descendants.

Barrow elevated Barbados over the other BWI colonies in ways that echoed Grantley Adams's 1952 speech (quoted above), when Barrow reminded "Mr. Secretary of State" that Barbadians had enjoyed "the solid comforts of representative government" from 1639 to 1966 (quoted in Holder 2007, 65). Barrow declared:

> In 1651, when Englishmen were cowering in their homes under the whip of Cromwell's major-generals, and when they who had lopped off the head of a king sought to enmesh the people of Barbados in their "saintly" tyranny, Barbadians stubbornly defended their respective institutions from Cromwell and in the famous Charter of Barbados which they signed, they . . . managed to preserve for three centuries the supremacy of parliaments and the liberty of the subject. (65)

He elaborated, "In our country . . . the supremacy of Parliament is zealously upheld and a Government of Barbados, like its counterpart in Britain, would never resort to any subterfuge designed to frustrate the clearly expressed desires of a duly elected

Parliament" (65). Barrow's emphasis on the "supremacy of Parliament" reflected his anxiety about notions the British might have harboured that an independent Barbados led by his Democratic Labour Party might degenerate into an autocracy. He defended English royal absolutism in Barbados over the prospect of a republican government under Oliver Cromwell, ignoring the fact that the "liberty of the subject" did not extend to the mass of bonded toilers. "The people" did not constitute the sovereign body politic, given that his way of employing the term masked the location of power in the state in order to give the untenable impression that the colonial "capitalist social control formation" (Perry 2010) in Barbados was democratic. Barrow also skirted the 1937 working-class rebellion, which resulted in the reforms that made it possible for him to deliver the pro-independence speech at Lancaster House.

He offered as an example of the "autochthonous" Barbados constitution, the event where the legislature of Barbados asserted its "sovereign" right to resist British colonial encroachments in the 1876 attempt to "force our country into a federation which . . . would have given the Colonial Office greater control over Barbadian affairs" (Holder 2007, 57). He failed to acknowledge that a federation based on the 1876 British proposals carried the potential for fostering BWI integration. The high point of Barrow's notion of constitutional autochthony was the creation in 1966 of the Constitutional Monarchy of Barbados as a sovereign state, with the appointment on his recommendation of the last colonial governor of Barbados to be the first governor general of sovereign Barbados. Barrow's "No Loitering on Colonial Premises" speech was instrumental in establishing a conservative accommodation with the United Kingdom's battered post-imperial masculinity and the US-led hegemonic Cold War project.

Eric Barrow and Grantley Adams embraced exceptionalism as the official nationalist ideology of Barbados (see also Clarke 2001);[6] they eschewed any substantive relationship with working-class political interests by superimposing bourgeois nationalist ideology, the politically divisive ideology of party politics and trade union authoritarianism as political components of the dominant "capitalist social control formation" (Perry 2010). Adams and Barrow differed by degree rather than kind on the fundamentals of decolonization and they exploited the hegemonic ideology of Barbadian exceptionalism to establish and affirm control over Barbadian society. Barrow, unlike Adams, did not openly represent himself as an ostensible Anglophile; however, he related to his colonial status in ways that reflected deference to imperial authority, without being necessarily uncritical of the colonial order. He knew that the constitutional autochthony of which he spoke freely was merely nominal, as it could not invest Barbados with the constitutional authority to act autonomously towards the United Kingdom (see W.A. Lewis 1978, 97) or the United States.

Exceptionalism, Citizenship and Immigration in Contemporary Barbados

Sovereign states force individuals to become national persons in the process of nationalizing societies, creating citizenship and subsuming individual and group subjectivity under the state. Agnew argues that the "globalizing world is marked by a crisis of governance because existing national-state–scale institutions cannot offer the spatial reach needed to regulate increasingly worldwide and world-regional transactions, but existing global-scale institutions are still creatures of the most powerful states and dominant business interest groups from them" (Agnew 2005, 170). States that have to rely on juridical sovereignty are not equipped to mediate the contradictions Agnew mentions.

The judicial ruling by the Caribbean Court of Justice[7] in favour of Shanique Myrie and against Barbados poses questions about what state security and order imply for freedom of movement,[8] which is not definitively covered by the Revised Treaty of Chaguaramas (Sanders 2013; Jones 2013; Foreman and Powell 2014). The handling by Barbados of the Myrie case also raises issues of governance, with reference to citizenship and belonging that are works in progress at the level of CARICOM (the Caribbean Community and Common Market). Natalie Jones argues that the development of CARICOM "community law" (2013, 2) can strengthen a sense of the regional "cultural consciousness" (3) of belonging to member societies. Jones notes that the "CARICOM mobility regime" will not "catch up with the cultural practices which have become entrenched with the region vis-à-vis migration", considering that the crisis of governance that "national governments like Barbados" face, tends to force them to "sacrifice the mobility component of the integration project . . . to manage migration" (2). The fact is that the contradictions arising from global capitalism condition those "cultural practices" to which Jones refers.

Where production for private accumulation is the norm, state security and order always take precedence over justice. In the CARICOM context insular nationalism and xenophobia add to concerns about security, order, difference and exclusion, especially where governance issues are compounded by pressures arising from the economic motivation towards the free movement of people. Citizens of CARICOM countries developed a sense of "regional" belonging and identity that predates the sovereign state and its cultural institution, the nation state. The sovereign state with its exclusionary predisposition, which fosters a feeling that a nation is an end in itself rather than a means to an end, could hardly bolster substantive regionalism without a viable regional economy, which CARICOM does not represent.

Sir Ronald Sanders interprets the Myrie case as a CARICOM issue, arguing that "while the case gave redress to Myrie for her grievances, it was far more significant for its establishment of the rights of the people of Caricom and for eliminating misconceptions of the supremacy of 'national sovereignty' over 'Community Law' under the Revised Treaty of Chaguaramas" (2013, 2; see Jones 2013, 2; Brewster 2003). All citizens do not experience citizenship and belonging equally, due to the ways the contradictions arising from the economic organization of society play out via class, gender, ethnicity, religion, national origin and language (see Kaplan 2013).

The fact that no single state exercises absolute sovereignty over borders suggests that the chance of any state achieving total control over immigration is very remote. Trends in international migration under global capitalism also put into question "traditional conceptions of citizenship" (Agnew 2009, 180). Bruno Gullì argues that sovereignty is poorly equipped to encompass "notions of freedom, autonomy, and subjectivity", emphasizing that when we subsume "liberation, autonomy, independence, and self-determination" under state sovereignty we invariably mask sovereignty's core contradictions and risk depriving those values of their "fundamentally progressive . . . character" (2010, 72). The fact that territory is the physical container of the territorial state does not protect certain members of the resident labour force from being obligated to migrate to reproduce themselves (and others). The transnational spatial organization of capitalist production, the unevenness of the productive forces and the resultant pressures that force workers to migrate to improve their condition also means that sovereignty and wage labour must coexist in a contradictory relationship that is compounded by the primacy accorded by their own governments to the mobility of capital.

The state's immigration policy is important for regulating the average global price of labour power and maintaining the subordination of labour to capital. Labour, which is forced to reproduce itself via the operation of the law of value, is subject to the "violence that creates the law" (Gullì 2010, 130). This is where the power of the state – what Ellen Wood calls the "moments of coercion" (2002, 21–22, 29–31) – and the power of capital in the market – the economic compulsion – converge. The "mode of domination and superexploitation amounts to a violation of basic human rights, and . . . cannot be remedied by the same system that produces it. . . . In fact . . . learning to labor in a regime of domination . . . is a path to injustice, poverty, unhappiness, unfreedom and illness" (Gullì 2010, 130). Immigration issues generate contradictions that test the capacity of the state and civil society and expose the myth that each sovereign territory includes a "culturally homogeneous population" (Agnew 2009, 144) that determines who belongs to the nation, who qualifies to enter and who is alien. The data from managed immigration contradict claims about the existence of a "self-evident identification between one culture and a singular territory" (144, 145).

The Barbadian state treats immigration as part of a larger security problem because it lacks effective control over the economic process with reference to price inflation, an almost expired sugar industry, sluggish tourism, problems in offshore financial services, structural unemployment, serious imbalances in trade and balance of payments, and a rising debt-to-GDP ratio, all compounded by the impact of the global economic and financial crisis on the society. Globally, the transnational capitalist class forces are replacing throngs of white-collar and blue-collar workers with "smart tools" to reduce the cost of production, while leading transnational state apparatuses – the International Monetary Fund, World Trade Organization and World Bank – demand that national states like Barbados adopt austerity measures to comply with the requirements for building an integrated global economy. Most Barbadian workers are not positioned to weather the effects from the global economic and financial crisis in a society with a narrow production and skills base in relation to what constitutes globally defined productivity and competitiveness, especially keeping in mind low-wage, high-productivity global mass-production platforms like China and India.

The fact that Barbados and Barbadians have a very long history of dependence on emigration to mediate structural and protracted economic problems receives hardly any consideration in the anti-immigrant calculations of the ruling Democratic Labour Party government. Any realistic attempt to map the political and ideological terrain of anti-immigrant sentiment in contemporary Barbados (or in any other CARICOM country) must consider that CARICOM is not a viable space for substantive regional economic integration – which helps to explain why its member states emphasize "irreducible sovereignty" (Bishop and Payne 2010) when it comes to dealing with contradictions arising from intra-CARICOM immigration issues and other regional problems.

Annalee Davis (2009) draws attention to the predicament that CARICOM immigrants residing in Barbados often face, highlighting the contradictory relationship between sovereignty, labour and residency in Barbados with attention to how the bureaucratic process frustrates legal immigrants. Davis notes that it is normal for certain CARICOM immigrants, with children born in Barbados and attending school there, to be required to wait up to fifteen years to have their immigration status resolved. Davis stresses that the Barbadian state subjects immigrants to indeterminacy, uncertainty and insecurity of status, routinely fostering or exploiting divisions between the "national" population and so-called "foreigners" (2009, 1). She emphasizes that anti-immigrant ideology in Barbados operates through the state and civil society, with immigrants routinely blamed for high unemployment; crime; polluting the "nation's" water; undermining the country's economic, social and political stability; smuggling drugs into Barbados; prostitution and otherwise undermining the country's "high" standard of living (2).

Norman Girvan argues that the anti-immigrant outlook in Barbados deflects attention from the fact that Barbados benefits disproportionately from access to the CARICOM market. He says, "Caricom is the largest single market for Barbadian manufactured exports. Caricom visitors are the second-largest category of Barbadian tourism. Barbados derives benefits from being an airline travel hub for the Eastern Caribbean. A large number of regional organizations are based in Barbados.

Barbados is both recipient and source of foreign investment with the rest of Caricom" (Girvan 2009). Girvan's account contrasts with how the Honourable Dennis Kellman (then Barbados's ambassador to CARICOM) painted the threat immigration poses to Barbados, claiming that that "Barbados had reached maximum capacity because of immigration" and asserting that "any further opening of the floodgates to immigration under the guise of free movement . . . would lead to the suffering of all concerned" (Oscar Ramjeet, caribbeannetnews.com, 2009), with negative implications for the health system, transportation and traffic congestion, unemployment, housing, education and much more (*Jamaica Observer*, "Myrie Judgement a Turning Point, Regional Experts Say", 2 November 2013). The rhetoric about what the Caribbean Court of Justice ruling represents in terms of people's freedom of movement, human rights and the rights of sovereign states to protect their self-interest discounts the fact that the CARICOM economic space lacks the deep inner structures of capital necessary for promoting a viable regional economic space in the global economy.

Cuba in the Cross Hairs of US Hegemonic Strategy

The US security strategy in the Caribbean reflects the contradictions of hegemony that are evident in the inability of the United States to banish certain forms of resistance by those states like Cuba that it treats as subordinates. The US pursues its foreign policy in keeping with updated versions of Thomas Jefferson's declaration that the US constitution was uniquely "calculated . . . for extensive empire and self-government" (quoted in Landau 1988, 13). The United States carried out "103 interventions in the affairs of other countries between 1875 and 1895" (Love 2004, 13) and a much larger number by the end of World War II (Rosenfelder 1996; Chomsky 1993). The US leaders are convinced that the world should be thankful for the processes and consequences of its expansionist deeds because manifest destiny ordains it to function permanently as "empire of liberty" (see Foner 2002). Put differently, Washington must not permit any territorial boundaries to constrain its right to project its sovereign power globally.

The US annexation of Puerto Rico (1898), invasion of Cuba (1898, 1906 and 1912), military occupation of the Dominican Republic (1915–24 and 1965) and of Haiti (1916–34) and invasion of Grenada (1983) and of Panama (1989) and the role the United States played in the removal of Jean-Bertrand Aristide from power in Haiti (2004) are exemplary of the US quest for absolute (though elusive) hegemony in the Caribbean. In 1916, when the US occupation of the Dominican Republic and Haiti was underway, Smedley Butler said, "We were all imbued with the idea that we were trustees of a huge estate that belonged to minors."[9] In 1915 US secretary of state Robert Lansing informed President Woodrow Wilson of US motives for acquiring the Danish Virgin Islands from Denmark. Lansing said, "I make no argument on the ground of benefit which would result to the people of these republics by the adoption of this policy. . . . The argument based on humanitarian grounds does not appeal to me" (24 November 1915, from Link 1980, 246–47). Lansing reminded Wilson that "the integrity of other American nations is an incident, not an end" (246–47) of American policy, and he let the Danish minister know that Denmark had two options in the matter: sell the islands to the United States for a decent price or watch the United States take them and receive no compensation (FRUS 1940, 501–2, cited in Fernandez 1994, 104n33).

The United States began to draw Cuba into the cross hairs of its Jeffersonian "empire of liberty" project (Foner 2002, 63–64) as early as 1823, when Thomas Jefferson said, "We will oppose, with all of our means, the forcible interposition of any other power, as auxiliary, stipendiary, or under any other form or pretext, and most especially, [Cuba's] transfer to any power by conquest, cession, or acquisition in any other way" (63–64). Secretary of state John Forsyth reiterated the Jeffersonian doctrine in 1840, declaring that the United States would "at all hazard" block any attempt by Spain to transfer Cuba to "any other power" (quoted in Pérez 1998, 49). In 1898, Yale University law professor Theodore Woolsey argued that US control of Cuba was indispensable for the security of the eastern "approach to the canal" (49). In 1902, US senator Stephen Elkins exulted that when

> Cuba shall become a part of the American union and the isthmian canal shall be completed . . . Porto Rico [*sic*], Cuba, Hawaii and the Philippines shall be outposts of the great republic, standing guard over American interests in the track of the world's commerce in its triumphant march around the globe. . . . This splendid chain of island possessions, reaching half-way around the world would not be complete without Cuba, the gem of the Antilles.[10]

Under the Platt Amendment (1903) Washington claimed the right to occupy Cuba, updating the security strategy that began with the Monroe Doctrine (1823) which signalled that the United States was not bound by any principle to respect the sovereignty of any republic in Latin America or the Caribbean. US post-war involvement in the Caribbean region from British Guiana (1953) to Haiti (2004) confirms that liberal democratic peace theory – according to which democracy is a force for peace in the world – lacks a supporting empirical foundation (Layne 2006; Bilgin and Morton 2002; Barkawi and Laffey 1999). In 1962, as the Cuban Revolution was unfolding, the United States fabricated a plan to launch a pre-emptive war against Cuba. The creation of the Alliance for Progress (1961), the abortive Bay of Pigs incident and the Cuban Missile Crisis (1962) were emblematic of US attempts to treat the Cuban Revolution as a challenge to its Cold War hegemonic strategy to achieve total economic and geopolitical dominance in the Western Hemisphere.

When the sovereign state of Cuba nationalized capitalist property located on Cuban soil, the United States declared that capitalist property rights must take precedence over the sovereign power of any state.

Details of the 1962 US plan to invade Cuba are contained in a Joint Chiefs of Staff (JOS) Memorandum for the Secretary of Defence that enumerates "pretexts which would provide justification for US military intervention in Cuba".[11] The JOS would assume "responsibility for . . . overt and covert military operations" and "provide justification for US military intervention in Cuba". The JOS invasion plan called for fabricating "heightened US-Cuban tensions which place the United States in the position of suffering justifiable grievances. World opinion and the United Nations forum should be favorably affected by developing the international image of the Cuban government as rash and irresponsible and as a[n] . . . unpredictable threat to the peace of the Western Hemisphere." The JOS memorandum identifies three reasons for US scepticism that the Soviet Union might be drawn into a "US military intervention in Cuba": (1) Moscow and Havana did not have a bilateral security agreement; (2) Cuba was not a member of the Warsaw Pact and (3) the Soviet Union did not have military bases in Cuba "in the pattern of US bases in Western Europe".

The JOS memorandum suggested that neither the US military officers assigned to NATO nor the US delegation or United Nations military staff committee, should be informed of the plan, which emphasized provocation, harassment and "deceptive actions to convince the Cubans of imminent invasion". Specific tactics included "rumors"; use of "friendly Cubans" to attack the US base at Guantanamo Bay;[12] deployment of "friendly Cubans" inside Guantanamo as saboteurs; and capturing and using the "friendly Cubans" to start riots near Guantanamo Bay, blow up ammunition, burn aircraft, lob mortar shells inside Guantanamo Bay from outside, sink ships in or near the harbour entrance, stage funerals for "mock-victims" and initiate "offensive operations to secure water and power supplies, destroy[ing] artillery and mortar emplacements which threaten the base", followed by "large-scale United States military operations". The plan also provided for blowing up "a US ship in Guantanamo Bay", recalling the Maine incident of 1898[13] to provoke Cuba to "attack from the air or sea or both."

The United States would stage "air/sea rescue operations covered by US fighters to 'evacuate' remaining members of the non-existent crew. Casualty lists in US newspapers would cause a helpful wave of national indignation." There were also plans to create international sympathy for a justifiable invasion by carrying out attacks inside other "Caribbean countries like Haiti or the Dominican Republic and blame them on Castro-supported" groups, using "US pilots to fly Cuban 'MIG type aircraft' " for additional provocation.

Other "complementary actions" were to include "destruction of US military drone aircraft by MIG type planes" and use of fabricated "Cuban MIGs" to destroy "a USAF aircraft over international waters in an unprovoked attack". The plan provided for fomenting "an internal Cuban rebellion", failing which the United States would "develop a Cuban 'provocation' as justification for . . . US military action". The Department of State would contribute to "courses of action to develop justification for US military intervention in Cuba" (see also Bamford 2001).

Cuba survived a number of concerted US efforts to isolate it in the Western Hemisphere and globally and also survived the economic blockade, which European allies helped to fracture (Hennessy and Lambie 1993). Cuba was effective in providing military and non-military support that helped to bring national liberation movements to power in parts of Africa. It contributed to strengthening the non-aligned movement and received important diplomatic support from Commonwealth Caribbean states in the face of intense US opposition.

Undeniably, Cuba's relationship with the United States since 1959 highlights the contingent nature of state sovereignty and of hegemony, even in the face of the "migratory propensities of sovereignty" (Agnew 2009, 122), where the footprint of US hegemony is unmistakable.

Conclusion

Ruling forces in Caribbean societies respond to contradictions arising from global capitalism by asserting the primacy of territorial (national) sovereignty as an organic (irreducible) form. I dispute this ideological perspective by emphasizing the historical nature of state sovereignty, historicizing the body politic, patriarchy, gender, citizenship and belonging in order to part with illusions of what Agnew calls "epistemological territorialism" (2009). I conclude that postcolonial states in the Commonwealth Caribbean preserved the institutional basis of the principle of sovereignty inherited from British imperialism with its authoritarian propensities. I argued that sovereign statehood and civil society are designed to accommodate neo-patriarchy, which facilitates the integration of growing numbers of females while leaving male dominance in place, and with the neo-liberal demand for equity taking precedence over legitimate political struggles for working-class power across the gender spectrum.

My focus on Barbados shows how Grantley Adams and Errol Barrow worked to modernize the retrogressive nationalist-populist ideology of Barbadian exceptionalism in the process leading up to independence. I hope that this way of looking at the decolonization process in Barbados might provide a fruitful path for other scholars interested in why all BWI colonies – allowing for territorial peculiarities – came to independence as monarchies within the British Commonwealth rather than as republics. My argument makes it easier to appreciate how and why Barbadian exceptionalism frames the subtle or explicit xenophobic disposition that Barbadians exhibit towards neighbouring CARICOM immigrants, and how the myth of irreducible sovereignty plays an ideological role in mediating CARICOM's unattainable regional integration project.

On the question of contingent sovereignty I examined Cuba's relationship with the United States to show that absolute sovereignty and hegemony remain elusive for the United States in dealing with Caribbean states. All Caribbean states cling to sovereignty myths. Contextually, even if an integrated Caribbean of sovereign states were possible to achieve it would reproduce the domination, exclusion and insecurity that are built into sovereignty, which remains a fundamental problem of world order. An increasingly globalized, deterritorializing world also opens up space to think about ways to struggle for a post-national, post-sovereign, post-capitalist world – the outlines of which are already taking shape in ways that help us to appreciate that a goal of achieving our universal humanity is not romantic; it is utopian in a materialist sense.

Notes

1. In 1904 US custom agents were dispatched to the Dominican Republic to assume control of the sovereign state's customs, ostensibly to ensure payment of the external debt, which depended on labour exploitation. US intervention in Cuba in 1912 and 1917 involved protecting the capitalist owners of the sugar industry and subjugating rebellious sugar workers to the rule of capital. In 1953 attempts at radical social democratic reform in British Guiana were met with hostile responses by the United Kingdom and United States (Rabe 2005). Between 1960 and 1962 the United States attempted to subvert the Cuban Revolution and its anti-imperialist and socialist aims. In 1963 the United States backed a coup that overthrew Juan Bosch in the Dominican Republic and invaded the country in 1965 to prevent Bosch's return to power in order to neutralize popular democratic working-class assertiveness. The BWI colonies achieved sovereign autonomy in a hostile anti–working-class, Cold War–dominated environment (Horne 2007).
2. Having addressed in considerable detail issues of structural and non-state violence in the Caribbean elsewhere (see Watson 2013), I will not emphasize that analysis here.
3. Translation: "I am neither Carib nor creole, Massa! – I am true Barbadian born."
4. Publius Cornelius Tacitus (56–117 CE) was a senator and a historian of the Roman Empire.
5. See Holder 2007 for discussion of Barrow's speech. All references to this speech, including all passages quoted from it, are taken from Holder 2007.
6. Barrow entered politics as a member of Grantley Adams's Barbados Labour Party in 1950–51 and was a founding member of the Democratic Labour Party, which was formed in 1957. He and other parliamentarians broke with Adams and the Barbados Labour Party on the technical grounds that Adams and the Barbados Labour Party were following too gradualist an approach to constitutional decolonization.
7. The Caribbean Court of Justice was established in 2001 to replace the Privy Council (based in the United Kingdom) as the final court for CARICOM member states. Largely,

CARICOM signatories to the Caribbean Court of Justice recognize it as their court of original jurisdiction; however, Barbados, Guyana and Belize are the only signatories to the appellate jurisdiction of the Caribbean Court of Justice, which "also serves as an international tribunal interpreting the Revised Treaty of Chaguaramas that governs the integration movement" (*Jamaica Observer*, 2 November 2013).

8. The dean of the University of the West Indies, Cave Hill, Faculty of Law, David Berry, argues the Treaty of Chaguaramas does not grant freedom of movement. Under Article 46 "it grants freedom of movement . . . to CARICOM Skilled Nationals, certain categories of persons. So what the revised treaty does have is another provision which says towards the goal of free movement we will try to do these things" (*Jamaica Observer*, "Myrie Judgement a Turning Point, Regional Experts Say", 2 November 2013).
9. On Smedley Butler, see IOHSD 1921, 517; see also Fernandez 1994, 406.
10. From the Congressional Record, 57th Cong., 1st Sess., 1902, 35:7639–40, quoted in Pérez 1998, 49.
11. The JOS Memorandum for the Secretary of Defense, Subject: Justification for US Military Intervention in Cuba (TS) was signed by L.L. Lemnitzer, Chairman, Joint Chiefs of Staff, on 13 March 1962 (JOS 1969/321, 2165). All other passages quoted in the section "Cuba in the Cross Hairs of US Hegemonic Strategy" are taken from JOS 1969/321 1962.
12. The naval base at Guantanamo Bay, Cuba, is the "oldest overseas naval base . . . and the only US naval facility in a country with which the US has no formal diplomatic relations. The naval base in Cuba represents a broader struggle between remnants of a former colonialist government that was entirely submissive to Washington and a post-revolutionary . . . government that refuses to let the United States interfere in silence as the rest of the Cuban political sphere boils in dissent" (Keen and Gioia 2015, 1).
13. The US acquisition of a naval base at Guantanamo signalled the disintegration of the remnants of the "Spanish Empire" and the expansion of the "American empire" (Keen and Gioia 2015, 2). The Platt Amendment of 1901 effectively subsumed Cuban independence under US hegemony and gave the United States the right to intervene militarily and otherwise in Cuban affairs and to annex Cuban territory at Guantanamo Bay. A treaty signed between the United States and Cuba in 1909 provided for a "lease agreeement" that "authorized the use of Guantanamo for naval and coaling stations" (2). In 1934 a second treaty between the United States and Cuba was ratified to allow "for greater autonomy of the US Guantanamo base by cancelling the termination date of the lease" (2). Guantanamo is a concrete expression of what John Agnew calls the "migratory propensities" (2009, 144) of US sovereignty at the expense of Cuban territorial sovereignty.

References

Agamben, Giorgio. 2005. *State of Exception*. Translated by Kevin Attel. Chicago: University of Chicago Press.

Agnew, John. 2005. *Hegemony: The New Shape of Global Power*. Philadelphia: Temple University Press.

———. 2009. *Globalization and Sovereignty*. Lanham: Rowman and Littlefield.

Alleyne, Frederick. 2012. "Barbadian Migration to British Guiana, 1840–1960: The Search for El Dorado". Paper presented at the History Forum, University of the West Indies, Cave Hill. 2 March.

Arendt, Hannah. 1973. *The Origins of Totalitarianism*. New York: Harcourt.

Aumeeruddy, Aboo T., Bruno Lautier and Ramon G. Tortajada. 1978. "Labour Power and the State". *Capital and Class* (6): 41–66.

Bakhtin, Mikhail. 1965. *Rabelais and His World*. Cambridge: Massachusetts Institute of Technology Press.

Balibar, Etienne. 1991. "The Nation Form: History and Ideology". In *Race, Nation, Class: Ambiguous Idenitites*, by Etienne Balibar and Immanuel Wallerstein, 86–106. London: Verso.

Bamford, James. 2001. *Body of Secrets: Anatomy of the Ultra-Secret National Security Agency: From the Cold War to the Dawn of a New Century*. New York: Doubleday.

Barkawi, Tarak, and Mark Laffey. 1999. "The Imperial Peace: Democracy, Force and Globalization". *European Journal of International Relations* 5 (4): 403–34.

Beckles, Hilary. 2004. *Great House Rules: Landless Emancipation and Workers' Protest in Barbados 1838–1938*. Kingston: Ian Randle.

Bilgin, Pinar, and Adam David Morton. 2002. "Historicising Representations of 'Failed States': Beyond the Cold-War Annexation of the Social Sciences?" *Third World Quarterly* 23 (1): 55–80.

Bishop, Matthew, and Anthony Payne. 2010. "Caribbean Regional Governance and the Sovereignty/Statehood Problem". *Caribbean Papers* (8) 29 January. https://www.cigionline.org/publications/2010/1/caribbean-regional-governance-and-sovereigntystatehood-problem.

Bolland, Nigel. 2001. *The Politics of Labour in the British Caribbean: The Social Origins of Authoritarianism and Democracy in the Labour Movement*. Kingston: Ian Randle.

Brewster, Havelock. 2003. "CARICOM: From Community to Single Market and Economy". In *Governance in the Age of Globalization: Caribbean Perspectives*, edited by Kenneth Hall and Denis Benn, 499–508. Kingston: Ian Randle.

Castoriadis, Cornelius. 1991. *Philosophy, Politics, Autonomy: Essays in Political Philosophy*. New York: Oxford University Press.

Chibber, Vivek. 2013. *Postcolonial Theory and the Specter of Capital*. London: Verso.

Chomsky, Noam. 1993. *Year 501: The Conquest Continues*. Boston: South End.

Clarke, Richard. 2001. "Roots: A Genealogy of the Barbadian Personality". In *Nationalism: The Empowering Impulse*, edited by Glenford Howe and Don Marshall, 301–49. Kingston: Canoe.

CO (Colonial Office) 32/127. 1952. Supplement to the *Official Gazette*. Vol. 87, no. 43, 29 May.

CO (Colonial Office) 1031/5219. 1966. Interview between Lord Longford and Sir Grantley Adams of Barbados. File no. WIS ZX2.

Connolly, William E. 1991. "Democracy and Territoriality". *Millennium: Journal of International Studies* 20 (3): 463–84.

Davis, Annalee. 2009. "Thoughts on Prime Minister Thompson's New 'Amnesty'". *Stabroek News*, 25 May. http://www.stabroeknews.com/.

Elden, Stuart. 2009. *Territory and Terror: The Spatial Extent of Sovereignty*. Minneapolis: University of Minnesota Press.

Fernandez, Ronald. 1994. *Cruising the Caribbean: US Influence and Intervention in the Twentieth Century*. Monroe, ME: Common Courage.

Foner, Eric. 2002. *Who Owns History?* New York: Hill and Wang.

Foreman, Jeffrey, and K. George Powell. 2014. "Maybe We Should Scrap CARICOM after All". *Gleaner*, 19 October.

FRUS (Foreign Relations of the United States). 1940. *The Lansing Papers, 1914–1920*. Vol. 2. Department of State, Washington, DC: US Government Printing Office.

Gill, Stephen. 2003. *Power and Resistance in the New World Order*. New York: Palgrave Macmillan.

Girvan, Norman. 2009. "Xenophobia: Where Will It End?" http://www.normangirvan.info/caribbean-xenophobia-where-will-it-end-norman-girvan/.

Gullì, Bruno. 2010. *Earthly Plenitudes: A Study on Sovereignty and Labor*. Philadelphia: Temple University Press.

Harvey, David. 2005. *A Brief History of Neoliberalism*. New York: Oxford University Press.

Hennessy, Alistair, and George Lambie. 1993. *The Fractured Blockade: West European–Cuban Relations during the Revolution*. London: Macmillan.

Hobsbawm, Eric. 1992. *Nations and Nationalism since 1780: Programme, Myth, Reality*. Cambridge: Cambridge University Press.

Holder, Jean. 2007. *The Right Excellent Errol Walton Barrow National Hero and Father of Independence: A Souvenir*. Bridgetown: Jean Holder.

Holloway, John. 2002. *Change the World without Taking Power: The Meaning of Revolution Today*. London: Polity.

———. 2005. "Stop Making Capitalism". In *Human Dignity: Social Autonomy and the Critique of Capitalism*, edited by Werner Bonefeld and Kosmas Psychopedis, 173–80. Aldershot, UK: Ashgate.

Horne, Gerald. 2007. *Cold War in a Hot Zone: The United States Confronts Labor and Independence Struggles in the British West Indies*. Philadelphia: Temple University Press.

Horsman, Reginald. 1981. *Race and Manifest Destiny: The Origins of American Racial Anglo-Saxonism*. Cambridge: Harvard University Press.

IOHSD (*Inquiry into Occupation of Haiti and Santo Domingo: Hearings Before a Select Comm. on Haiti and Santo Domingo*). 1921. Senate, 67th Cong., 1st Sess. Vol. 1.

Jahn, Beate. 1998. "One Step Forward, Two Steps Back: Critical Theory as the Latest Edition of Liberal Idealism". *Millennium Journal of International Studies* 27 (3): 613–41.

———. 2000. *The Cultural Construction of International Relations*. New York: Palgrave Macmillan.

Jones, Natalie Dietrich. 2013. "In Defence of Barbados?" *Gleaner*, 13 October.

JOS (Joint Chiefs of Staff Memorandum to the Secretary of Defense) 1969/321. 1962. Top Secret, 12 March. Report by the Department of Defense and Joint Chiefs of Staff Representative on the Caribbean Survey Group to the Joint Chiefs of Staff on Cuba Project (TS). Unclassified.

Kantorowicz, Ernst H. 1957. *The King's Two Bodies: A Study in Medieval Political Theology*. Princeton: Princeton University Press.

Kaplan, Marty. 2013. "Textism: Is Spelling Over? Are We Witnessing the Death of Proper Language?" Alternet.com. 10 October. http://www.alternet.org/culture/textism-spelling-over.

Keen, Timothy, and Paul Gioia. 2015. "The Guantanamo Base: A US Colonial Relic Impeding Peace with Cuba". 12 February. http://www.coha.org/the-guantanamo-base-a-u-s-colonial-relic-impeding-peace-with-cuba/.

Koenigsberg, Richard. 2009. *Nations Have a Right to Kill*. New York: Library of Social Science.

Lamming, George. 1953. *In the Castle of My Skin*. London: Michael Joseph.

Landau, Saul. 1988. *The Dangerous Doctrine*. Boulder: Westview.

Layne, Christopher. 2006. *American Grand Strategy from 1940 to the Present*. Ithaca: Cornell University Press.

Lerner, Gerda. 1986. *The Creation of Patriarchy*. New York: Oxford University Press.

Lewis, Linden. 2004a. "Masculinity, the Political Economy of the Body and Patriarchal Power in the Caribbean." In *Gender in the 21st Century: Caribbean Perspectives, Visions and Possibilities*, edited by Barbara Bailey and Elsa Leo-Rhynie, 236–61. Kingston: Ian Randle.

———. 2004b. "Caribbean Masculinity at the Fin de Siècle". In *Interrogating Caribbean Masculinities: Theoretical and Empirical Analyses*, edited by Rhoda Reddock, 244–66. Kingston: University of the West Indies Press.

Lewis, W. Arthur. 1978. *Evolution of the International Economic Order*. Princeton: Princeton University Press.

Link, Arthur S., ed. 1980. *The Papers of Woodrow Wilson*, vol. 35, *1915–1916*. Princeton: Princeton University Press.

Losurdo, Domenico. 2011. *Liberalism: A Counter History*. London: Verso.

Love, Eric. 2004. *Race over Empire: Racism and US Imperialism, 1865–1900*. Chapel Hill: University of North Carolina Press.

Maritain, Jacques. 1951. *Man and the State*. Chicago: University of Chicago Press.

Mawby, Spencer. 2012. *Ordering Independence: The End of Empire in the Anglophone Caribbean, 1947–1969*. Basingstoke, UK: Palgrave Macmillan.

McGrew, Anthony. 2007. "Organized Violence in the Making (and Remaking) of Globalization". In *Globalization Theory: Approaches and Controversies*, edited by David Held and Anthony McGrew, 15–40. Malden, MA: Polity.

Mills, Charles. 2010. *Radical Theory and Caribbean Reality: Race, Class and Social Domination*. Kingston: University of the West Indies Press.

Neocleous, Mark. 2008. *Critique of Security*. Montreal and Kingston, ON: McGill-Queens University Press.

Newton, Melanie J. 2008. *The Children of Africa in the Colonies: Free People of Color in Barbados in the Age of Emancipation*. Baton Rouge: Louisiana State University Press.

OG (*Official Gazette*, Barbados). 1951a. Vol. 84, no. 4, 5 July.

———. 1951b. Vol. 86, no. 79, 1 October.

———. 1952. Vol. 86, no. 49, 19 June.

Oldfield, Adrian. 1990. *Citizenship and Community: Civic Republicanism and the Modern World*. London: Routledge.

Osiander, Andreas. 2001. "Sovereignty, International Relations and the Westphalian Myth". *International Organization* 55 (2) Spring: 251–87.

Pérez, Louis A., Jr. 1998. *The War of 1898: The United States and Cuba in History and Historiography*. Chapel Hill: University of North Carolina Press.

Perry, Jeffrey B. 2010. "The Developing Conjuncture and Some Insights from Hubert Harrison and Theodore W. Allen on the Centrality of the Fight against White Supremacy." *Cultural Logic: Marxist Theory and Practise.* 2–117.

Prozorov, Sergei. 2010. "The State of Nature as a Site of Happy Life: On Giorgio Agamben's Reading of Hobbes". In *International Political Theory after Hobbes,* edited by Raia Prokhovnik and Gabriella Slomp, 123–46. New York: Palgrave Macmillan.

Rabe, Stephen G. 2005. *US Intervention in British Guiana: A Cold War Story.* Chapel Hill: University of North Carolina Press.

Richards, David A.J. 2010. *Fundamentalism in American Religion and Law: Obama's Challenge to Patriarchy's Threat to Democracy.* Cambridge: Cambridge University Press.

Robinson, Tracy. 2000. "Fictions of Citizenship, Bodies without Sex: The Production and Effacement of Gender in Law". *Small Axe* (March): 1–27.

Robinson, William I. 2004. *A Theory of Global Capitalism: Production, Class and State in a Transnational World.* Baltimore: Johns Hopkins University Press.

———. 2014. "The Political Economy of Israeli Apartheid and the Spectre of Genocide". Truthout.org. September 19. http://www.truth-out.org/news/item/26254-the-political-economy-of-israeli-apartheid-and-the-specter-of-genocide.

Rosenberg, Justin. 2000. *The Follies of Globalization Theory: Polemical Essays.* London: Verso.

Rosenfelder, Mark. 1996. Zompist.com. "U.S. Interventions in Latin America". http://www.zompist.com/latam.html.

Sand, Shlomo. 2009. *The Invention of the Jewish People.* London: Verso.

Sanders, Sir Ronald. 2013. "Shanique Marie [*sic*] Case before the CCJ: A Landmark for Free Movement of Caribbean People?" *Sir Ronald Sanders* (blog), 8 February. http://www.sirronaldsanders.com/viewarticle.aspx?ID=353.

Santner, Eric. 2011. *The Royal Remains: The People's Two Bodies and the Endgame of Sovereignty.* Chicago: University of Chicago Press.

Schmitt, Carl. (1932) 1996. *The Concept of the Political,* translated by George Schwab. Chicago: University of Chicago Press.

Sharabi, Hisham. 1988. *Neopatriarchy: A Theory of Distorted Change in Arab Society.* Oxford: Oxford University Press.

SOG (*Supplement to the Official Gazette* [Barbados]). 1950. "Barbados Annual Report of the Department of Labour for the Year 1950".

———. 1952a. Vol. 87, no. 2, 7 January.

———. 1952b. Vol. 87, no. 3, 10 January.

Stepan, Nancy. 1982. *The Idea of Race in Science: Great Britain 1800–1960.* London: Macmillan.

Thompson, Alvin O. 1997. *The Haunting Past: Politics, Economics and Race in Caribbean Life.* Armonk: M.E. Sharpe.

UNDP (United Nations Development Programme). 2012. *Caribbean Human Development Report 2012: Human Development and the Shift to Better Citizen Security.* New York: United Nations Development Programme. http://www.regionalcentrelac-undp.org/en/hdr-caribbean.

Wallerstein, Immanuel, Randall Collins, Michael Mann, Georgi Derluguian and Craig Calhoun. 2013. *Does Capitalism Have a Future?* Oxford: Oxford University Press.

Watson, Hilbourne A. 2007. "Materialist Praxis and Nationalist Aesthetics: A Perspective on George Lamming's Contribution to Caribbean Intellectual Culture". Typescript. Department of International Relations, Bucknell University, Lewisburg, PA.

———. 2013. "Transnational Capitalist Globalization and the Limits of Sovereignty: State, Security, Order, Violence, and the Caribbean". In *Caribbean Sovereignty, Development and Democracy in an Age of Globalization*, edited by Linden Lewis, 35–67. New York: Routledge.

Welch, Pedro L.V. 1992. "In Search of a Barbadian Identity: Historical Factors in the Evolution of a Barbadian Literary Tradition". *Journal of the Barbados Museum and Historical Society* 40: 37–47.

Williams, Michael C. 2006. "The Hobbesian Theory of International Relations: Three Traditions." In *Classical Theory in International Relations*, edited by Beate Jahn, 253–76. Cambridge: Cambridge University Press.

Wood, Ellen Meiksins. 1995. *Capitalism against Democracy*. Cambridge: Cambridge University Press.

———. 2002. "Global Capital, National States". In *Historical Materialism and Globalization*, edited by Mark Rupert and Hazel Smith, 17–39. London: Routledge.

Yuval-Davis, Nira. 2011. *The Politics of Belonging: Intersectional Contestations*. London: Sage.

Zavarzadeh, Mas'ud. 2003. "The Pedagogy of Totality". In *Red Critique: Marxist Theory and Critique of the Contemporary* (Fall–Winter): 1–53.

Žižek, Slavoj. 2001. *Did Somebody Say Totalitarianism? Five Interventions in the (Mis)Use of a Notion*. London: Verso.

———. 2012. "Why Obama Is More than Bush with a Human Face". *Guardian*, 14 November.

3 From Revolutionary Slaves to Powerless Citizens

The Unresolved Contradictions of the Haitian Revolution

ALEX DUPUY

Haiti was born as a sovereign state in 1804 after a unique and successful revolutionary war against French colonial rule, much as the United States was created after the 1776 American Revolution. However, unlike the new United States, the new Republic of Haiti abolished racial slavery and declared all citizens, men and women, to be equal. As I will argue in this chapter, this extraordinary achievement by the revolutionary slaves would prove to be a pyrrhic victory for the labouring classes that soon became subordinated to and exploited by a new but divided dominant ruling class. The victory would also lead to what I call the stalemate for the new Haitian ruling class. There were two primary reasons for these outcomes.

First, the dominant class became divided between those factions whose power was derived from the ownership of property and the commercial sectors and those who controlled state power. Given the specific configuration of the dominant class that emerged during and after the revolution, the state itself became a primary site of conflict between factions of that class. Thus, rather than acting to promote the development of the productive forces of the economy in order to expand the scope of production and of private capital accumulation, the holders of state power did the opposite: they stifled such expansion by competing directly with the private sector to accumulate wealth. Rather than serving as an instrument for the development of the economy as a whole, the wielders of state power used the state as a primary site for the promotion of the interests of a faction of the dominant class that used the state's resources for its private enrichment. It is in this sense, then, that

I speak of the Haitian bourgeoisie comprising two factions – one which accumulates wealth through its private ownership of capital in the means of production and the other which accumulates wealth through its control of the state and its various apparatuses. These are the two dominant factions of the bourgeoisie, one economic and the other state based. Substantively, the competition and conflict between the holders of state power and the economically dominant class notwithstanding, the two always formed a bargaining relationship, or a pact of domination, with each other. Largely, if the economically dominant class always had to pay its "dues to the state to maintain [its] dominance" (Trouillot 1990, 28), the holders of state power also found it necessary to reach compromises with the economically dominant class, "even while it limit[ed] the reach of representative institutions, including those that represent the dominant classes" (28).

An important distinction between these two factions of the dominant class needs to be made. If the state bourgeoisie could operate relatively autonomously and at times even be contrary to the interests of the private-sector bourgeoisie, it nonetheless remained dependent on the latter, as well as on the relations between that class faction and the governments and bourgeoisies of the dominant capitalist powers with which Haiti interacted. This fact made the private-sector bourgeoisie the primary accumulators of capital in Haiti and thus gave them greater leverage over the state bourgeoisie. Moreover the economic bourgeoisie reproduced itself by bequeathing its wealth to its descendants and through its continued participation in the world market. By contrast, the state bourgeoisie could not as a matter of right transfer power to its offspring – hence the tendency of those who control the state apparatuses to prolong their hold on state power as long as possible and sometimes even make it hereditary (a practice that could endure as long as dictatorships and coups d'état were the principal means of acquiring power). This was the case throughout the nineteenth and most of the twentieth century, until a mass movement in the mid-1980s toppled the thirty-year Duvalier dictatorship and ushered in a transition to democracy.

However, the institutionalization of democratic governance and transfer of power is not to be equated with the empowerment of "the people" and their ability to determine the public (economic and political) agenda. The reason is that in a capitalist society the fiscal health or well-being of the state usually depends on the growth and well-being of the economy, and the latter in turn depends on the extent to which the capitalists – those who own or control the principal means of production – invest their capital to generate economic growth to accumulate more wealth. As many have argued, this fact grants the private owners of capital – domestic or foreign – much greater sway over state policies than non-owners – the majority of citizens – have, which means that a capitalist democracy must disempower the people if it is to serve the interests of (private) capital. The point here is that there is an inverse relationship between capitalism and democracy (Przeworski 1985; Wood 1995; Held 1995).

The second factor that led to the stalemate of the bourgeoisie, on the one hand, and the pyrrhic victory of the labouring classes, on the other, was the inability of the bourgeoisie to transform the slave masses into proletarians because of the former slaves' success in gaining access to land, either as outright owners (with or without legal land titles) or sharecroppers. At the same time, the former slaves who became subsistence farmers could not block their subordination to and exploitation by the dominant classes, which occurred through the imposition of taxes (direct and indirect) and other mechanisms of extortion, rents on lands leased by sharecroppers or the buying and selling of the cash crops sold on the world market. For its part, unable to proletarianize the peasant classes, the new bourgeoisie could not revitalize the sugar plantations that had been the basis of Saint-Domingue's wealth in the eighteenth century, or lay the groundwork for the development of national industries. This development limited the ability of the dominant-class forces to accumulate wealth mainly from the circulation of commodities (commerce and trade) rather than the production of commodities (capital and consumer goods) for domestic and export markets. In other words, the Haitian bourgeoisie became primarily a rentier and a commercial rather than an industrial-manufacturing bourgeoisie. This fact, as we will see, also facilitated the return and reassertion of foreign capital's dominance over the national economy, in the form of commercial capital in the nineteenth century and industrial-manufacturing capital in the twentieth and twenty-first centuries.

Revolution and the Rise of a New Ruling Class[1]

Toussaint Louverture was not among the original leaders of the slave revolution that erupted in August 1791; however, his appearance on the political stage and the instrumental role he would play in creating an indigenous revolutionary army, which would ultimately defeat the French colonial forces and lead to the declaration of independence and birth of the Republic of Haiti in January 1804, marked the first major phase of the transformation of Haiti. The transformation of Haiti was characterized by the rise of a new ruling class, which comprised two factions: the *affranchis* (or "free people of colour") property-owning class of the ancien régime, most of whom were, on the one hand, mulattoes and, on the other, a newly formed, predominantly black landed class, which comprised mostly military officers of the revolutionary army that appropriated properties from the former French planters and new lands that fell under the domain of the new state-to-be.

Mulattoes, as blacks, were not a homogeneous group; they differed in terms of skin colour (from lighter to darker skin complexion) as they did in their social status. The "line" between those who were considered mulatto or black was fluid, but in general mulattoes were those of mixed African and European ancestry, who had lighter skin complexions, and blacks were those of predominantly African ancestry, who tended to have darker skin complexions. There tended also to be a correlation between skin colour and social status, such that in colonial Saint-Domingue a higher percentage of mulattoes than blacks were part of the population of *affranchis*. Many among the mulattoes owned property, including slaves, and others engaged in occupations ranging from artisans to plantation overseers, professional soldiers in colonial militia to semi-skilled and unskilled workers. The vast majority of slaves were black; however, a small number of mulattoes were slaves. In short, mulattoes did not share similar class positions, similar relations or similar interests on the burning questions of the day with either whites or blacks. Most wanted equality with whites, but not all of them supported equality for blacks or the abolition of slavery. Thus, when I speak of "mulatto" interests here, I am referring primarily to the interests of mulatto property and slave owners, their leaders and, after the revolution, those mulattoes who comprised the dominant faction of the bourgeoisie and their spokesmen/intellectual defenders.

Louverture joined the rebellious slaves around November 1791 when they defected to the Spanish army in neighbouring Spanish San Domingo which, along with the English, were fighting the French in Saint-Domingue. But once the French government decreed the emancipation of the slaves in 1794, Louverture and his now seasoned slave army switched over to the French side to help them expel the Spanish and English forces from French Saint-Domingue. By mid-1800, Louverture and his army of ex-slaves emerged as the dominant force in control of Saint-Domingue. Though his army included a number of mulattoes, most of the high-ranking officers and military commanders of the new revolutionary army led by Louverture were black. Once in full control of the colony in 1801, Louverture formed a nine-member Central Assembly that included white colonial planters and mulattoes chosen for their loyalty to him. The assembly produced the constitution of 1801 that reorganized the colony and proclaimed Louverture governor general for life, with the right to name his successor. Despite its republican and liberal principles based on juridical equality of all citizens and the elimination of social distinctions based on race or colour, the 1801 constitution in fact sanctioned the military dictatorship of Louverture. It also introduced the practice of political absolutism and permanence of office, in addition to the use of public office as the private property of those who held it – that is, what I and others have called the prebendal or predatory state in Haiti (see Dupuy 1989, Fatton 2002).

Louverture did not trust the French and knew that they would attempt to retake the colony and re-enslave its population. But he also realized that declaring the independence of Saint-Domingue would sever its economic ties with France, which he felt were essential for its prosperity. Thus he opted for a compromise that allowed him to exercise the greatest amount of autonomy over the colony, short of declaring its independence. But for this option to have any chance of success, and for the economy to recover on a sustainable basis from the tremendous losses suffered during ten years of revolutionary war,[2] Louverture had to maintain the plantation system established by the French, allow the French planters to retain control of their plantations and compel the former slaves to continue to work on the plantations as paid wage labourers.

Following the outbreak of the revolution many planters had fled the colony. The government then decided to take over the properties of those who refused to return and either leased or sold them to the high-ranking officers of the revolutionary army who were now in charge of managing those properties. Through such means Louverture and many other high-ranking military officers, including Jean-Jacques Dessalines, acquired several plantations.

Military officers and administrators of the new political order did not only appropriate properties from former French planters; they also despoiled the public treasury. It was on that basis that a new black propertied class was created alongside the old class of white and free mulatto and black property owners under the old regime. Herein lay the raison d'être and the historical-material base of the predatory state system and of generalized corruption of public office in Haiti: the formation, promotion and reproduction of a faction of the dominant class made up of both those who had social origins generally not from the traditional propertied classes and those who had property, which helped them obtain special privileges, exemptions or other favours from office holders. This mutually dependent relationship was also the basis for the pacts of domination between state rulers and the economically dominant classes.

To maintain order and the plantation system, Louverture imposed harsh discipline on the labourers and confined them to their plantations. Since many of the former slaves had fled to the mountainous hinterland and were opposed to returning, Louverture contemplated increasing the plantation labour force by importing slave workers from Africa bought from English and American slave traders, with the intention of freeing them once they arrived in the colony. At the same time, he adopted a conciliatory attitude towards those French planters who remained in the colony. As C.L.R. James points out, Louverture was not naive. He understood that the whites had no choice but to accept his regime, that the planters hated the labourers and that the planters and the mercantile bourgeoisie in France were anxious for the return of the old regime.

James maintains that Louverture "set his face sternly against racial discrimination. He guarded his powers and the rights of the labourers by an army overwhelmingly black. But within that wall he encouraged all to come back, mulattoes and whites. The policy was both wise and workable, and if his relations with France had been regularized he would have done all he hoped to do" (James 1963, 261).

The labourers that Louverture compelled to return to the plantations did not see things that way. They equated plantation labour with slavery and aspired to become independent, landowning farmers.[3] They therefore opposed Louverture's policies, and his intention to import new workers from Africa deepened their distrust. So profound was the resentment of the labourers against Louverture that they rebelled against him with the aim of overthrowing Louverture's government and massacring the whites. Louverture moved quickly and swiftly to suppress them; however, he never succeeded in preventing them from gaining access to land, especially uncultivated lands in the hills and mountains of Haiti – a practice that had its origins in the rebellious tradition of *marronage* (fugitive slaves) – that haunted the slave owners throughout the colonial period and played a key role in instigating the general slave uprising in 1791 (see Fouchard 1972). At issue here, then, was the fundamental class question that was being decided: who would dominate the colony and in whose interest it would be reorganized.

Along with the class question, the issues of independence from France and what policies to adopt towards the French colonists in Saint-Domingue were also coming to a head. These conflicts put Louverture in opposition to Jean-Jacques Dessalines and other high-ranking officers of the rebel army and reached their decisive moment when Napoleon Bonaparte sent an expedition to Saint-Domingue in 1802, led by his brother-in-law General Victor Emmanuel Leclerc, to recapture the colony from Louverture and restore slavery. Faced with this imminent threat to his revolutionary government and to the liberty of the former slave masses, Louverture equivocated. As James (1963) argues, instead of declaring independence immediately, raising the population against Bonaparte's army and giving the French planters and white colonists the choice of either leaving the colony or accepting the new order and defending it, Louverture tried to maintain order and reassure the whites that they and their properties were safe. Moreover, at the same time that he sought to appease the whites, Louverture ignored the masses, when, as James points out, he needed them most. For James, this was a regrettable and fatal error that stemmed from his misunderstanding of the significance of the race question at this specific juncture in the conflict. As James's frequently quoted, but often misunderstood, passage states: "The race question is subsidiary to the class question in politics, and to think of imperialism in terms of race is disastrous. But to neglect the racial factor as merely incidental is an error only less grave than to make it fundamental" (James 1963, 283). James believed that Louverture understood this, but that his mistake was to still deal with it in that way – ignoring the fears and feelings of the black masses while at the same time appearing to be taking the side of the whites.

James's argument would have been more convincing if, in fact, Louverture shared the same interests as the former slave masses, but this was not the case. As I have argued (Dupuy 1995), Louverture had become part of an emerging new landowning class whose interests demanded the preservation of the plantation system and hence the suppression of the aspirations of the former slaves. Louverture's error was not that he took the masses for granted, as James suggests, but rather that he believed he could convince the French government and the colonial planters who had remained in the colony to accept the new social order he had created because he preserved Saint-Domingue's colonial status and defended the properties of the whites.

Unlike Louverture, Dessalines had a different objective: to get rid of the French and declare the colony's independence – to achieve which Dessalines knew that he had to get rid of Louverture. That opportunity came soon after Louverture, whose military position had been weakened with the prior submission of several of his top general officers, decided to submit as well, but not until he signed an agreement with Leclerc that freedom would be guaranteed to all and that all the officers of the revolutionary army would maintain their grade and their functions (James 1963, 327; Pluchon 1979, 340). Once Louverture submitted, however, Leclerc intended to arrest and deport him to France. He approached Dessalines with the idea, and the latter signalled to him that he would not oppose such a move, and that in fact it would serve his interests. Christophe and Clerveaux, two other general officers of the revolutionary army, told Leclerc the same thing (Madiou 1989, 2, 321–22, 329; James 1963, 332–33; Dubois 2004, 274–75). In June 1802, the French general Brunet, under Leclerc's orders, arranged to meet with Louverture and then proceeded to arrest and deport him to France.[4] As the insurrection against the French continued, and word reached Saint-Domingue that slavery had been restored in the other French colonies, Dessalines and the other black and mulatto officers left the French army and organized the war that drove the French out for good and won Haiti its independence, in January 1804.

Pyrrhic Victory of the Peasantry

The conflicts between the dominant class and the former slave masses in deciding the land question and between the factions of the dominant class to control the state would characterize the second major social and economic transformation of Haiti in the nineteenth century. These conflicts would result in what I called the stalemate of the bourgeoisie and the pyrrhic victory of the agricultural labourers and peasants – factors that contributed significantly to the underdevelopment of the Haitian economy and its subservience to foreign capital.[5]

No sooner had Haiti declared its independence on 1 January 1804 than the struggle between the black and mulatto factions of the new ruling class erupted into a full-blown civil war that led to the partition of the country from 1806 to 1807 into the State of Haiti in the north, under the black general-turned-king Henri Christophe, who renamed the territory the Kingdom of Haiti in 1811, and the Republic of Haiti in the west and south, controlled by the mulatto general-turned-president Alexandre Pétion. The mulatto Jean-Pierre Boyer assumed the presidency of the republic after Pétion's death in 1818 and reunified the country after Christophe's death in 1820. The internecine conflicts between the two factions of the new ruling class for control of the state would continue throughout the nineteenth century and well into the twentieth, a period in which military coups d'état would become the principal mechanism for removing governments and forming new ones led by one faction or another. These practices gave rise to the predatory anti-developmental state by systematizing corruption, by establishing the non-equivalence of state power and the power of the ruling class and by separating state power from the general interests of the ruling class, while simultaneously creating a contradictory interdependence between them.

Those internecine conflicts also had their ideological expressions as "colour" conflicts between "mulattoes" and "blacks", which consisted of "reappropriating the white racist ideology of black inferiority . . . [to] propagate hatred and contempt [between] mulattoes against blacks and vice versa [to] establish an incommunicability between them and erase the problematic of social injustice" (Péan 2007, 112–13). The mulatto variant of that ideology justified mulatto dominance by claiming that being in "closer proximity" to whites, mulattoes were the "most advanced" and, therefore, the "most capable" and "natural" leaders (Paul [1882] 1976, 37). By contrast, the black nationalist variant claimed that their "likeness" to the black majority made them "the most authentic" representative of that majority, and that "a government of the majority by the majority and those who respect the majority is the only one possible in Haiti" (Janvier 1885, 248).

In short, the ideologies of colour expressed not only a struggle for power between the two factions of the dominant class but, most importantly, a struggle for a share in the exploitation of the subordinated classes in terms of which faction controlled, on one hand, the apparatuses of the state and their prebendal yields and, on the other, the private sector and its links to the world market and foreign capital. And although the "colour question" cannot be reduced to class relations, it cannot be understood independently of those relations. Though classifications of colour or race are ideological expressions and means of justifying the unequal positions of members of such colour or racial groups in the social division of labour, their significance can also diminish or become politically if not socially irrelevant when there are changes in the structural location of and in the relations of power between the contending groups (see Dupuy 2013).

The conflicts between the black and mulatto elites can be understood better through an examination of the class configuration of Haiti in the nineteenth century and the articulation of the Haitian economy with the global capitalist economy. As mentioned above, the former slave masses successfully resisted the attempt by Toussaint Louverture to compel them to return to work on the sugar plantations as wage labourers. They also resisted such attempts by the governments of Jean-Jacques Dessalines (1804–6) and Jean-Pierre Boyer (1818–43). The former slaves fought against the consolidation of landed property by the dominant class and succeeded in gaining effective ownership of or access to land, thereby controlling the means and processes of food production for the domestic market. With the demise of sugar production, coffee emerged as Haiti's main export crop; here, too, the peasant farmers controlled production but not sale or export (as I will explain below).

Three categories of landed-peasant farmers emerged: those who owned land (that is, who had legal titles), those who possessed land but did not own it (that is, they had de facto control but not de jure ownership), and those who leased land from large landowners through the *métayage*, or sharecropping, system. Those who owned or possessed land were also those who had larger (though still relatively small) farms of approximately ten to seventeen acres. Sharecroppers, however, leased their land from the bourgeoisie, who owned properties larger than sixty-three acres and subdivided their estates into smaller units. And below the categories of landowning or land-possessing peasants or sharecroppers were those who did not own land – a proletariat – who were thus compelled to hire themselves out as day labourers to those who owned or possessed land. The changes in the pattern of land ownership and the rise of a landed peasantry had significant effects on the relations between the dominant and subordinate classes, on the one hand, and between the dominant classes and foreign powers (France in particular), on the other.

First, because the majority of the rural population were farmers with access to land, they controlled the means and processes of production and, hence, the rate of their exploitation. This was the case even where the landed bourgeoisie tried to extract more surplus from the sharecroppers.[6] Second, unable to defeat, expropriate from and proletarianize the majority of the peasantry, the bourgeoisie was stymied in its efforts in the mid-nineteenth century to develop a national infrastructure in both the rural and urban areas; expand public, technical and professional education; diversify agriculture; promote the growth of small- and medium-sized industries; establish a textile industry and create a coastal maritime service, among other ventures. Consequently, the dominant classes were limited to accumulating wealth primarily from the circulation rather than the production process. They became a commercial and a rentier bourgeoisie that engaged in commercial and trade relations with other countries to which they could export Haitian agricultural products (principally coffee) and from which they could import durable and consumer goods that they resold on the domestic market.

Establishing and extending trade, commercial and financial relations with other countries, especially the major powers of western Europe and the United States, required first and foremost those countries' recognition of Haiti as a sovereign republic; however, all of them steadfastly refused to do so until France did. For the United States in particular, recognizing Haiti's independence would have legitimized the slave revolution that achieved it, thus undermining the United States' own slave regime and ideology of white supremacy. The United States also pushed to prevent the other independent states of Latin America from recognizing Haiti's independence at the Panama Congress of 1825. France's position was thus strengthened, and it demanded that Haiti pay it an indemnity of 150 million francs (later reduced to 60 million francs) calculated on the estimated value of the properties French planters owned before the outbreak of the revolution in Saint-Domingue, as well as demanding other concessions in its favour on duties imposed on French goods and Haitian goods exported to France.

As Pétion and Christophe had done before him, Boyer considered such demands blackmail and refused to go along, but, knowing that Haiti was isolated diplomatically and had nowhere else to turn, he ultimately accepted the French conditions. This event was a major turning point in Haiti's post-revolutionary history that represented a major defeat for the ruling class and whatever aspirations Haiti had to have its sovereignty recognized and respected by the community of states. The indemnity would prove to be the Achilles heel of the Haitian ruling class, politically and economically. To start paying the indemnity Boyer had to borrow money from foreign banks – French in particular, adding insult to injury – and since Haiti's trade and fiscal balances would almost always be negative, all subsequent Haitian governments would incur sovereign debts as well. Foreign lenders and their governments would henceforth use Haiti's debts to wrench concessions for their businesses that sought to establish a foothold in Haiti. It was through such means that foreign commercial interests would re-enter Haiti in the nineteenth century, begin to supplant Haitian businesses and pave the way for the penetration of foreign capital in other sectors in the twentieth century, from agricultural to financial, extractive and industrial activities.

Herein also lay Haiti's vulnerability to the return and dominance of foreign capital, as well as its subordinated rural and urban classes' ultimate political weakness and defeat. Unable to accumulate capital directly from the production of commodities, the dominant-class factions enriched themselves by other means. Those who owned land or had commercial interests controlled the sphere of circulation – that is, through the rents extracted from their lands, by buying the export crops (primarily coffee) and selling them on the international markets and by reselling imported goods on the domestic market. Those who controlled the state apparatuses used political means – that is, taxes, corruption and other means of exploitation.[7] This explains why the state became the site of intense internecine conflicts between the factions of the dominant class and why that conflict expressed itself as a "colour conflict" between the mulatto elite, who tended to control the commercial and import-export sectors, and the predominantly black landed elite, who sought to solidify their control of the state. That is also why the parliamentary or democratic form of government could not take hold during the nineteenth century and why the coup d'état became the principal means of forming and removing governments.

Between 1804 and 1915 (the year the US occupation of Haiti started), there were twenty-nine insurrections to overthrow or install a government led by a leader from one of the two factions of the ruling class.

For all their ability to block the expropriation of their land and limit their exploitation, the peasant farmers remained powerless economically and politically. They could never effectively block the different mechanisms of exploitation or surplus extraction to which they were subjected, such as the derisive prices they received from the coffee speculators (middlemen between the peasants and urban merchants) for their crops, the direct and indirect taxes imposed by the state and the corvée rural state officials forced them to perform for public-works projects – and the pain of fines or imprisonment for those who refused. Peasants resisted these measures and even revolted against particularly abusive or corrupt governments during the nineteenth century; however, those movements remained disorganized and decentralized, and never coalesced into national movements that articulated the aspirations of "the peasantry" as a whole. The reason for this outcome was that the primary interest of the peasants was safeguarding their property rights or their right to have access to land as the sine qua non of their independence and freedom. In short, while the peasants waged a successful struggle to become a landed peasantry, they remained generally poor, subsistence producers subordinated to and exploited by a dominant class. For its part, the bourgeoisie, unable to proletarianize the peasants and preoccupied with endless internecine conflicts to control the state, was stalemated in its ability to lay the foundation for industrial development. It therefore remained a parasitic class whose wealth derived from land rents, extortion, exporting coffee and other goods (such as lumber) and reselling imported manufactured and consumer goods on the national market.

Democratization, Proletarianization and Powerlessness[8]

The twentieth century began with the nineteen-year US occupation (1915–34),[9] which led to the third major transformation of the economic, social and political landscape of Haiti. That process of transformation was characterized by: (1) the substitution of US dominance for European, primarily French, dominance; (2) the proletarianization of Haitian peasants combined with the export of Haitian workers to other parts of the Caribbean and North America and (3) a transition to a weak or minimalist democracy and the disempowerment of the majority of the people to effect substantive change. As I have argued elsewhere (Dupuy 1989, 129–42), the US invasion and occupation of Haiti must be understood in the context of the projection of US power in Central America and the Caribbean since the 1820s in order to displace its European rivals, establish its hegemony and facilitate the penetration of US capital throughout the region. Far from being peaceful, this process was often preceded by military interventions and occupations of many countries in the region between 1853 and 1916, including Nicaragua, Honduras, Guatemala, Mexico, Cuba, Haiti and the Dominican Republic. Under the threat of having the Virgin Islands seized by the United States if the Danish government refused to sell them, the Danes sold the islands to United States in 1916. In short, since peaceful trade alone would not guarantee the dominance of US capital in the region, military power became its necessary support (Dupuy 1989, 129–30).

Once the United States crushed the five-year guerilla war against the occupation, it replaced the old Haitian army with a new army and police force that became the dominant political force in Haiti until former president Jean-Bertrand Aristide disbanded them in 1995.[10] The United States also drafted and imposed a new constitution that, for the first time since Haiti became independent, allowed foreigners to buy and own commercial property, without the need to marry Haitians as required by previous constitutions. It also created a centralized public administration, expanded technical education and developed a modern infrastructure of roads and other transportation and communication networks to facilitate foreign, primarily US, investments and expand capitalist production. Though US businesses had been established in Haiti before 1915, many new ones followed on the heels of the occupation, including those involved in electricity, port and railroad construction, mining, banking and large-scale plantation production of such things as pineapple, sisal and sugar. The occupation definitively uprooted France as the dominant power in Haiti, economically and politically. Haitian banking and finance were placed under the control of US banks, the Haitian currency was henceforth pegged to the US dollar rather than the French franc, and the United States became the single most important market for Haitian exports and imports.

The intensification of foreign capital investments in Haiti necessitated the proletarianization of farmers. From the outset that process had a dual aspect: creating a supply of labour for businesses operating in Haiti and exporting Haitian workers to other parts of the Caribbean and Central and North America. First, to supply the labour force for the businesses that came to Haiti, US occupation forces and Haitian authorities evicted tens of thousands of peasant farmers from the lands they had leased from the government and ceded it to the companies. Between 1917 and 1955 hundreds of thousands of acres of land were transferred to foreign companies. The authorities adopted other measures to expropriate farmers from lands they leased or rented, such as imposing a tax on alcohol that forced hundreds of small distillers out of business or not renewing leases or increasing their costs to farmers on rented state lands. Agricultural companies, such as those producing sisal and pineapple, foreclosed the provision grounds of the farmers on their large estates or, as did the newly formed Haitian American Sugar Company, contracted small farmers to sell the company their crop at low prices and eventually ended up hiring them as wage labourers. Thus, just as US military power served to implant US capital throughout the region, the occupation authorities used their power to proletarianize Haitian peasants and accomplish in short order what the Haitian bourgeoisie could not do for over one hundred years. Force, in other words, is the intermediary of capital accumulation.

Once unleashed, this process continued unabated after the occupation. From the 1930s to the 1950s, foreign companies came to Haiti to produce bananas, rubber, lumber and bauxite for export. Starting in the 1970s, the United States, through the United States Agency for International Development, the World Bank and the Inter-American Development Bank championed the export assembly industries as Haiti's main capital accumulation strategy. Though initially these industries produced electronic components, baseballs and garments, the latter has become the only activity sustaining the export assembly platform today. And, as it did then, garment assembly today relies on the constant supply of an unskilled labour force that is the lowest-paid in the Caribbean. This is made possible by the decline of agricultural production, a large reserve army of unemployed labour that swells the informal sector and the dogged resistance of the United States Agency for International Development, the World Bank and foreign investors and their subcontracting Haitian partners to raising wages in that sector, combined with the suppression of labour unions. The proletarianization of Haitian peasants was not limited to supplying a labour force for the businesses operating in Haiti only. During the occupation Haitian workers were also recruited to work on US-owned sugar and other agricultural plantations in Cuba, the Dominican Republic and Central America. Though Haitians stopped migrating to Cuba after the Cuban Revolution, migration to the neighbouring Dominican Republic, the wider Caribbean and North America increased dramatically.

The US occupation also modified the class structure and balance of power in Haiti beyond the proletarianization of the peasantry, which still constitutes the majority of the population. The most significant change was the rise of a small but significant urban middle class of professionals and white-collar workers spawned by both the expansion of job opportunities in the private sector and the growth of a civil bureaucracy and state institutions (for example, education, public works, sanitation and health), in addition to the new Haitian army and police. The political significance of the rise of the middle class was the growth within its ranks of an intelligentsia and various currents and political tendencies that expressed the new class forces and interests that would form broad coalitions with factions of the dominant class as well as with working-class organizations and trade unions.

Two broad political and ideological tendencies crystallized during the 1930s and 1940s that would have great significance for subsequent political developments in Haiti. On the left were communist, socialist, social democratic and populist parties, which, along with some progressive trade unions, prioritized the "class question", democracy and social justice. On the right were those parties, organizations and trade unions that were staunchly anti-socialist, anti-communist, nationalist and populist, and prioritized the "colour question" and the conflicts between the mulatto and black bourgeoisies. The US occupation authorities exacerbated that conflict by installing or supporting mulatto presidents and placing mulattoes, already dominant economically, in the top administrative and civil service positions, as well as in the top echelons of the new Haitian army.

Though both mulattoes and blacks belonged to the middle class and the subordinate stratum of the bourgeoisie, blacks predominated in both and were intensely conscious of the correlation between skin colour and upward social mobility. Thus, when mulattoes regained control of the government and monopolized key positions in the various state apparatuses, including the military, they directly challenged the black middle class's traditional means of social ascension, thereby elevating the "colour question" to the centre stage, ideologically and politically. The struggle between those two factions reached a decisive turning point in 1946, when the black-nationalist forces succeeded in electing Dumarsais Estimé as president.[11] Though Estimé's presidency was short-lived, it allowed the black middle class, in alliance with the provincial and urban black bourgeoisie, to regain its dominance in the government and public administration. But it was in 1957 that the black-nationalist forces reached their apogee with the election of François Duvalier to the presidency,[12] which he soon transformed into a thirty-year dictatorship that included transferring power to his son Jean-Claude before his death in 1971. Jean-Claude then ruled until he was overthrown and exiled in 1986.

Here I will focus on three essential aspects of the Duvalier regime that were consequential for future political and economic developments in Haiti. First, the principal objective of the regime under François Duvalier was not to alter the class structure and economic dominance of the predominantly mulatto bourgeoisie;[13] rather, the aim was to recapture political power for the black bourgeoisie and middle class. It achieved this by purging most, but not all, mulattoes from the top positions in the government, public administration and military.[14] Never fully trusting the military even after having chosen officers to run it, the Duvalier regime created a parallel military force to the Haitian army called the Volunteers for National Security (popularly known as the Tontons Macoutes) that he controlled directly and which was used as the regime's security and terror apparatus.

Second, once in place, the Duvalierist state unleashed a reign of terror unprecedented in Haiti's history. Going beyond the repressiveness of previous dictatorships, the regime spared no one from its violence. Men, women, children, families from all classes and even entire towns were subject to the regime's ruthless and unpredictable terror. No major state or civil society institutions were left untouched or allowed to function independently: the legislature, judiciary and civil administration were all brought under the direct control of Duvalier, and the regime suppressed all hitherto independent political, trade union, media and other civil society organizations by arresting, exiling or killing their leaders who were considered a threat to the regime. Even the Catholic Church came under the regime's control when Duvalier expelled all foreign clergy and replaced them with Haitians. As Michel-Rolph Trouillot observed succinctly, Duvalier's governement "did not seek the physical intervention of the State in the battlefield of politics; it aimed to create a void in that field to the benefit of the State. It wanted an end to that struggle for a lack of combatants in the sphere occupied by the totalitarian executive" (1986, 189).

The cost of capturing and consolidating power for the black-nationalist bourgeoisie and middle class was quite high. In addition to the tens of thousands of citizens killed by the regime, the economy and the standard of living of the majority of the population deteriorated. The regime had alienated the mulatto bourgeoisie as well as the United States and other western European powers, which suspended direct military and financial aid but made no effort to topple the regime. To attract new foreign investments and financial and military aid, the regime made overtures to the mulatto bourgeoisie and offered advantages to foreign investors – such as tax exemptions, an abundance of cheap labour, and a climate of labour peace occasioned by the suppression of all independent labour organizations and the banning of strikes. These measures led US president Richard Nixon to resume full financial and military aid in 1969.

But it was not until after Jean-Claude Duvalier assumed power in 1971 that foreign businesses began to invest in Haiti. This third aspect of the regime was characterized by a triple alliance among the Duvalier regime: the black bourgeoisie and middle class, the mulatto bourgeoisie and foreign capital, with the first two components functioning as junior partners. Substantively, the Haitian government turned over the formulation of economic policy to the United States and the international financial institutions – the World Bank, the International Monetary Fund and the Inter-American Development Bank. Capitalizing on Haiti's poverty, a climate of labour peace achieved through brutal repression and a large, unskilled labour force, those institutions proceeded to transform Haiti into a supplier of the cheapest labour in the Western Hemisphere for the export assembly industries established by foreign investors and domestic entrepreneurs as subcontractors.

Though they would not be fully implemented until after the overthrow of the second Duvalier regime in 1986 and the transition to democracy in the 1990s, a set of "structural adjustment" policies – reductions on tariff and trade restrictions, tax incentives to investors, privatization of public enterprises, reduction of public spending and reduction of the size of the public-sector labour force – would destroy Haiti's near-sufficiency of food and turn it into the largest importer of US-produced foods, especially rice, in the Caribbean. Rather than generating sustainable economic development, these policies exacerbated poverty and income and wealth inequalities and spurred more emigration. An estimated 19 to 20 per cent of the Haitian population (that is, about two million) now lives abroad, the majority of whom are in the Dominican Republic, the United States and Canada. Migration is not only a safety valve or an alternative to unemployment and poverty; it has become an increasingly important lifeline to the economy itself. The remittances by Haitian emigrants are estimated at around 20 per cent of Haiti's gross domestic product – which is more than what Haiti earns from its exports.

Even though it was not as brutally repressive as his father's, the Duvalier son's regime could not reform itself sufficiently to accommodate the popular demands for democratic reforms and civil and human rights that emerged in the early 1980s. As those movements grew and became more radical, Jean-Claude Duvalier was finally forced to leave Haiti in 1986 and went into exile in France. The fall of Duvalier unleashed a power struggle among the neo-Duvalierists and the military for the next four years to regain control of the state.

But the relentless fight of the democratic movement prevented any of the successive military governments from imposing a dictatorship and led instead to the elections that resulted in the landslide electoral victory of the then radical liberation theology priest, Jean-Bertrand Aristide, in December 1990.

The democratic movement fought to rid the country of dictatorship, democratize the government, eliminate corruption in public office, reform the military and police and create a just and equitable society. It comprised many different political, religious, civic, human rights, neighbourhood, women's, student, professional, labour, peasant and media organizations that gave voice to the vast majority of the people and formulated their collective aspirations. Although no single political organization, individual or group of individuals controlled the popular movement, its aggregate demands amounted to nothing short of a call for a maximalist egalitarian democracy in Haiti (Dupuy 2007).

Vowing to carry out the popular mandate for change, Aristide earned the enmity of the neo-Duvalierists, the military, the Haitian bourgeoisie and the United States. Once in power, however, the Aristide government pursued a twofold and contradictory strategy. On the one hand, the government encouraged the people to remain mobilized and to press their demands and incorporated many of them in the programme of government it presented to parliament in February 1991, including greater access to education, health care and land reform and a higher minimum wage. On the other hand, while it called on the bourgeoisie to cooperate with the government to bring about change, it also threatened to unleash the power of the people against them if they refused. The bourgeoisie responded by backing a military coup against Aristide in September 1991 that sent him into exile until US president Bill Clinton returned him to power in October 1994 with the support of twenty thousand US troops (Dupuy 1989; Ballard 1998; Girard 2004; Deibert 2005; Shacochis 1999; Sprague 2012).

By the time Aristide returned to finish the eighteen months left in his first five-year term, he had abandoned his radical views and broken with the interests of the majority of Haitians he championed in 1990. As quid pro quo for returning him to power, Aristide accepted the neo-liberal programme drafted by the international financial institutions in 1994, but managed to avoid implementing them fully by the time he left office and transferred power to the newly elected government of René Préval in February 1996.

When Aristide won re-election for a second and final five-year term in November 2000,[15] the balance of class forces had shifted even more in favour of the bourgeoisie and the organized political opposition. The popular movement that brought him to power in 1990 had been decimated after three years of brutal repression under the junta (1991–94), and Aristide never attempted to revive it. Moreover, the left-of-centre or social democratic parties that had coalesced around him in 1990 and 1991 had broken with him and now opposed his new Lavalas Family Party created in 1996. Thus, in the absence of a strong popular movement to back him, Aristide pursued an accommodation with the bourgeoisie and foreign capital, but they rebuffed him and supported the opposition instead.

Aristide pursued the recommended neo-liberal policies by privatizing public enterprises, reducing tariffs to their lowest levels and negotiating deals with the World Bank and the Inter-American Development Bank to create a free-trade zone in northern Haiti that required the expropriation of farmers and the appropriation of more than a thousand acres of their farm land in the region. But none of these measures won him the support of the international community (especially the United States under the Bush administration), the Haitian bourgeoisie or his political opponents. Fully backed by the United States, France and Canada, the Haitian bourgeoisie and the opposition coalition blocked any and all negotiated solutions that would allow Aristide to remain in power until the end of his second mandate in 2006, and they succeeded in removing him once more from power in February 2004 – and again exiling him – with the help of an armed uprising by former members of the Haitian army that Aristide had dissolved in 1995. An interim government installed by the international community succeeded Aristide,[16] and its main task was to pacify the country – that is, to neutralize the remnants of Aristide's more militant, and sometimes armed, supporters known as Chimères. René Préval was then re-elected for a second and final term in 2006 and ceded power to the elected government of Michel Martelly in 2011. But neither of these two governments challenged the policies outlined above that were dictated by the international community. The dominant political and economic classes of Haiti have become more subservient to and dependent on the international community since the devastating earthquake that hit Haiti in January 2010 and from which it is still far from recovered.

Immediately after the earthquake, the Préval government surrendered the decision-making process to an Interim Haiti Recovery Commission co-chaired by former US president Bill Clinton and then–Haitian prime minister Jean-Max Bellerive. Though the commission comprised equal numbers of representatives from Haiti and the international community, the latter made all the key decisions from which most of the Haitians were excluded (Dupuy 2012). Predictably the commission and the international community pursued the same policies discussed above that exacerbated Haiti's poverty, inequalities and dependence on foreign aid and foreign capital. The objective of those policies had never been to generate sustainable and equitable development in Haiti but to serve the interests of foreign investors to take advantage of the lowest-cost labour for garment production in the hemisphere, as well as US agricultural exports for which Haiti has become the largest importer in the Caribbean region (of rice in particular). The mandate of the Interim Haiti Recovery Commission expired in October 2011; however, the government of President Michel Martelly, which came to power in May of that year, had already made clear its intention to pursue the agenda laid out by the international community.

But if the Haitian bourgeoisie (economic and political) has accepted its subservience to foreign capital, it has in turn gained the support of the latter in suppressing the popular demands for a more just and more equal society. Nowhere can this be seen more clearly than in the struggles of Haitian workers to improve their standard of living by pushing for a higher minimum wage in both Haitian industries and those operating as subcontractors for foreign companies (such as Kmart, Walmart, the Gap, Banana Republic and Levi Strauss & Co.). The gap between the wages of Haitians and those of workers in other Caribbean countries is and has always been high enough to offset transportation, tariffs and other costs to the investors, but the World Bank, the United States Agency for International Development and the Association of Haitian Industries (representing those Haitian entrepreneurs involved in subcontracting production for companies) fought continuously to keep them low.

Whenever a government tried to raise the minimum wage of workers in these industries, as the Aristide government tried to do in 2002 and the Préval government tried to do in 2008, the Haiti business–international financial institutions partnership mentioned above intervened to make sure that did not happen. Consequently, the tens of thousands of workers in the garment industry today, the vast majority of whom are women, receive on average five dollars a day, which, accounting for inflation, is one-third less than the value of the wages they were paid under the Duvalier dictatorship in 1982, when the assembly industries were at the height of their operation. Such a wage covers less than half of the most basic needs of the workers and their families for housing, food, clothing, schooling and transportation. According to the American Federation of Labor and Congress of Industrial Organizations' (AFL-CIO) Solidarity Center, a worker would need to be paid at least five times as much to meet the basic needs for a family of four (Haitigrassrootswatch .squarespace.com, "Haiti: 'Open for Business' ", 29 November, 2011).

Haitian and foreign employers understand all too well the advantages they have over their employees and how to maximize them. As the Haitian owner of one of the largest garment industries in Haiti acknowledged recently, "When you have a country where 80 percent of the people don't work, anything is good" (Haitigrassrootswatch .squarespace.com, "Anti-Union, Pro-'Race to the Bottom' ", 29 November 2011). The manager of another plant justified the low wages in this way: "If you don't work, you don't have anything. [With the wages they get] at least [they] can survive. . . . It's better than nothing" (ibid.). Expressed theoretically, the two employers are saying that Haiti's large reserve army of labour allows employers to have maximum advantage in exploiting their workers by paying wages below subsistence and denying them the most elementary labour rights because the workers have no other means of reproducing themselves other than selling their labour power. In explaining the role the reserve army of labour plays in the accumulation of capital, Marx said:

> [T]he greater this reserve army in proportion to the active labour-army, the greater is the mass of a consolidated surplus population, whose misery is in inverse ratio to the amount of torture it has to undergo in the form of labour. The more extensive, finally, the pauperized sections of the working class and the industrial reserve army, the greater is official pauperism. *This is the absolute general law of capitalist accumulation.* (Marx 1977, 798)

The alternative to unemployment and starvation, then, is either employment in Haitian-owned firms, domestic labour, employment the informal sector where wages are even lower or, failing all this, emigration.[17]

Conclusion

Popular and grassroots organizations in Haiti have fought against these conditions. In addition to calling for the rejection of the neo-liberal policies, they proposed prioritizing the rebuilding and expansion of Haiti's infrastructure, communication, transportation, public schools, public health and public housing; promoting Haiti's food security and sovereignty by launching an agrarian reform and subsidizing production for the local market as well as for export; subsidizing the development of industries that use domestic inputs to produce consumer and durable goods; protecting the rights of workers to form trade unions and to strike; and providing a living wage to all workers, including those in the export assembly industries. But to achieve these goals these organizations, and the working people in general, would need to mobilize themselves on a scale not seen since the days – years – of relentless struggles to overthrow the Duvalier dictatorship and bring to power a government that, at least for a short time in 1991, raised the spectre of an alternative – as the government of 1800 had done for the slaves who overthrew colonialism and racial slavery.

Acknowledgements

I would like to thank Hilbourne Watson for his comments and suggestions on previous drafts of this essay.

Notes

1. Recommended further readings on the subject of this section include Dupuy 1989, chapter 3; Dupuy 1995; Dubois 2004; James 1963; Cabon 1929; Madiou 1989; Pluchon 1979; Brutus, n.d.; Fick 1990; Schoelcher 1889; Bell 2007 and Lacroix 1820.
2. Between 1789 and 1801, the two major exports of Saint-Domingue declined: white sugar production by 99 per cent and raw sugar by 80 per cent. Coffee production, the next largest export, declined by 44 per cent (Dupuy 1989, 54).
3. As Sidney Mintz shows, what he called a "proto-peasantry" emerged during the slave era when slaves began to use the plots of land the sugar planters allowed them to cultivate to produce not just their own food but also other goods (for example, cooking wares, cloths, handicrafts), which they sold or exchanged in local markets that they controlled (see Mintz 1974, 152). Slaves also fled the plantations to set up Maroon communities in the hills and mountains of Saint-Domingue, which represented a constant threat to the slave regime. The best and unsurpassed study of this latter practice and its role in instigating the slave revolution is that of Jean Fouchard (1972).
4. There are different interpretations as to why Louverture agreed to meet with Brunet when he thought this might be a trap to arrest him (see, for example, Césaire 1960, 266–67; Madiou 1989, 2, 323–25; Dubois 2004, 277–78; James 1963, 325–35; Bell 2007, 265).
5. For more on this subject, see Dupuy 1989 (especially chapter 4), Dupuy 1989 (especially chapters 3–5), Fatton 2002, Trouillot 1990, Péan 2000 and 2007, Labelle 1978, Nicholls 1979, Luc 1976, Moral 1961, Joachim 1979 and Bellegarde-Smith 1990.
6. Sharecroppers did not own the land they worked and lived on, but they owned the tools and animals and therefore controlled when and how they worked.
7. Normally taxes appropriated by the state cannot be considered exploitation in the strict sense of the word, insofar as these revenues are used to provide social and welfare services or to build infrastructures – that is, public goods – to the population as a whole, especially the poor, the working classes and the most vulnerable sectors of the population. However, such has never been the case in Haiti.
8. Recommended further readings on the subject of this section include Dupuy 1989, 2005, 2007 and 2012; Fatton 2002; Trouillot 1990; Péan 2000; Delince 2000; DeWind and McKinley 1986; Anglade 1982; Corten 1986 and Lundahl 1983.

9. For more on this subject, see Bellegarde 1929, Gaillard 1973–85, Schmidt 1971, Millet 1978, Labelle 1978, Nicholls 1979, Renda 2001 and Smith 2009.
10. Elected in 1990, Aristide was toppled by the Haitian army and exiled in 1991. In October 1994 the United States led a UN multinational force to remove the military junta from power and return Aristide to finish the eighteen months left in his first term as president.
11. Until 1957, Haitian presidents were elected indirectly by the legislature, which itself was elected by popular vote. But as I mentioned previously, such elections were meaningless since the coup d'état was the primary means of creating and undoing governments during the nineteenth and twentieth centuries.
12. Contrary to most accounts, the first universal election in Haiti was in 1957, when François Duvalier was elected, not 1990 when Jean-Bertrand Aristide was elected president. Despite a heavy military presence during the 1957 election and its support for Duvalier, he won 71 per cent of the popular vote.
13. When I speak of the Haitian bourgeoisie, both mulatto and black, as it evolved during the twentieth century, I am referring to 1 to 2 per cent of the population, which included among its ranks some of the Levantine immigrants who had come to Haiti early in the twentieth century and many of whom (and their descendants) had married Haitians. The economic base of this class consisted of those in import-export firms and manufacturing industries (often in partnership with foreign investors), those with landed estates and high public functionaries and professionals (especially those in the medical and legal professions who originated from that class). In the 1960s and 1970s that class controlled about 45 per cent of the national income; today it controls approximately 26 per cent of the country's wealth and nearly 50 per cent of the national income.
14. Though they were small in numbers, several high-ranking officers and members of the bourgeoisie were among the strongest defenders of the Duvalier regime in its early years. Duvalier also had support from members of the Levantine business groups who were despised and socially excluded by the haute mulatto bourgeoisie.
15. To prevent the possibility of consecutive and unlimited presidential terms, the Haitian constitution of 1987 allowed an elected president to be re-elected to a second and final five-year term separated by an interval of a five-year term by a different president.
16. By "international community" here I mean the dominant powers – principally the United States, France and Canada – and the international organizations – principally the International Monetary Fund, the Inter-American Development Bank, the World Bank and the United Nations – involved in designing and implementing policies for Haiti. The international organizations, however, do not operate autonomously, but do so in accordance with the interests of the major powers, principally the United States in the case of Haiti.
17. Migration may have some possible and as-of-yet unrecognized positive effects for the working class as a whole. There is good evidence that the remittances Haitian migrants send to Haiti help reduce poverty, provide for about 25 per cent of Haitian families and even allow them to have bank and saving accounts (see Fajnzylber and López 2008, 4, 8). This fact, then, may well reduce the need for individuals to work for low wages and reduce the labour force – and hence put upward pressure on wages. This, actually, was a conclusion reached by a World Bank study: "The impact of remittances on labor supply is

in principle ambiguous. For individuals in households with migrants, the net additional income derived from remittances could have the 'income effect' of increasing the demand for leisure and reservation wages, with a consequent reduction in labor force participation. However, out-migration also has the direct effect of reducing the size of the labor force, and the ensuing upward pressure on local wages could in turn create a 'substitution effect' away from leisure, with a consequent increase in labor supply for those living in areas with high migration rates" (World Bank 2006, 41).

References

Anglade, Georges. 1982. *Éspace et liberté en Haïti.* Montréal: Groupe d'études et de recherches critiques d'éspace, et Centre de recherche caraïbes, Université de Montréal.

Ballard, John R. 1998. *Upholding Democracy: The United States Military Campaign against Haiti.* Westport, CT: Praeger.

Bell, Madison Smartt. 2007. *Toussaint Louverture: A Biography.* New York: Pantheon.

Bellegarde, Dantès. 1929. *l'Occupation américaine d'Haïti et ses conséquences morales et économiques.* Port-au-Prince: Chéraquit.

Bellegarde-Smith, Patrick. 1990. *Haiti: The Breached Citadel.* Boulder: Westview.

Brutus, Edner. n.d. *Révolution dans Saint-Domingue.* 2 vols. Brussels: Les Éditions du Panthéon.

Cabon, Adolphe. 1929. *Histoire d'Haïti.* 4 vols. Paris: Congrégation des Frères de Saint-Jacques.

Césaire, Aimé. 1960. *Toussaint Louverture: La Révolution française et le problème colonial.* Paris: Club Français du Livre.

Corten, André. 1986. *Port au sucre: Prolétariat et prolétarisations: Haiti et République dominicaine.* Montréal: Les Éditions du CIDIHCA.

Deibert, Michael. 2005. *Notes from the Last Testament: The Struggle for Haiti.* New York: Seven Stories.

Delince, Kern. 2000. *l'Insuffisance de développement en Haïti: Blocages et solutions.* Plantation, FL: Pegasus.

DeWind, Josh, and David H. McKinley III. 1986. *Aiding Migration: The Impact of Development Assistance on Haiti.* New York: Columbia University Immigration Research Program, Center for the Social Sciences.

Dubois, Laurent. 2004. *Avengers of the New World: The Story of the Saint-Domingue Revolution.* Cambridge: Harvard University Press.

Dupuy, Alex. 1989. *Haiti in the World Economy: Class, Race, and Underdevelopment since 1700.* Boulder: Westview.

———. 1995. "Toussaint-Louverture and the Haitian Revolution: A Reassessment of C.L.R. James's Interpretation". In *C.L.R. James: His Intellectual Legacies*, edited by Selwyn R. Cudjoe and William E. Cain, 106–17. Amherst: University of Massachusetts Press.

———. 2005. "Globalization, the World Bank, and Haiti". In *Contemporary Caribbean Cultures and Societies in a Global Context*, edited by Franklin W. Knight and Teresita Martinez-Vergne, 43–70. Chapel Hill: University of North Carolina Press.

———. 2007. *The Prophet and Power: Jean-Bertrand Aristide, the International Community, and Haiti*. Lanham, MD: Rowman and Littlefield.

———. 2012. "Class, Power, Sovereignty: Haiti before and after the Earthquake". In *Caribbean Sovereignty, Development and Democracy in an Age of Globalization*, edited by Linden Lewis, 17–34. New York: Routledge.

———. 2013. "From François Duvalier to Jean-Bertrand Aristide: The Decline of Color Politics in Haiti". In *Politics and Power in Haiti*, edited by Kate Quinn and Paul Sutton, 43–63. London: Palgrave Macmillan.

Fajnzylber, Pablo, and J. Humberto López, eds. 2008. *Migration and Development: Lessons from Latin America*. Washington, DC: World Bank.

Fatton, Robert. 2002. *Haiti's Predatory Republic: The Unending Transition to Democracy*. Boulder: Lynne Rienner.

Fick, Carolyn. 1990. *The Making of Haiti: The Saint-Domingue Revolution from Below*. Knoxville: University of Tennessee Press.

Fouchard, Jean. 1972. *Les marrons de la liberté*. Paris: Éditions de l'École.

Gaillard, Roger. 1973–85. *Les blancs débarquent*. 7 vols. Port-au-Prince: Imprimerie Le Natal.

Girard, Philippe R. 2004. *Clinton in Haiti: The 1994 U.S. Invasion of Haiti*. NY and Houndsmills: Palgrave Macmillan.

Held, David. 1995. *Democracy and the Global Order*. Stanford: Stanford University Press.

James, C.L.R. 1963. *The Black Jacobins: Toussaint Louverture and the San Domingo Revolution*. New York: Random House.

Janvier, Louis-Joseph. 1885. *Les affaires d'Haïti (1883–1884)*. Paris: Marpon et Flammarion.

Joachim, Benoît. 1979. *Les racines du sous-développement en Haïti*. Port-au-Prince: Imprimerie H. Deschamps.

Labelle, Micheline. 1978. *Idéologies de couleur et classes sociales en Haïti*. Montréal: Les Presses de l'Université de Montréal.

Lacroix, Joseph Pamphile de. 1820. *Mémoire pour servir à l'histoire de la révolution de Saint-Domingue*. 2 vols. Paris: Pillet Amé.

Luc, Jean. 1976. *Structures économiques et lutte nationale populaire en Haïti*. Montréal: Les Éditions Nouvelles Optiques.

Lundahl, Mats. 1983. *The Haitian Economy: Man, Land and Markets*. New York: St Martin's.

Madiou, Thomas. 1989. *Histoire d'Haïti: Tome 2, 1799–1803*. Port-au-Prince: Éditions Henri Deschamps.

Marx, Karl. 1977. *Capital: A Critique of Political Economy*, vol. 1, translated by Ben Fowkes. New York: Vintage.

Millet, Kethly. 1978. *Les paysans haïtiens et l'occupation américaine, 1915–1930*. La Salle, QC: Collectif Paroles.

Mintz, Sidney. 1974. *Caribbean Transformations*. Chicago: Aldine Publishing.

Moral, Paul. 1961. *Le paysan haïtien: Étude sur la vie rurale en Haïti*. Paris: G.P. Maisonneuve.

Nicholls, David. 1979. *From Dessalines to Duvalier: Race, Colour and National Independence in Haiti*. Cambridge: Cambridge University Press.

Paul, Edmond. (1882) 1976. *Les causes de nos malheurs: appel au people*. Kingston: George Henderson. Reprint, Port-au-Prince: Les Éditions Fardin.

Péan, Leslie. 2000. *Économie politique de la corruption: De Saint-Domingue à Haïti 1791–1870.* Port-au-Prince: Éditions Mémoire.

———. 2007. *Haïti, économie politique de la corruption: Tome IV, l'Ensauvagement macoute et ses conséquences 1957–1990.* Paris: Maisonneuve et Larose.

Pluchon, Pierre. 1979. *Toussaint Louverture: de l'esclavage au pouvoir.* Paris: l'École; Port-au-Prince: Éditions Caraïbes.

Przeworski, Adam. 1985. *Capitalism and Social Democracy.* Cambridge: Cambridge University Press.

Renda, Mary A. 2001. *Taking Haiti: Military Occupation and the Culture of US Imperialism.* Chapel Hill: University of North Carolina Press.

Schmidt, Hans. 1971. *The United States Occupation of Haiti, 1915–1934.* New Brunswick, NJ: Rutgers University Press.

Schoelcher, Victor. 1889. *Vie de Toussaint Louverture.* 2nd ed. Paris: Paul Olendorff.

Shacochis, Bob. 1999. *The Immaculate Invasion.* New York: Viking/Penguin.

Smith, Matthew. 2009. *Red and Black in Haiti: Radicalism, Conflict, and Political Change, 1934–1957.* Chapel Hill: University of North Carolina Press.

Sprague, Jeb. 2012. *Paramilitarism and the Assault on Democracy in Haiti.* New York: Monthly Review Press.

Trouillot, Michel-Rolph. 1986. *Les raciness historiques de l'état duvalierien.* Port-au-Prince: Henri Deschamps.

———. 1990. *Haiti: State against Nation.* New York: Monthly Review Press.

Wood, Ellen Meiksins. 1995. *Capitalism against Democracy.* Cambridge: Cambridge University Press.

World Bank. 2006. *The Development Impact of Workers' Remittances in Latin America: Main Findings* (Report No. 37026, Vol. 1). Washington, DC: World Bank.

4 Citizenship and the Politics of Belonging in the Caribbean

Linden Lewis

Perhaps it is the mutability of the concept of citizenship that gives this most fundamental of social identities its enduring quality. Despite the ponderous discourses about the impact of globalization and neo-liberalism on the state and the nation – two entities which are crucial to the reproduction of the idea of citizenship – we discuss this concept, envisioning ways of tracking its expanding vistas. Globalization may appear to some to have annihilated time and space, but it simply changes the way we experience the enormity of the global community. It may even have led us into the murky territory of viewing ourselves as cosmopolitans who claim to be global citizens. The idea of cosmopolitanism is summarily dismissed by Etienne Balibar most eloquently: "Modern cosmopolitanism is to real politics what the rights of man are to the rights of citizens: a utopian future, nourished by the memory of a lost unity" (2011, 110).

Irrespective of the changing geopolitical environment, the issue of citizenship continues to engage our political consciousness. This continuing significance may also have to do in part with the role played by the myriad civil society organizations in the public sphere, both within and outside of the Caribbean, that promote the notion of civic engagement, which resonates with ideas associated with active citizenship. As Charles Tilly points out: "At a national scale effective citizenship is a necessary condition of democracy" (2005, 196). At its most basic level, citizenship embodies the relationship between an individual and the state, but it is more than just a bond of territory and belonging. The ostensible goal of citizenship is to create a deep and enduring sense of a social and political community. Citizenship is a process through which the state socializes the nation into imagining a sense of belonging. It is, as suggested earlier, very much also about creating a consciousness around a sense of a common community – a sense of sharing similar values, history and culture.

Though there is a general understanding of this nationalist goal, the meaning of citizenship has to be placed in a historical context, where different social agents have laid claims to the concept for fundamentally different reasons. Immediately, we can anticipate the problem that plagues the concept: namely, that citizenship is not a uniform concept (Turner 2001, 189–209). Indeed, the concept of citizenship means many different things to different people. It is therefore important to define the term in the interest of clarity. I concur with Bryan Turner when he argues, "Rather than define citizenship within a static framework of rights and obligations, it is valuable to conceptualize citizenship as a process" (192).

This chapter therefore seeks to move away from an approach that is rooted in identity, to see how citizenship is constructed in specific historical moments and to observe how such moments change over time and occasion corresponding changes, which serve to include and exclude people in the process. In essence, the argument that is being developed here is that citizenship is not a fixed status, merely conferred by virtue of birth or through the procedure of naturalization. It is a dynamic process with shifting boundaries and criteria of eligibility, calculated to reproduce the privilege of membership, while socially and politically excluding those considered variously as strangers, foreigners and aliens.

Ironically, it is precisely this exclusion of others that, at least in part, generates the sense of community. Nira Yuval-Davis recently distinguished between the idea of belonging and the politics of belonging. This distinction is rather useful. For Yuval-Davis: "Belonging is about an emotional (or even ontological) attachment, about feeling at home" (2011, 10). The experience of belonging is normalized and becomes commonplace. The politics of belonging, however, revolves around particular strategies designed to effect belonging in specific collectivities or categories, which are themselves undergoing construction. "Belonging" implies, therefore, a more generalized sense of connection to place, while "the politics of belonging" marks a more specific affinity to clearly identified groupings. The boundaries with which the politics of belonging are concerned are those of the political community of belonging – the boundaries which, sometimes physically but always symbolically, separate the world population into "us" and "them" (20).

Some, such as Anthony Smith (1991, 118), have noted that this distinction, which revolves around the boundaries of the political community, is usually associated with strong moral and economic implications. Morality here is a marker of a certain character of what is considered good and responsible citizenship. Tilly's insights (2005, 175) on the issue of the role of boundaries and responsibilities to the political community are worth noting here. We begin to see that conceptions of national boundaries have strong implications for the creation of citizenship – namely, the establishment of categorically defined (rather than particular) rights and obligations connecting subjects of a given state to that state's agents.

It is in the general terrain of the politics of belonging that some of the most intense contestations take place. It is in this location where disputations are manifold and claims of authenticity are made and at times rendered invalid. Separating these two concepts for analytical purposes is useful, but one should not conclude that in reality such a neat distinction is possible. Citizenship and the politics of belonging are not so much separate features as highly intertwined phenomena; hence in the context of the Caribbean, we can begin to discern the boundaries that designate the nature of citizenship. Who legitimately has claims to the region, outside of it merely being one's territory of origin? Who continues to claim a sense of belonging and citizenship, even though they do not live in the region, by actively seeking to shape the social and political contours of a society from which they have migrated? These are critical issues raised by the notion of citizenship and the politics of belonging in the Caribbean. They are not issues that are already resolved; they are issues currently being negotiated at the same time that global and local developments – in many ways overdetermined by economic, political and social factors – shape how we view the Caribbean and its people.

In conceptualizing citizenship as process and using an historical approach to do so, the dynamics of our understanding can help to explain how, for Caribbean people, the idea of citizenship moves from a notion of freedom to the ways in which freedom is circumscribed by property ownership, race and colour. It can also help to explain how, in the realm of the social, the continuing struggles for broadening and deepening the democratic process demand the expansion of the rights of marginalized social classes and demand addressing, in a fundamental way, the issues of gender and sexual orientation.

Citizenship as Freedom

Given the specific history of enslavement in the Caribbean, citizenship in its earliest manifestation resonated with the expectation of freedom. The revolutionary act of liberation of the enslaved in Haiti, beginning in 1791 and culminating in independence in 1804, very clearly sent a message to the rest of the world, but especially to France, that considerations and adjustments had to be made about the breadth of understanding the notion of citizenship. The Haitian Revolution confounded European claims of universality, especially as it related to the enslaved, who were not considered human in the context of the Declaration of the Rights of Man and of

Citizen of 1793. Addressing this issue, Laurent Dubois observes: "The transformation of citizenship by slave insurgents brought major challenges for Republican administrators" (2004, 172).

Dubois also very dramatically recounts this understanding of citizenship-as-freedom in relation to a revolt in April 1793 in Trois-Rivières, Guadeloupe. Having revolted, the enslaved proceeded to kill twenty-two whites. They then very purposefully looted specific plantations before locking up those same plantations and placing guards to prevent further pilfering. They then proceeded to the capital, Basse-Terre, where they encountered soldiers who, having knowledge of the massacre, inquired: "Who goes there?" The enslaved responded: "Citizens and friends" (Dubois 2004, 25).

In essence, before seizing their freedom, the enslaved had already made the calculation that they were entitled to it, and had begun to see themselves as the equal of other citizens of the republic. Much of this is captured in the eyewitness account of the incident reported by Dubois: "One of the slaves began to speak and asked if we were citizens, patriots; the response came yes, we were; in that case, he said, we are friends" (Dubois 2004, 25). Moreover, the implication of this eyewitness's account is that the enslaved man demonstrated a clear knowledge of the scope and meaning of citizenship, for he continued: "We have no bad intentions; we want to fight for the Republic, the law, the nation, order" (25).

What is noteworthy here also, is that the enslaved men and women were all freed and declared citizens in the French Antilles by 1794; however, this status was summarily revoked by 1802 when slavery was once again imposed on these colonies of France. Dubois's remark on the revocation of citizenship is once again instructive: "During this period, those who had been re-enslaved were stripped of any property they might have gained while emancipated" (Dubois 2004, 269). The issue of the crucial relationship between private property and citizenship will be discussed more fully subsequently, particularly in relation to the free coloureds. Elsa Goveia's conclusion in relation to the free coloured in the British Leeward Islands is poignant: Although the slaves were more feared, it was the free coloured, not the slaves, who most effectively challenged the system of inequality that the whites had built up to protect their power and privileges in the society of the Leeward Islands (1980, 99).

One of the best examples of a comprehensive understanding of the idea of freedom is personified in the experiences of the maroons or runaway slaves. Not only did the enslaved seek to free themselves from the oppression and exploitation of the plantation system but they also encouraged many other enslaved persons to flee their plantations and join Maroon communities. Furthermore, the maroons established parallel communities, which were so powerful and so destabilizing to colonial rule, that the British, in the case of the anglophone Caribbean, were forced to enter into treaties with the maroons to stop these rebel slaves from undermining the plantation productive system, its authority and its control of labour. As oppressive a system as slavery was, there was always resistance, and marronage became a principal strategy of securing freedom in Suriname, Jamaica, Cuba, Martinique and Guadeloupe. In the case of Jamaica, Edward Kamau Brathwaite notes: "The Maroons had been in successful armed conflict with the British/Jamaican forces for 85 years: 1655 to 1740; and continued after the treaties of 1738/40 in a state of increasing dissatisfaction for another 55 years" (1977, 9). The Saramaka of Suriname followed a similar trajectory as the maroons of Jamaica. By the end of the seventeenth century, the increasing number of enslaved individuals in Suriname began their quest for freedom when many of them started running away.

Richard Price noted: "The colonists fought back, sending countless militias in pursuit of the runaways and handing out gruesome punishments for recaptured slaves – hamstringing, amputation of limbs, and a variety of deaths by torture" (2011, 5). In due course, the planters realized the futility of the exercise of pursuing the runaways. The Saramaka, like the Jamaican maroons, had established secure communities and had proven to be adept in the defence of their freedom and their community.

The colonists eventually came to the conclusion that pursuing the Surinamese maroons was too costly, too time-consuming and too taxing to their human resources: "After several great battles between Saramakas and colonial armies during the 1750s, a peace treaty was at last negotiated" (Price 2011, 8). The treaty between the Dutch colonial government and the Saramaka was eventually agreed upon in 1762, after a century of warfare. The Saramaka had indeed won their freedom and forced the Dutch to recognize their autonomy. It should be noted, however, that although running away had a negative economic impact on the plantation and could not be ignored, not all those escaping the grasp of their plantations were doing so as a demonstrated act of defiance. Some were simply going in search of other members of their family who were sold to other plantations.

In essence, however, what is sometimes described as "grand marronage" weakened the plantation, flouted its authority and amounted to industrial sabotage. This type of practice of marronage was not only evidence of an expressed desire for freedom from oppression and exploitation but of the development of a sense of a specific understanding and consciousness of community, a sense of shared values and of civic responsibility to the immediate Maroon community and to those still enslaved. Moreover, the maroons understood that their act of resistance was important to the reclamation of their humanity, which the system of enslavement had attempted to deny. The act of running away and establishing a fully functioning parallel community contributes to our understanding of the concept of citizenship as freedom in the Caribbean. It moves beyond a mere formal notion of access to rights and obligations, and inhabits the sphere of human dignity and a new sense of belonging.

The Colour of Citizenship

At the end of the eighteenth century in the British Leeward Islands, the population consisted of a majority of enslaved blacks, a minority of free people of colour and a powerful minority of whites. The colour of citizenship was clearly demarcated by the enormous role race, among other factors, played in determining the exercise of political rights, namely that of citizenship. Given their economic and political power, political participation in the Leeward Islands was the prerogative of whites. The enslaved were precluded from political participation insofar as "they were regarded primarily as property to be represented by their white owners" (Goveia 1980, 82). In addition, people classified as "free coloured" were also excluded from any type of political rights: "Elsewhere [other than Antigua], the free coloured were held to be merely slaves who had been freed from the power of their masters, not free men entitled by their freedom to participate in the public life" (Goveia 1980, 82).

Whites viewed enslaved blacks as intellectually and morally unfit for citizenship. In similar fashion, they viewed free coloureds as equally unsuitable for such political rights. To many whites, admission of the free coloured to the rights of citizenship appeared not only repugnant but dangerous. It was therefore to be expected that when the free coloured demanded political equality, their demand would be opposed by the group of whites unwilling to accept an extension of political rights without regard to colour. Whatever its eventual outcome, the resultant struggle upset the long-established relationships of racial inferiority and superiority between the dominant whites and the other classes, which characterized the slave society (Goveia 1980, 97).

The free coloured of Haiti embraced a feeling of entitlement to citizenship, which rested on the bourgeois European notion of claiming property. During the 1760s they were able to establish themselves as property owners as a result of their profits from the "coffee revolution". Despite their higher status than enslaved blacks in the social hierarchy of plantation society, the free coloured were not allowed to hold any public office, nor were they permitted to serve as jurors. The *gens de couleurs* were also precluded from such occupations as medicine and law and excluded from officer ranks within the military. They were made to pay taxes from which whites were exempted. Mulattoes who were assaulted or injured by whites could not obtain redress in courts, nor could mulattoes adopt European names, walk alongside or eat with whites, wear the same clothes as Europeans or be buried in European cemeteries (Antoine de Abbè Cournand, cited in Dupuy 1989, 29–30).

It was the case in most of the Leeward Islands in the eighteenth century that the right to vote was restricted to free white Protestant males, as long as they were twenty-one years of age or older and owned at least ten acres of land or "a house and land to the yearly value of £10 currency" (Goveia 1980, 90). In all other public spheres of life, there was a property requirement attached as a condition of eligibility.

In other words, at this historical juncture, private property was critical to the establishment of citizenship. As we will see later in this chapter, although this requirement does not loom as largely as it once did, other forms of exclusion remain. At the end of the eighteenth century, however, privileging the rights of property owners was crucial. As Kenan Malik points out, the defence of private property requires a defence of inequality (1996, 59). Of course, the institution of slavery exposed the liberal presumptions of a universal equality, since the enslaved were considered property that was owned by others. The enslaved were therefore not viewed as being worthy of liberty; moreover, the free coloured, even though already legally free, did not meet the other requirements necessary for participation in the political systems as citizens. Race was also important, therefore, for the exclusion of the free coloured from the political process.

In the end, however, the position of the free people of colour approached the question of citizenship in ways that were different from those of the enslaved. In Haiti, for example, the free people of colour were more focused on equality with whites. They were of the view that they had basically met all of the requirements of citizenship and were as qualified, if not more so, than their white rivals, the *petits blancs* (Knight 1990, 206). While the free people of colour thought of themselves as equal to whites, the whites in the colonies knew that their own position of power in the social structure of the colonies was predicated on the exclusion of both free people of colour and the enslaved. To grant equal rights to the free people of colour would delegitimize the entire social order and would inevitably bring about the emancipation of the slaves. It should come as no surprise then that Le Noir de Rouvray, who represented the colonial establishment, would conclude the following: "Mulattoes today, slaves tomorrow!" (Le Noir de Rouvray, cited in Dupuy 1989, 44).

But there were harsher penalties than exclusions from the rights of equal citizenship: it is important to bear in mind that in 1791 Vincent Ogé and Jean-Baptiste Chavannes were executed because of their demand for equal citizenship rights for free people of colour (Girard 2011, 13). With respect to the Leeward Islands at the end of the eighteenth century, Elsa Goveia's concluding remarks about the free people of colour are an important coda: "In challenging the whites, however, the free coloured had strictly limited political aims. They were not trying to revolutionise the whole society, as the slaves needed to do if they were to be freed from subjection. Like the whites, the free coloured had important interests in slave holding. They rejected their own subordination, but they did not completely reject the social structure of which it had been a part" (1980, 99).

For all intents and purposes, citizenship in the Caribbean in the seventeenth and eighteenth centuries was limited to one skin colour only, to the exclusion of other members of society. An important lesson to be gleaned from this historical experience in the Caribbean – and contrary to the liberal discourse about citizenship serving as an agent of equalization in society – is that the exclusion of certain disfavoured groups has always been built into the concept of citizenship. If in the end the rights of citizenship devolve to a broader and more inclusive grouping of people, such expansion of benefits results not because of some idealistic notion of equality but from struggles waged by the disenfranchised against the state, in order to broaden the scope of freedom and entitlements.

In a recent work, Mimi Sheller (2012) drives home an important and often neglected dimension of the subject that should accompany the foregoing historical discussion of the making of Caribbean citizenship: citizenship does not stand outside of all social relations; "citizen" is already interpellated as a subject in concert with other subjectivities. Indeed, the very mutability of citizenship (mentioned at the beginning of this chapter) is a consequence of such struggles, and it is particularly in the realm of the social that these rights are best observed. As Sheller muses, to become a citizen is also to become a gendered, racialized and sexed subject; thus, citizenship is fundamentally connected to the discursive history and scientific understanding of the human body and how the state regulates such bodies (2012, 26).

This observation is quite apposite to an understanding of who, at least initially, is considered the archetypal citizen – although one should be careful to locate the subject within the context of social relations, insofar as social class is also important to the notion of citizenship. Again, Sheller is insightful in this regard. Citing Michel Laguerre, she notes: "Indeed, Article 9 of the first constitution [of Haiti] stated, 'no one is worthy of being a Haitian if he is not a good father, a good son, a good husband, *and above all a good soldier*' (emphasis added), foreshadowing the militarization of the state, the marginalization of women and the depiction of citizens as male protectors of family and nation" (2012, 150).

Sheller is at pains to make this point not only in her argument but for further development by future historians and social scientists who have not been as attentive to the issue of gender and sexuality in the area of citizenship and freedom: "Within the power structure of slave societies, freed men's armed service connoted respectability, citizenship and public service; women's freedom, on the other hand, often came at the price of sexual vulnerability, non-citizenship and dependence on private relationships. Freed men and freed women thus experienced very different paths to freedom and different kinds of insertion into the public political process once there" (2012, 153).

In short, the interpellation of the Caribbean individual as citizen not only encompasses the important considerations of nation and belonging but incorporates specific – if not always immediately recognizable – rules and regulations of gender and sexuality as criteria of eligibility. (The issue of sexuality is elaborated upon in a subsequent section of this chapter.) Citizenship was enacted differently according to gender; in fact, its very validity could be challenged in the case of nineteenth-century Haitian women who chose to marry foreign men (see Sheller 2012, 153). Despite the motivational goals of liberation and freedom that informed citizenship in various parts of the Caribbean, such status did not always include women as agents in the construction of the nation. Moreover, as I have indicated elsewhere (Lewis 2000), even in the postcolonial period, when the opportunity to choose an alternative path to the hierarchical and authoritarian political form of rule in the Caribbean was made available, this was not the path taken. Although they contributed significantly to the struggles for decolonization in the region, women were not represented at the level of the prestigious opportunities opened up by the success of the decolonizing efforts, nor were they a part of the glory and symbolism of the emerging nation. They were essentially marginalized for many years to come, until the first wave of feminism and feminist activism began to push back the boundaries of patriarchy in the Caribbean.

Social Experience of Citizenship in the Caribbean

Complicating the issue of citizenship in the Caribbean is its colonial legacy. Different colonial powers have clearly left their mark on their former, as well as their current, Caribbean territories. Citizenship in the anglophone Caribbean permits travel without a visa throughout the English-speaking region, the Dutch Antilles, Suriname and the Dominican Republic but not to Puerto Rico or the US Virgin Islands, which require an American visa. To enter the French Caribbean islands (except Haiti) from the anglophone Caribbean is the equivalent of entering the European Union in that it requires a Schengen visa for the French overseas departments of Guadeloupe, Martinique and French Guiana. A Schengen visa is also required for the French overseas collectivities of Saint-Martin and Saint-Barthélemy, even though all of these French islands are neighbouring countries of the Caribbean.[1] These French islands are dependencies of France and function as overseas departments. The fact is that the legal entanglements of citizenship, labour certification and residency all create tremendous tension between the ideals of national citizenship and Caribbean regionalism.

The free movement of labour within the Caribbean Single Market and Economy has been a major stumbling block for the regional organization of the Caribbean Community and Common Market (CARICOM).

Everyone acknowledges the small size of the Caribbean and its population; however, some countries fare better than others economically and prefer not to be overrun by additional migrant labour from other parts of the region. This attitude, which is at times officially sanctioned, results in tensions between neighbouring islands, creating an unwelcoming and often hostile environment for those who are merely in search of a better life for themselves and their family.

The social experience of citizenship in the Caribbean is also in part shaped by the very powerful influences of neo-liberalism and capitalist globalization. Both the uneven and contradictory process of globalization and the accompanying economic strategy of neo-liberalism raise troubling issues for those who believe in the certitude of citizenship, the inviolability of boundaries and the practice of democracy. The blurring of territorial boundaries benefits capital and is not necessarily open to labour's mobility. Nevertheless, it places into sharp relief the need to rethink how we conceive and understand the phenomenon of immigration and immigrants. There is a need to reimagine the notion of citizenship in terms that are broader than the customary sense of belonging to a bounded territory and localized community of the nation. In many ways these considerations reconfigure the rules of citizenship that inform our sense of belonging. They also place on the agenda the major social issues of contemporary society, providing an impetus for social and class resistance movements and for a potentially more robust practice of democracy. This broader sense of the social experience of citizenship is one that opens up a space for a type of citizens' engagement that extends far beyond the current limitation of democracy to, essentially, a populace simply voting into office one set of professional elites as opposed to another set of elites, every five years.

The social engagement of citizens also means that they do not have to rely so heavily on those specific civil society (namely non-governmental and non-profit) organizations to offer relief from social, economic and political ills. They can begin to act more broadly on their own behalf, by becoming more involved in trade union activity, in matters of environmental concerns and in relation to the challenges posed by climate change in an area so prone to hurricanes and earthquakes. The daily experience of citizenship removes the concept from a theoretical abstraction and forces Caribbean people to examine their social priorities. In effect, to view citizenship in this light is to provide the social infrastructure for broadening the scope of rights. Group rights in this context therefore elicit collective struggle on the part of ordinary men and women in the Caribbean.[2]

Also increasingly important to consider are those who claim a dual allegiance including an allegiance to a Caribbean territory, regardless of their geographical location (in or outside of the Caribbean). Of those persons with citizenship in more than one country there are two types.

The first type comprises those who, usually after a considerable period spent in North America or Europe, have acquired citizenship in other parts of the world but who reside in the Caribbean. These are sometimes referred to as "the returnees". The importance of these citizens has captured the attention of Caribbean governments, which have established offices to facilitate their re-entry into the region and have been positioning themselves, albeit mostly unsuccessfully, to benefit from the returnees' investments in the region. Specialists on migration in the region have been closely observing these citizens for some time now (see Plaza 2008, 115–37; Basch, Glick Schiller and Szanton Blanc 1994; Potter, Conway and Phillips 2005).

The other type of dual citizen comprises those Caribbean persons who have become naturalized citizens in North America or Europe (among other places), but who retain a very strong interest in and connection to not only the society in general but the political life and direction of their country of origin. These diasporic Caribbean persons have over the years sustained relatives back home through remittances, which according to a World Bank estimate for 2012 was expected to be US$400 billion (*Jamaica Observer*, "Caribbean to Receive over US$400 Billion in Remittances", 22 November 2012).

What is evident, however, is that these diasporic Caribbean people, who enjoy either dual citizenship or legal residence in another country and citizenship in their country of origin, are no longer satisfied simply with contributing to the reproduction of relatives in their countries of birth; they are demanding a greater say in the political and economic life of their countries of origin. No longer are they content to financially support their political parties; they are arguing for the opportunity to vote in national elections. To date, Honduras, the Dominican Republic, Panama and Venezuela permit overseas voting, and the practice is currently under consideration in the Bahamas.[3]

A more intriguing development is that, quite apart from the counting of overseas ballots in the Dominican Republic, Dominicans living in the United States (who in the past have heavily backed political candidates financially) have begun to demand a seat at the table. This development is evident in the election of three Dominican men from New Jersey, who were elected in 2012 to serve in the Chamber of Deputies of the Dominican Republic government. These were the first persons to be elected from abroad. Indeed, seven members of the Dominican Republic's Lower House were elected from overseas: three from the United States and Canada, two from Europe and two from the Caribbean and Latin America.

This development is indeed very significant. It forces us to adjust our understanding and reconfigure the geography of citizenship. It brings us to the realization that the notion of citizenship cannot be restricted to space of territory and that the term "diaspora" means more than those who are "not here but over there" – scattered elsewhere in the world. "Diaspora" is a more dynamic label about those who are both there and here and who are part of that culturally imagined community. In short, the American-based new members of the Chamber of Deputies in the Dominican Republic also confound narrower definitions of the nation and nation-building and in the process raise some challenging questions about the relationship between state and nation.

Whispers of Xenophobia and Non-Belonging

The ill-treatment of Guyanese has become commonplace in the Caribbean. Citizens of the Republic of Guyana, who for a myriad reasons leave their country of origin for greener pastures in Barbados or Antigua, have found out all too harshly that their presence in these countries is not welcome. Even as fellow Caribbean residents, they do not belong in places other than that of their birth. They have become strangers at the gate of those places to which they seek entry – places that were sources from which people were sent to Guyana in an earlier historical period. Holders of Guyanese passports – one of the symbols of citizenship – tend to be given short shrift from immigration officials in Trinidad, Jamaica and the Bahamas; however, the perceived chief offenders seem to be those officials in Barbados. The actions taken in relation to Guyanese persons residing in Barbados have created tensions not only between the governments of Barbados and Guyana but, more importantly, between Barbadian and Guyanese people, whose genealogies often interest each other at various points.

As the economic situation in Guyana deteriorated while the economic fortunes of Barbados remained stable, many Guyanese began moving to Barbados and setting up residence, legally and illegally. It is believed that there are some 34,000 Guyanese living in Barbados (Herweg, 2009). As a result, a number of fault lines have emerged. Many Guyanese coming into Barbados are prepared to sell their artisanal labour power, either in carpentry or agriculture, below the wages that Barbadian workers would accept. Generally, not many Barbadians are open to taking menial jobs, but they insist, nevertheless, that Guyanese labour is forcing down the value of Barbadian labour by lowering wages. Barbadian employers have argued that, besides settling for lower wages, Guyanese workers are more dependable and work harder and longer hours.

There is also a claim made by some Barbadian women that Guyanese women marry Barbadian men out of convenience, in a bid to remain in the country, and thus reduce marital options for Barbadian women. Indeed, sometimes the status of "foreigner" creates (or is imagined to create) new forms of sociability, which create conflict and compete with the sociability of citizens – those who "belong". There is a tendency for this difference to manifest itself uncomfortably at the level of interpersonal relations, where competition for sexual and romantic partners intensifies.

There is also a pernicious racial dimension to these tensions that is expressed at times in an anti–East Indian sentiment. On many of the call-in radio programmes, and in letters to the daily newspapers, many in Barbados voiced the opinion that Guyanese were responsible for crimes ranging from drug trafficking to prostitution and theft. In general, Barbadians viewed Guyanese nationals as interlopers, who, if not checked by the government, would overrun their island paradise.

The late prime minister of Barbados David Thompson's political campaign, which brought him and his Democratic Labour Party government to power in 2008, ran on promises to address the issue of the "out-of-control" immigration problem of the island, which a high-powered Cabinet Subcommittee on Immigration had concluded was detrimental to Barbadian society. When he assumed office as prime minister, Thompson presided over the enactment of a "Barbadian First" amnesty law announced on 1 June 2009 (Herweg, 2009). In effect, the amnesty applied only to those CARICOM residents who had been residing in Barbados illegally prior to 31 December 1998. This was a less generous amnesty than that granted under the previous Barbados Labour Party administration, which required only a five-year window of being undocumented before qualifying for the official pardon. Under the amnesty introduced by Thompson, illegal residents who qualified were given six months to regularize their immigration status or face deportation. Those residents who arrived after 1998 would be subject to immediate deportation.

Not only did this iteration of an amnesty seem incompatible with the spirit of regionalism and regional solidarity, but the unceremonious execution of the deportation process was considered inhumane, even to those who were wary of the non-nationals in their midst (*Stabroek News*, "Consulate Instructed to Follow-Up Reports of Barbados Raids", 25 June 2009). Shortly after the amnesty law was enacted, Barbadian immigration officials were reported to have engaged in early-morning raids of the homes of suspected undocumented Guyanese workers and illegal residents. Some were put on the first available plane out of Barbados; among these were parents who had Barbadian-born children. In many cases, some unscrupulous Barbadian men, including employers, exploited women who were made vulnerable by virtue of their immigrant status. These men engaged in the practice of threatening to report the undocumented status of non-Barbadian-born women to immigration authorities, if they could not otherwise secure sexual favours from the women.

In short, Guyanese were made to feel as though they did not belong in Barbados. The culture and social structure of Barbados did not offer Guyanese people any sense of a feeling or connection to a home away from home. It did not provide them with any space for forging alliances with other groups – including legal residents from Guyana, who were either cowed into silence or were prevailed upon to demonstrate that they legitimately belonged in Barbados. Others were reminded of their outsider status if they dared to object to any harsh treatment of their compatriots.

In the Caribbean then – whether the issue is that of Guyanese in Barbados or in Antigua or Dominicans in Puerto Rico, *cocolos*[4] from Saint Kitts in the Dominican Republic or Haitians in the Bahamas – it is clear that various forms of exclusion, xenophobia and non-belonging index citizenship. Given the immigration problems for Guyanese and Haitians in the wider Caribbean, what is really revealed in the din over the need for greater integration are the day-to-day limitations of the ideas of Caribbean unity and the sense of belonging.

Citizenship, Gender and Sexual Orientation in the Caribbean

The language of citizenship is misleading insofar as its universality conjures the idea of equal membership in the community of the nation but, as has been demonstrated so far, this is not accurate. Using the lens of gender allows us to discern the difference in the status of men and women. We know that even though women in the Caribbean may in several areas enjoy the same rights as men, they are not always offered the same level of legal protection. Indeed, as the 2012 report from the United Nations Development Programme has stated: "Women have made important advances in education, labour force participation, political participation and equality before the law, but gender inequalities persist" (UNDP 2012, 18). It is an all-too-familiar story in places such as Guyana and Jamaica, where the prosecution of violence against women lags way behind the crimes visited upon the bodies of women. As the report states: "Across the Caribbean, rape rates are relatively high, and clearance rates on cases are low; so by extension, conviction rates are also low" (26). Rape, including in the context of conflict and disaster, is one type, but crimes against women further range from sexual harassment to sexual assault and domestic violence. Women in the region and all over the world deserve lives free of violence, but this is certainly not always the case in the Caribbean.

Accurate and up-to-date data on violence against women in the Caribbean is not always easy to come by; however, the recent outcome document for Latin America and the Caribbean prepared for the Commission on the Status of Women, sheds some light on this problem in the region (CSW 2012).[5] The incidence of violence against women, including femicide (the feminist term for the murder of women by their intimate partners), is generally on the increase in the region. The Commission on the Status of Women document reports:

> The frequency of femicides has seen an alarming increase in many countries in Latin American and the Caribbean in recent years. Of the 25 countries worldwide with the highest femicide rates, more than half are in this region: 4 in the Caribbean (Jamaica, Lesser Antilles Region, Bahamas, Dominican Republic), 4 in Central America (El Salvador, Guatemala, Honduras, Belize) and 6 in South America (Guyana, Colombia, Bolivia, Venezuela, Brazil, Ecuador). It has also been found that the regions with the highest femicide levels largely correspond to the regions with the highest overall rates of lethal violence, among these South America, the Caribbean and Central America. Two contributing factors to the increase in femicides are the high level of tolerance of violence against women and the absence and/or negligence and impunity of state actors to guarantee and protect the rights of women and girls. (5)

The situation in specific parts of the anglophone Caribbean has been a cause for concern over the last decade:

> Available data shows that in Jamaica in 2008, 60 of the 160 murders of women were related to domestic violence. In Grenada, between 2005 and 2008, only 8 cases of women killed in situations of gender based violence were reported, but this number climbed between 2011 and September 2012, during which time 5 more women were

> killed in intimate partner violence. In Trinidad and Tobago on average over the last 10 years, there were between 17 and 35 cases a year, depending on the year, in which a woman was killed, linked to situations of domestic violence. (8)

The situation in Haiti is a special case, in which the devastation of the infrastructure from the 2010 earthquake left women even more vulnerable, although "even before the earthquake, 40% of the 500 rape cases were among girls under the age of 18" (UNDP 2012, 5). The United Nations Development Programme report also indicates that, regionally, the burden of violence against women is disproportionally borne by youths and significantly so by girls (26).

An example of the widespread nature of the problem of violence against women can be seen from the case of the Dominican Republic. In July 2011, the public prosecutor of Santo Domingo Province described the scale of domestic violence in the Dominican Republic as "alarming" (AI-USA). The General Prosecutor's Office noted that there was a "20 per cent increase in the number of women killed by their partners or former partners between January and July 2010, compared with the same period in 2009" (AI-USA 2011). According to Amnesty International, "A report entitled *Critical Path of Dominican Women Survivors of Gender Violence*, issued in June jointly by several Dominican women's rights NGOs, found that the great majority of survivors of gender-based violence were re-victimized by the justice system. It found that a high percentage of victims abandon the legal process and highlighted the lack of judicial personnel trained to deal with the issue" (AI-USA). Equally alarming is the practice of what has become known as "corrective" gang rape of lesbians in Jamaica.

These are all abuses that women face on a daily basis as citizens of various parts of the Caribbean. In short, it is difficult to enjoy the full benefits of citizenship when one is confronted by the constant threat of violence in the public and private spheres and when one carries the burden of knowing that there is little redress to be had through the judicial system.

Poverty poses many challenges for the practice of citizenship. In many ways, full participation of citizens is predicated on people's material conditions of existence. Poverty exposes the level of deprivation of rights of certain individuals who, by virtue of their marginalization and social exclusion, are rendered incapable of fully participating as citizens. Women generally tend to be over-represented among the poor. Indeed, according to a recent International Trade Union Confederation report, the current economic crisis has had a profound impact on the lives of women. This impact is felt both in terms of diminishing opportunities for employment and by virtue of their responsibility for the care of their households (ITUC 2011, 7). The impact of the current global economic crisis on women serves to aggravate historically pre-existing conditions of disadvantage: "The gender inequalities and power imbalances that predate the current crisis have resulted in the effects of the global crisis falling disproportionately on those who are already structurally disempowered and marginalised" (7). Job loss for women is of particular concern in the Caribbean. The International Labour Organization found that in Latin America, the Caribbean and Asia, job losses for women are expected to exceed those of men. This is particularly worrisome given the large percentage of female-headed households – almost 40 per cent in the Caribbean (8).

The lens of gender helps us to better see some of the limitations of an uncritical embrace of the concept of citizenship in the Caribbean. What is true of gender is equally valid for the practice of sexual orientation. Sexual minorities in the Caribbean for the most part live out their daily lives as second-class citizens. They are not given protection from discrimination in the same way that heterosexual people in the region enjoy other types of protection. Martha Nussbaum's thinking about this matter is relevant in this context. She observes: "As long as no laws protect gays against discrimination in other areas of life and guarantee their equal citizenship, as long as their sex acts can be criminalized, as long [as] they are disparaged as second class citizens, we may expect the rights they do have to go on being underenforced, and violence against them to remain a common fact" (Nussbaum 2001, 581–82).

A very clear statement in the region, then, is that citizens have rights as long as they operate within the heterosexual norms of Caribbean culture (although this is not to say that all heterosexuals enjoy equal rights to citizenship – as indicated in the foregoing discussion on freedom, national origin, gender and race). Nussbaum is also insightful in pointing out the extent to which a society inflicts shame on its citizens or offers protection from such shame. This shame manifests itself in the form of taunting, teasing, ridicule and what Nussbaum (2004) describes as an assault on a person's human dignity and individuality. She argues that the law plays an important part in both aspects of the process. Using a similar perspective, Tracy Robinson (2012) recently outlined the constitutional dilemma that such a position holds for Caribbean states. Robinson points out that Caribbean constitutions are framed in such a way as to recognize the need that certain minorities may require rights protection in circumstances of hostility, violence and threats to these rights by majority groups. Herein lies a fundamental constitutional contradiction, as Robinson (2012) elaborates: "Laws in the Commonwealth Caribbean that criminalize sexual activity between adults of the same sex fall afoul of fundamental values and norms expressed in Caribbean constitutions, especially the core principle of respect for human dignity. Although these laws focus on certain sexual acts, like anal sex, and not homosexuality per se, they disproportionately and negatively impact on the lives of gay men, lesbians and transgender persons."

Caribbean governments not only face constitutional challenges such as that described by Robinson above, but these issues get at the heart of the colonial past, which continues to burden the present, even though the metropolitan systems upon which Caribbean law is based have long abandoned anachronistic regulations about private sexual practices.

New legislation to reflect modern thinking about matters of sexuality and privacy has to be enacted; however, this must be accompanied by changes in attitudes about belonging and who benefits from full citizenship. Changes at the juridical level and at the level of modern, progressive thinking should prevent such absurdities as the 2009 conviction of seven people under the Summary Jurisdiction (Offences) Act in Guyana, who were charged for cross-dressing in public. Even more disturbing than the convictions and fines was the admonishment of the magistrate who told the convicted individuals that they were "confused" about their sexuality and gender and concluded: "it's a curse on the family" (USDS 2010, 17). A change in the thinking about the politics of belonging of sexual minorities in the Caribbean may go a long way in avoiding such remarks as the above and the one made in 2008 by the former prime minister of Jamaica, Bruce Golding, on the BBC programme *HARDtalk*, that he could not conceive of a gay person being a member of his cabinet (see *Jamaican Gleaner*, 21 May 2008). Despite such truculent attitudes, there are signs of gradual change occurring, with the establishment of Caribbean human-rights organizations, and organizations of gay, lesbian, bisexual, transgendered and queer people.

Citizenship, as we have seen, is much less fixed and settled a concept than it might be thought. As argued throughout this chapter, citizenship is more a process than an unchanging status. Not only is there a changing and adapting relationship between the individual and the state but, in some ways, the relationship is a contradictory one marked by shifting standards of inclusion and exclusion. There is a tendency to see social exclusion as a sort of collateral damage of the politics of belonging, but we must view such marginalization more critically. It is incumbent upon us to be cognizant of such exclusion in order to better resist the deprivation of the rights of marginalized groups, to ensure the safety of those who face the threat of violence on a daily basis and, finally, to act as a bulwark against other forms of discrimination. In short, we must move beyond purely territorial and narrowly defined, nationalist preoccupations when we think about the lived experience of citizenship in the Caribbean. There is much more at stake than what appears in its phenomenal form.

Conclusion

The foregoing discussion centres around an argument concerning the importance of the condition of freedom to an understanding of the phenomenon of citizenship. Meaningful citizenship can only flourish in an environment of freedom, not in an authoritarian context or in a context that is hostile to change. If we understand change as an ever-dynamic process, which facilitates expanding the boundaries of inclusion and the full participation of all, then freedom has to be a sine qua non of citizenship. Attendant to the idea of freedom is the notion of social justice. What has been traced throughout this chapter is the journey of the marginalized, the excluded, "the wretched of the earth" (in Franz Fanon's phrase), who were able to resist or are still engaged in an ongoing struggle against an oppressive and discriminatory system. These forms of resistance are motivated by the ideal of social justice. Social justice is at the heart of an embrace of citizenship, insofar as it addresses the issue of human dignity, and human dignity, in the words of Martha Nussbaum, is about ensuring equal worth of persons (2004, 338). In the final analysis, it is important that we recognize that citizenship operates within specific historical contexts, and its meaning is constructed within such contexts, depending on the space permitted by their conjuncture and seized by progressive forces for the expansion of democratic rights.

Though citizenship is often simply seen as a bundle of rights and entitlements, these rights are not gifts from the state but, rather, the result of struggles waged by individuals and social groups in society. A more inclusive type of citizenship that embraces equality and dignity is only possible in the context of a robust democratic environment. The issues of human dignity and social justice mentioned above, the expansion of rights for sexual and racial minorities, and the creation of greater equality between men and women can only take place in a genuinely democratic society. Thus democracy has to move beyond neo-liberal notions of civic engagement and embrace a more radical democratic practice of people's power in the Caribbean.

Notes

1. On 28 May 2009 Barbados, the Bahamas, Saint Kitts and Nevis, Antigua and Barbuda signed a Short-Stay Visa Waiver Agreement, with most of the Schengen visa areas of the European Union (the exceptions are England and Ireland). The acceptance of this arrangement by these designated Caribbean countries while the residents of other Caribbean countries continue to have difficulty gaining access to the European Union is both troubling and in conflict with the spirit of Caribbean regionalism.
2. Worth mentioning here but requiring an essay of its own is the issue of race and citizenship in the contemporary Caribbean. A study of this issue would be an appropriate complement to the discussion, earlier in this chapter, of the role of race and citizenship in the eighteenth- and nineteenth-century Caribbean. The issue looms large in places such as Guyana, Trinidad, the Dominican Republic and Haiti, as well in other parts of the region. All of the different racial fault lines have the effect of producing differently privileged citizens (see Hinds 2009; Yelvington 1993; Oostindie 1996; Kwayana 1988).

3. Guyana introduced overseas voting in 1968 and continued the practice until 1985. This voting was generally regarded as corrupt and contributed in no small manner to the political rigging of the general elections during those years (see Latin American Bureau 1984; Thomas 1984; Morrison 1998)
4. *Cocolos* is a Spanish vernacular word used in the Spanish-speaking Caribbean to refer to non-Hispanic people of African descent.
5. My thanks to Taitu Heron for bringing this document to my attention.

References

AI-USA (Amnesty International USA website). "Dominican Republic Human Rights". http://www.amnestyusa.org/our-work/countries/americas/dominican-republic.

AI-USA (Amnesty International USA website). 2011. "Annual Report: Dominican Republic 2011". 28 May. http://www.amnestyusa.org/research/reports/annual-report-dominican-republic-2011.

Balibar, Etienne. 2011. *Politics and the Other Scene*. London: Verso.

Basch, Linda, Nina Glick Schiller and Cristina Szanton Blanc. 1994. *Nations Unbound: Transnational Projects, Postcolonial Predicaments, and Deterritorialized Nation-States*. New York: Gordon and Breach Science.

Brathwaite, Edward Kamau. 1977. *Wars of Respect: Nanny and Sam Sharpe and the Struggle for People's Liberation*. Kingston: Agency for Public Information, for National Heritage Week Committee.

CSW (Commission on the Status of Women). 2012. "NGO CSW Outcome Document for Latin America and the Caribbean (An Open Discussion Paper)", December.

Dubois, Laurent. 2004. *A Colony of Citizens: Revolution and Slave Emancipations in the French Caribbean, 1787–1804*. Chapel Hill: University of North Carolina Press.

Dupuy, Alex. 1989. *Haiti in the World Economy: Class, Race, and Underdevelopment since 1700*. Boulder: Westview.

Girard, Philippe. 2011. *The Slaves Who Defeated Napoléon: Toussaint Louverture and the Haitian War of Independence, 1801–1804*. Alabama: University of Alabama Press.

Goveia, Elsa. 1980. *Slave Society in The British Leeward Islands*. Connecticut: Greenwood.

Herweg, Andrew. 2009. "'Barbadian First' Policy Flogs Guyanese in Barbados". *Council on Hemispheric Affairs*. 5 August. http://www.coha.org/barbadian-first-policy-flogs-guyanese-in-barbados/.

Hinds, David. 2009. "Ethnopolitics and Fractured Nationalism in Guyana". In *Anthropologies of Guyana: Cultural Spaces in Northeastern Amazonia*, edited by Neil Whitehead and Stephanie Alemán, 154–66. Tucson: University of Arizona Press.

ITUC (International Trade Union Confederation). 2011. "Living With Economic Insecurity: Women in Precarious Work". March. http://www.ituc-csi.org/living-with-economic-insecurity?lang=en.

Knight, Franklin. 1990. *The Caribbean: The Genesis of a Fragmented Nationalism*. 2nd ed. Oxford: Oxford University Press.

Kwayana, Eusi. 1988. *Guyana: No Guilty Race*. Georgetown, Guyana: N.p.

Latin American Bureau. 1984. *Guyana: Fraudulent Revolution*. London: Latin American Bureau (Research and Action).

Lewis, Linden. 2000. "Nationalism and Caribbean Masculinity". In *Gender Ironies of Nationalism: Sexing the Nation*, edited by Tamar Mayer, 261–81. London: Routledge.

Malik, Kenan. 1996. *The Meaning of Race: Race, History and Culture in Western Society*. London: New York University Press.

Morrison SJ, Fr Andrew. 1998. *Justice: The Struggle for Democracy in Guyana, 1952–1992*. Guyana: Red Thread Women's Press.

Nussbaum, Martha. 2001. "Lesbian and Gay Rights". In *The Philosophy of Human Rights*, edited by Patrick Hayden, 574–97. St Paul: Paragon House.

———. 2004. *Hiding from Humanity: Disgust, Shame, and the Law*. Princeton and Oxford: Princeton University Press.

Oostindie, Geert, ed. 1996. *Ethnicity in the Caribbean*. London and Basingstoke: Macmillan Education.

Plaza, Dwaine. 2008. "Transnational Return Migration to the English-Speaking Caribbean". *Revue européenne des migrations internationales* 24 (1): 115–37.

Potter, Robert, Dennis Conway and Joan Phillips. 2005. *The Experience of Return Migration: The Caribbean Perspectives*. Aldershot, UK: Ashgate.

Price, Richard. 2011. *Rainforest Warriors: Human Rights on Trial*. Philadelphia: University of Pennsylvania Press.

Robinson, Tracy. 2012. "Caribbean Constitutional Standards and the Rights of Sexual Minorities". UN AIDS Caribbean website, 14 January. http://unaidscaribbean.org/node/165.

Sheller, Mimi. 2012. *Citizenship from Below: Erotic Agency and Caribbean Freedom*. Durham: Duke University Press.

Smith, Anthony D. 1991. *National Identity*. London: Penguin.

Thomas, Clive. 1984. *The Rise of the Authoritarian State in Peripheral Societies*. New York: Monthly Review Press.

Tilly, Charles. 2005. *Identities, Boundaries and Social Ties*. Boulder: Paradigm.

Turner, Bryan S. 2001. "The Erosion of Citizenship". *British Journal of Sociology* 52 (2): 189–209.

UNDP (United Nations Development Programme). 2012. *Caribbean Human Development Report 2012: Human Development and the Shift to Better Citizenship Security*. New York: UNDP.

USDS (US Department of State). 2010. *Human Rights Country Reports*. Washington, DC: US Department of State.

Yelvington, Kevin. 1993. *Trinidad Ethnicity*. London and Basingstoke: Macmillan.

Yuval-Davis, Nira. 2011. *The Politics of Belonging: Intersectional Contestations*. Los Angeles: Sage.

5 Citizenship and Belonging
Forging a Caribbean Identity

Anton L. Allahar

This chapter will focus on the politics of identity and belonging in the English-speaking Caribbean. It will situate those politics historically, first, in the colonial context and, second, in the postcolonial context. To frame the analysis theoretically I will use the concept of "primordialism" and tie it to considerations of citizenship and belonging of different peoples in the English-speaking Caribbean. The main thrust of the argument is that while "citizenship" may be a clear-cut matter – one is either a citizen or not – "belonging" is a very fraught notion, especially as it touches the question of Caribbean regional nation-ness that is so complicated by class, ethnic and racial divisions.

The standard dictionary definition of citizenship says it is a legal status conferred on someone who, "by place of birth, nationality of one or both parents, or by going through the naturalization process, has sworn loyalty to a nation".[1] In the language of identity and belonging, the person in question "belongs" juridically to the nation in which he or she was born or naturalized as a citizen. In other words, it is that person's home by virtue of the fact that he or she was born there, and the person in question is said to "belong" to the nation and is entitled to all the rights – including the right to an official birth certificate, passport or other government-issued form of identification – accorded to any other citizen. Evidently, then, "belonging" has both a biological and a social-legal dimension.

But belonging to a nation or country extends beyond these to suggest that citizenship also has to be understood in emotional terms. This latter point is captured in the patriotic sentiment of "my country, right or wrong" and also touches on the psychological aspects of belonging when one invokes "the comforts of home" or the "home" in "homeland" (Allahar 1994, 20). In these renderings, "home is where the heart is" – it is a space that human beings crave and a place where they can feel safe, protected and loved.

This latter understanding of home and belonging is further complicated in the global age that has seen the uprooting of whole communities from their ancestral homes and the mass migrations, whether voluntary or forced, of all sorts of people. In this context citizenship is no longer equated simply with place of birth, especially given that today the notions of dual and even triple citizenship are not uncommon.

Finally, there is the more explicitly political and historical interpretation of citizenship that may be seen, for example, in the case of Zionism, where anyone who has at least one Jewish grandparent can gain the right of Israeli citizenship under the right-of-return laws (Atzmon 2011) or in the earlier German context in which "being German meant being born to German parents, hence children of immigrants born on German soil remained outsiders" (Lechner 2009, 206).

Given the generally social and gregarious make-up of human beings, their search for home is fuelled by a desire not to be left alone, for such aloneness is unnatural and leads to feelings of insecurity and vulnerability (Allahar 1994, 18–21). This is partly why Benedict Anderson could write that "nation-ness and nationalism command such profound emotional legitimacy" (1983, 13–14). Much like being a member of a family, being rooted in one's own land implies an unquestioned acceptance by others from that land and a sense of belonging that is both physically and emotionally reassuring. Speaking specifically about the individual in the group, Harold Isaacs wrote, "He is not only not alone, but here, as long as he chooses to remain in and of it, he cannot be denied or rejected" (1975, 43). He continues, "It is *home* in the sense of Robert Frost's line, the place where, when you've got to go there, they've got to take you in" (43). The exact sentiments are captured in the popular quote by Maya Angelou: "The ache for home lives in all of us, the safe place where we can go as we are and not be questioned" (1986, 196). In this poetic rendering, "home" represents safety and is associated with unconditional acceptance.

Citizenship and Loyalty

Citizenship and belonging also invoke the question of loyalty for they presume that belonging to a nation is synonymous with blind loyalty to it. Thus, Mark Purcell states adamantly: "Because each state is sovereign, a citizen's ultimate political loyalty must be to her nation state. She might be a member of other sorts of political community but they must all be subordinated to her membership in the nation state" (2003, 565). The difficulty presented by this stand is that it is not clear whether the loyalty in question is to a country or a government. So in the United States, for example, even those who were opposed to the Gulf War in 1991 and the Iraq War from 2003 to, arguably, the present as illegal invasions of Iraq, were instructed that although one may not have emotionally supported the initial decision of the Bush regime to go to war, once the troops were there, it is one's patriotic duty to support them, no questions asked. This obvious attempt to control and censor the public was very well documented by Nancy Snow (2003).

The idea that links citizenship with loyalty therefore becomes problematic if a person who is born in a certain country comes to display "disloyalty" to it (see discussion below of East Indians in the Caribbean who support the Indian cricket team over the West Indian team), for who or what is considered "disloyal" or "unpatriotic" is a deeply political and ideological question. How much can one disagree with her or his government without being seen as disloyal or seditious? We are all familiar with the communist witch-hunt in United States from 1938 to 1975, during which the so-called House Committee on Un-American Activities was established and served to persecute ordinary American citizens for their opposing political views and supposedly unsavoury political associations. What is the logic which says that one has to be loyal to the country into which one is born?

Primordial Belonging to One's Own "Kind"

When citizenship is tied to the sense of belonging to a nation it invokes a mutual psychological process in which an individual or group wants to be part of the whole and the whole wanting or accepting the individual or group as a part of it. Belonging is thus like assimilation: the individual or group in question wants to be a part of the host society and the host does not put obstacles in its path. Belonging also speaks to the primordial element in human relations that sees individuals as wanting to be with their own "kind". The problem, of course, is how "kind" is defined. Is it racial, national, regional, cultural, religious, linguistic or class-based?

One of the clearest descriptions and analyses of the origins of social attachment or belonging is presented by Emile Durkheim, who talks of a social solidarity through similarity or sameness. He writes that "we all know that a social cohesion exists where cause can be traced to a certain conformity of each individual consciousness to the common type" (1984, 60). Further, he notes that the similarity that is rooted in the collective consciousness automatically leads members to "love their country . . . to like one another, seeking one another out *in preference to foreigners*" (60; my emphasis). "Foreigners" in this context are best understood as belonging to the realm of "the other", real or imagined, according to Robert Miles (1989, 11–30).

On the basis of his review of the psychological literature on perception and aversion, Kenneth Gergen tells us, "The other appears strange, alien, and unknown. . . .

The common reaction to the unknown, the unpredictable, or the strange is aversion" (1968, 116). Merging these two perspectives, one can say that a total identification with the whole, born perhaps of xenophobia, binds the individual directly to his or her community or society. As a consequence, members are moved to react passionately against anything that threatens the whole's solidarity or cohesiveness. This is most relevant in the Caribbean context where many different "kinds" have come to define the region, as a whole and as discrete countries within that whole.

Colonialism and imperialism used race and class to divide those who would later become citizens; (legal) citizenship and (psychological) belonging do not always go hand in hand. This is my philosophical point of departure for asking some fundamental questions about the intertwined nature of individual and group identities in contemporary society, and it begins by problematizing the notion of "kind". In other words, is there a natural tendency for one to prefer one's own kind – however one defines "kind" – based on feeling more comfortable with those who are most like one? And if so, is this an indication that one might be a chauvinist or a racist?

In what follows, I want to question the presumed naturalness of human belonging and human roots (that is, biological ties among humans) versus their social constructedness. And to do so I will highlight the dialectical tension that may be observed in the make-up of all human beings.

I argue that this tension is tied to people's existential vulnerability and varies between the poles or extremes of (a) security and insecurity and (b) curiosity and uncuriosity. I trace the roots of existential vulnerability to human physical vulnerability. We know that the human infant is totally helpless and needs the support and protection of others, and we also know that in order to survive all humans must depend on others. While some are more independent and self-sufficient than others, no one is completely independent. Thus, to survive they must rely on others who may be said to be of their "kind" – whether family, clan, tribe, village or nation – and who may share racial, cultural or national attributes. This degree to which one feels secure or insecure is at the core of the sense of belonging.

While all humans have different degrees of a sense of security they also have different degrees or levels of curiosity, which I hypothesize is related to their sense of security. Secure people are curious people, and curious people tend to be more open to new things: new ideas, new friends, new adventures, new foods. Insecure people, in contrast, are fundamentally uncurious about the world. They are anxious and fearful of change and as a consequence tend to be more conservative and closed to new ideas, people, experiences and so on. Because of their sense of security, curious people have a desire to explore the unfamiliar, while the insecurity of the uncurious leads them to feel comfortable with the familiar, the routine and the predictable. Thus, as Kenneth Gergen reports, since positive feelings are experienced as less burdensome than negative ones, "similarity is said to breed mutual attraction. We can all attest perhaps to the inclination to feel friendly to 'one of our *kind*'" (1968, 115; my emphasis).

Stated differently, "belonging" is a nuanced concept and differs with context. Thus, the conservative impulse is seen in humans who cherish the personal and psychological comforts which come from being rooted in the familiar and the predictable terrain of "home", where those of their own kind abound and where they belong. Such familiarity calms their anxieties and fears and leads them to cling to what they know, be it ideas, foods, religion, books – even friends and spouses. For the conservative in all of us, home is a matter of social and spiritual location or belonging, a place within which lies a sense of security that is enhanced by rootedness. For many those roots may be a belief, dream, fiction or invention of what constitutes "home" – as captured in the Afrocentrists' embrace of Mother Africa and the Hinducentrists' embrace of Mother India (Allahar 2004). This manufactured notion of home as a spiritual place of belonging, escape or refuge has become much politicized in regions such as the Caribbean and in countries like Trinidad and Tobago and Guyana where the historical dividing lines drawn among the once-subordinate populations during colonial rule continue to have significant purchase.

Primordialism and "Natural" Community

Following Gergen's (1968) observation to the effect that positive affect or feelings are experienced less burdensomely than negative ones, it stands to reason that being with one's own "kind" produces positive feelings and a sense of comfort that comes from familiarity and predictability – the same familiarity and predictability that reduce feelings of insecurity and increase mutual attraction. It is in this context that I want to examine the themes of race, colour, nationality and primordial belonging and to suggest the possible link between these and social exclusion, ostracism and even racism.[2]

The term "primordialism" (or "primordial attachment") will be understood in two senses, which share a dialectical relationship. The "hard" sense of the term holds that human beings are attached to one another and to their communities of origin virtually, by mutual ties of blood and that such blood ties in turn somehow produce reciprocal feelings of trust and acceptance. We find comfort, security, belonging and unquestioned acceptance among our own blood relatives. It is the type of attachment that siblings or parents and their offspring are said to experience and implies an unconditional loyalty or devotion purely on the basis of the intimacy of the tie. Hence the sayings "we are blood" and "blood is thicker than water" – the latter using "thickness" as a metaphor for tight bonding and belonging. This is where the earlier reference to "disloyalty" and lack of patriotism among Trinidad's East Indian cricket fans is relevant.

The "soft" sense of primordialism stresses the social, non-biological bases of attachment and draws attention to the importance of social interpretation and symbolic meaning. In other words, feelings of intense intimacy and belonging do not have to be mediated by blood. Though socially constructed, such feelings can excite in adherents the same passion and devotion that are to be found among blood relatives, as is evidenced in wars or international sporting contests where patriotic sentiment unites soldiers on the battlefield or teammates at the Olympic Games.

But what is more, such sentiments usually spill over to the citizens at large and result in a national fervour among people who do not know one another, likely have never met and may not even care for one another personally. The national or regional passion and excitement generated during a cricket game featuring the West Indies against England is a clear case in point. Depending on the outcome of the game, West Indians in Guyana, Jamaica, Barbados, Trinidad and elsewhere in the region, who do not know one another, tend to come together in collective celebration of regional pride (or shame and disappointment) and react as a single people.

This "soft" primordialism can also be seen in allegiances that unify different populations within the Caribbean. The philosophies of Afrocentrism and Hindutva (Allahar 2004), for example, which certain African-descended and Indian-descended West Indians embrace, are made up of a complex mix of myth and make-believe that conjure up imagined communities of fellows "of the same kind" who live in Africa and India.

The solidarity associated with all primordial communities is steeped in make-believe and myth and tied to the notion of "retrospective illusion" (Bergson 1959, 1263–64), which may be seen to encompass the notions of a common territory of origin and residence, a common place of work or common lines of descent. In other words, primordial attachment can extend beyond that felt towards a parent, sibling or community to encompass a country, a race, a nation or a region, as is evident in the context of a general or specific type of Caribbean or West Indian identity.

There can exist a blind, even unquestioning, allegiance to the group or community, for no other reason than that it is said to be made up of one's own kind. Thus, since positive feelings are experienced as less burdensome than negative ones (Gergen 1968, 115), similarity is said to breed mutual attraction. People who are similar to each other – who are of the same "kind", be it in terms of attitudes, interests, values, personality or phenotype – feel more comfortable with one another, and feel more positively towards each other than those who are dissimilar. But for the "hard" primordialist, that attachment to one's kinship group, ethnic group, national group or regional group is attributed to the tie of blood (Shils 1957, 1968), or the lure of common ethnicity, colour or religion.

Thus, the actual existence of a blood tie between a given person and his or her community is less important than the fact that he or she believes it does and acts in accordance with such a belief (Thomas and Thomas 1928, 572). This is important for, as we shall see, even though class identity and consciousness are so crucial in the struggles against colonialism and capitalism, when there is a generalized sense of race consciousness among workers and the popular masses, as exists in today's Caribbean, race can come to trump class with the obvious consequences for such struggles. Because primordialism invokes a "corporate sentiment of oneness" (Geertz 1973, 260, 307) and a "consciousness of kind" (Giddings 1896, 17–19) that stem from the sharing of common physical features; common geographical space; common ancestors; common culture, language and religion; or common historical experience, Franklin Giddings wrote that "our conduct towards those whom we feel to be most like ourselves is instinctively and rationally different from our conduct towards others whom we believe to be less like ourselves" (18). While this is the stuff of hard primordial belonging, Giddings is also keen to point out that consciousness of kind "is not to be once and for all identified with consciousness of species, or of race, or of class, or of similarity of moral nature, although at any given moment it may, in fact, be identical with any one of these" (xiv).

Elaborating on this assertion, Nancy Boyd Willey and Malcolm Willey paraphrase Giddings and argue that the notion of "kind" comprises two phases of recognition that may be tied to acceptance and belonging: external physical resemblances and emotional and psychological resemblances (1924, 24). In other words, there are both objective and subjective elements involved in recognition of kind, and, whereas the objective element may speak to "a matter of race, size, color, stature, sex, age etc.", the subjective identification of kind rests on like-mindedness, common interest and mutual desires, feelings, sentiments and tastes (24). These authors do not think that a hard-and-fast rule based on "resemblance" applies when it comes to choosing those with whom we are most comfortable, yet they declare, "it appears that in selecting those with whom we would consort, a certain physical limit is set; white men do consort with white, blacks with blacks, yellow with yellow, etc. *Types go with types*" (25; my emphasis). This said, in what follows I will focus on some aspects of the regional, national and ethnic dimensions of citizenship, identity and belonging in the Caribbean.

Cricket and the Sense of West Indian Nation-ness

I use what is perhaps the greatest passion that has united the West Indies as a region: the game of cricket. The sport played a decisive role in the forging of the West Indian sense of nation-ness as a metaphorically black space. It was the cement or glue that sought to bridge the colonially imposed divisions of race, ethnicity and class as the region came together to pool its talents and do battle with the colonial masters. And, dialectically, the bridging in question would employ the very divisions of race and class that had been imposed, to energize players and the Caribbean public at large in the confrontation. Thus, one could only imagine the euphoria and pride, when, for the first time, the West Indian team defeated the English masters in the latters' own home, in 1950 at Lord's Cricket Ground. It was on the eve of independence for countries such as Jamaican, Trinidad, Guyana and Barbados, and because that independence was "black in complexion", the racial dimension of the victory was unmistakable. As a sport that is deeply raced and classed, the victory was to the ordinary West Indian what the 1937 boxing victory of the black fighter Joe Louis (the Brown Bomber) over his white opponent, James J. Braddock, was to the ordinary black American.

Ever since gaining their independence from Britain in the 1960s and 1970s, the countries of the English-speaking Caribbean have made several attempts at political, economic and cultural federation. To date none of these has been successful. Indeed, the only area in which the West Indies has seemed to be able to come together, albeit uneasily, as a united force in world matters, is cricket. The West Indian cricket team is therefore to be regarded as far more than a sporting body; cricket culture soon became "the mirror within which the modern Caribbean ontology could be viewed" (Beckles 1994, xvi). Or, as Richard Burton has observed, it is only "when they saw their cricket team locked in a combat with that of the English colonial masters that Jamaicans, Barbadians, Trinidadians and Guyanese came to see themselves as West Indians possessing a common historical, cultural and political identity" that transcended their otherwise insular visions of themselves and their world (1985, 179). That is to say, a sense of regional identity and belonging was born – and to this Tim Hector would add: "Cricket in the West Indies is more than a game, more than popular art"; it was the vehicle through which "West Indians overcame or sought to overcome the racism and consequent sense of racial inferiority and racial self-contempt in which the great majority of us were born" (1994, 113).

But cricket was not an uncomplicated regional or even national unifier. For when introduced into the colonies at the beginning of the nineteenth century, cricket – known generally as "the gentleman's game" – represented the most white, elite and upper class of English sporting engagements, which only later would become a crucial source of West Indian identity and belonging. Politeness was the order of the day, and such qualities as fairness, honesty, team spirit, integrity and good sportsmanship were hallmarks of the game and those who played it. Before long, cricket penetrated the ranks of the culturally insecure and dependent Euro-Creole elites,[3] who saw in the game an opportunity to emulate and approximate their metropolitan masters. They affected both the manners and the mannerisms of the English aristocratic elite to whom the game initially belonged: they dressed completely in white flannels, sipped tea, politely applauded good play with calculated reserve and spoke intensely and intellectually of "Cricket, lovely cricket!"[4]

But in the colonies where colour was currency, cricket also reflected colour and class divisions: it is an expensive game, and money decides who gets to play. Thus, a strain of cricket developed that was defined by the planter-merchant nexus, and in the racialized minds of the colonizers and their Euro-Creole cousins, no Afro-Creole was expected to exhibit the level of cricketing skill and leadership of a true Englishman.

This fact leads Hilary Beckles to admit that "cricket was at once an instrument of imperial cultural authority as well as a weapon of class and race domination" (1994, xiii–xiv). It was a cultural export from the mother country, and when it seeped down to the ordinary people at village levels of Caribbean societies, they embraced more than a just a game; cricket was a piece of English culture exported to the colonies complete with rules of "proper" play, "good" conduct and overall genteel respectability. L. O'Brien Thompson notes that the colonial subjects "learned to obey the umpire's decisions without question even though his judgement might have been obviously questionable" (1983, 24–25). And even if they were not treated with dignity when defeated, they were taught to be generous to their opponents in victory: "They were socialized to be modest. . . . They cultivated the habit of presenting a stiff upper lip in the face of adversity. They learned all about *esprit de corps*" (24–25). Furthermore, as cricket blended into the very character and personality of the colonial subjects, and as it became a popular passion, it served as a wonderful tool of distraction – and hence social control of the potentially volatile masses: "the game was considered to be crucial to maintaining control over colonial subjects" (St Pierre 1990, 14; see also Cummings 1990, 26–27).

But cricket also had the unintended consequence of giving a politicized identity to the local players and the masses they represented and of uniting the colonials and ex-colonials in ways that would extend well beyond the cricket field. Even though there is something amazingly democratizing about sport – where the richest and the poorest, the privileged and the disenfranchised, meet and engage one another on the same level playing field using the same rules – it was never part of colonial thinking that social equality was a value or a goal to be pursued. In other words, not all citizens were equal in status or in the sense of belonging. In fact, the colonial divisions of race and class also had national manifestations in discrete West Indian countries where local whites were able to use race and class privilege – they had access to the best grounds, pitches, equipment and coaches – to dominate the game locally. So on the eve of independence and right into its immediate aftermath, when it came to playing local-club cricket against their Euro-Creole compatriots or alongside those Euro-Creoles against a team of visiting English players, the working-class stars from the villages and poor neighbourhoods were daily becoming keenly aware of their own identities as West Indians belonging to the region. For in the larger colonial scheme of things, the body politic "was no more than the ideological superstructure of the plantation-based establishment that kept firmly in sight the concepts of white supremacy, the power and privilege of private property, and the attendant fear of, if not hatred for, racial/social egalitarianism" (Beckles 1994, xv).

This, however, was all to change by the middle of the twentieth century. After over 150 years of English political, economic, racial and cultural domination of the colonies (which included their cricketing supremacy) in the modified plantation society known as the Caribbean, a radical revolution took place in the white man's world of both politics and cricket. The British Empire was crumbling; colonies in Asia, Africa and the Caribbean were clamouring for, and winning, their independence, much to the chagrin of both the colonizers and many of their Euro- and Afro-Creole loyalists. Black Power politics began to enter the Caribbean scene, and cricket came to be seen as a metaphor for the independence movement and for the politics of identity and belonging. The West Indian cricket team – which up to 1961 had never been chosen on merit (St Pierre 1990, 17), owing to class and race prejudice and barriers, and which had never known a black captain – was to become an important site of the struggle for decolonization and served to condition much of the subsequent political culture of belonging in the region. But the struggle for decolonization was derailed as the class struggle came to be overshadowed by the race struggle.

By this time, cricket had grown immensely in popularity among the local whites and the black and the East Indian masses, and when the West Indies erupted onto the stage of world cricket by defeating England at Lord's the momentousness of the event was captured – albeit understated – thus by Burton: "After 1950 the 'mother country' would never be quite the same again in West Indian eyes" (1985, 180). Two questions arise from this important defeat: How did it serve to inform and to shape a West Indian identity and how did it speak to the issue of belonging to the region as a whole?

The 1950 victory ushered in an era that saw the transformation of the way the game was played, just as the politics of the era were serving to transform racial, national and regional pride. The West Indies batsmen were described by radio and newspaper commentators as savage hitters of the ball while their fast bowlers were repeatedly accused of intimidating tactics. This latter charge is clearly captured in a 2011 documentary about West Indian fast bowlers, *Fire in Babylon*, which depicts detractors characterizing them as angry and vicious and not very "sporting" (Riley 2011). Not unlike earlier attempts to neutralize the almost unplayable spin bowling of Sonny Ramadhin and Alf Valentine by changing the LBW (leg before wicket) rules, *Fire in Babylon* also features a segment in which there is talk by some previous players, rule makers and umpires of limiting the number of bouncers that can be bowled in an over, mandating a shorter run-up for fast bowlers and even lengthening the twenty-two yard cricket pitch in an effort to limit the impact of the West Indies pace bowlers. The West Indian players brought a flair to the game that was described as "calypso cricket", which, in the aftermath of the momentous victory at Lord's, was an identity marker they wore with pride. This is well captured by Garry Steckles (2009) when he wrote that, following that victory, "England had changed. Immigrants had found their voice, a sporting triumph had given them a vehicle to express themselves, 'without fear', and that voice was not about to be silenced. While all this was happening, calypso cricket would go on to triumphs that not even the jubilant fans who sang and danced around Lord's with Kitch could have envisaged." The players' antics on the field heralded a new dawning – one that saw the West Indian team become less "white", more integrated, far more cohesive and much bolder as they challenged the traditional rules and conventions of the game, just as in the wider society the traditional rules and conventions of colonialism and white supremacy were being challenged and transformed.

Race prejudice, which had kept any black player from becoming captain of the West Indian team prior to 1960, and which saw a long list of mediocre white captains with mediocre cricketing talent, was dealt a decisive blow with the hotly debated appointment of Frank Worrell to that position. Due largely to the political efforts of C.L.R. James (1963), the long-held idea that black men could not lead on the cricket field, let alone in politics, was finally put to rest. Worrell's considerable skill at captaincy was on par with his exceptional abilities as a player and his appointment "stood as a classic statement of the link between emergent nationalism, anti-colonial struggle and sporting culture" (Searle 1990, 35). Cricket, once an effective tool of colonial domination, was being refashioned by the colonized into a weapon of social, political and cultural liberation and used as a vehicle for the forging of a Caribbean identity that was black in complexion.

Under Worrell's captaincy, and subsequently under the captaincies of other black leaders such as Garfield Sobers, Clive Lloyd and Vivian Richards, the West Indies went on to become undisputed world champions for over two decades. They reinvented and revolutionized the rules and, by the 1980s, managed to redefine the game. By this time the empire was a remnant of its past, yet knighthoods had been conferred on several of the West Indian cricket revolutionaries: Sir Learie Constantine, Sir Clyde Walcott, Sir Frank Worrell, Sir Everton Weeks, Sir Garfield Sobers, Sir Vivian Richards, Sir Andy Roberts and Sir Curtly Ambrose.[5] Indeed, Richards summed up the implications of the process of changes in West Indian cricket in the very title of his autobiography: *Hitting across the Line* (1992). For cricketing purists, any batsman who hits "across the line" of the ball is playing an incorrect stroke. On his way to becoming one of the greatest batsmen the game has ever seen, however, Richards customarily hit across the line and, in the process, redefined this as proper stroke play. Burton captures the essence of the moment when he observes that "in the course of its transposition to the Caribbean, cricket, like so much else, has been comprehensively creolized" (1985, 180). To this Chris Searle would add, "Here was a cricket of resistance and assertion, which mirrored an entire people coming into their own, rejecting colonial divisions imposed upon them and bringing a new confidence and will for cultural construction" (1990, 36) and pointed out that these players transformed "cricket from a game played and controlled by white English and colonial elites, to a sport carrying the aspirations of national independence and democratic ownership" (34).

Blacks and Indians: The Other Dimension of Race, Cricket and Belonging

As noted earlier, when political independence came to the British Caribbean, it was black in complexion, for the blacks – whose residency in the Caribbean antedates that of the Indians by (in the cases of some countries) over three hundred years – came to see themselves as the rightful heirs of the newly independent states. In years to come this would lead to hotly contested politics of identity and belonging among these two ethnic groups in the cases of Trinidad and Tobago and of Guyana, the two Caribbean countries that played major roles as host to the indentured workers from India. Understandably this would figure prominently in the political culture of the new states, and since cricket is such an integral part of those societies and cultures, it is to be expected that the game would also reflect the tensions and conflicts engendered.

By the 1970s and 1980s, a politically independent Caribbean was simmering with class and racial unrest. The illusion that independence would bring prosperity, abundance and social equality was being shattered. Dependent capitalism, neo-liberalism and the ravages of structural adjustment policies imposed by the International Monetary Fund led to great social impoverishment for the working masses of the Caribbean (as elsewhere). Many felt betrayed by those once-charismatic leaders who were at the helm of the independence struggle (Allahar 2001).

But with the disappearance of the easy target – the white, English colonial master – people in the Caribbean began to look internally for answers and scapegoats. Here, then, the issues of class and race are not limited merely to a politically symbolic encounter between white, English slave masters and black slaves on the playing field. In the latter half of the twentieth century blacks comprised the bulk of the West Indian cricket team, which never really featured a consistently large number of players of Indian descent. And at the height of the team's success in the 1980s Captain Vivian Richards was to remark that that continuous success was achieved with an all-black team (Rohlehr 1994, 97). The implication for many Indian observers was that there was no longer any room on the West Indian team for Indians,[6] and in the racially sensitive climate of the day Indians would interpret this symbolically as saying also that West Indian societies had no room for Indians. The inference made them feel they did not belong. The incendiary remark had an obvious context.

The Black Power uprising in Trinidad in 1970 created a sense of insecurity among many Indians, who were already made to feel unwelcome. Indians were not politically in control of the country and numbered very few within the ranks of civil servants. But as a group they were perceived to be growing in economic prosperity and they began to dominate professions such as law and medicine, and all manner of business places bearing Indian names were, and still are, easily visible. But it was not all about race: the capitalist fraction of this group benefited financially from the policies of the black government but opportunistically played "the race card" when it suited their interests.

It was in this climate that a test team from India toured the West Indies in 1971 and in 1976. On both occasions the Indian team was victorious, and on both occasions Caribbean Indians, whose symbolic citizenship and sense of belonging to the local region were openly questioned, cheered wildly for the Indian team. This amounted to pouring gasoline onto a smouldering fire and incensed the black West Indian masses in the various Caribbean countries. In Trinidad, Selwyn Ryan tells us, "there were some ugly incidents between Africans and Indians whose behaviour was described as being treasonable" (1979, 10); here was the issue of "loyalty" as a key element of citizenship. How could these Indians claim to belong to the region when, in such a highly charged political encounter (a test cricket match), they clearly demonstrated their disloyalty? The game had spilled over beyond the boundary.

Kevin Yelvington explains the issue of the question of ethnic versus national identity and belonging in this way: "The majority of Trinidad East Indians are Hindus and many would have identified with India on these grounds alone. But the symbol of India would have been much more alluring, and its representatives seen as 'pure' in contrast to local 'creolized' East Indians" (1990, 10). In other words, the Indians' racial identity trumped their regional or national identity, and the open act of "treachery" of cheering on the Indian team clearly demonstrated to blacks that those Indians chose not to belong. Though commenting on a different context, Rhoda Reddock manages to make the point even more clearly: "Indian notions of Indian identity did not allow for being 'mixed' and retaining an Indian identity. Creole identity, and by extension, contemporary African identity allows for mixed identity alongside other identities" (1999, 192). Of course the notion of racial purity is built on myth and ideology, on "invented traditions" and "imagined communities", and the East Indian in the Caribbean is no less susceptible to it than is the African (Allahar 2004). The important point, however, is that, imagined or not, this is precisely the racialized baggage that one is likely to carry to the rum shop arguments, to the street corner courts of public opinion, to physical engagements with "the other" and to the polling booths on election day. The political culture of the Caribbean thus bears the unmistakable scars of empire even after the British Empire no longer exists, and, for many, a Caribbean identity continues to transcend legal citizenship in a given Caribbean country and problematizes the personal sense of belonging among the non-Afro-descended populations.

Steelband and Calypso: Whose Culture?

I move now to a specific assessment of identity and belonging as these are tied to class and race in Trinidad's popular culture as represented by the steelband and calypso.

The steelpan (also called pan or steel drum) is said to be the only musical instrument created in the twentieth century, and its origins, which date back to the late 1930s, were in the poor, black, urban areas of east Port of Spain in Trinidad. It was not until the American occupation of Trinidad between 1941 and 1945 that the steelband and the pan really started to assume the shape by which it is recognized today (Lee, 1997; Tarradath, 1991). In the beginning, this lower-working-class Afro-Creole invention came to reflect the values of its inventors, which were very much at odds with the values of the dominant classes, white, brown and black. It was a difficult time economically, and the rough conditions of existence gave rise to a rough social environment. The area in which steelband music took root was generally known as lying "behind the bridge", a location which implied a certain marginal or outcast identity. Patterning themselves after characters and gangs from American movies during the war years, the steelbandsmen took on military titles (captain, lieutenant, war horse) and gave their bands tough-sounding names (Desperadoes, Renegades, Invaders, Crossfire). The steelbands were territorial phenomena; they belonged to distinct communities, and residents of those communities identified closely with their respective bands. Members of steelbands also came to be seen as not only representing their communities but as protecting them. Thus, in the style of contemporary urban gang warfare in the United States, in which young men and women fight for the control of turf, steelband players and followers of their bands became self-appointed guardians of their communities. Rallying behind one's community's steelband was an intimate part of community identity and belonging.

By the 1950s, although steelbands had spread to most parts of Trinidad, the image of them as a black, lower-working-class, crime-prone movement persisted. The Mighty Sparrow's 1963 calypso "Outcast" captures the sense of social scorn best:

> Calypsonians really ketch hell for a long time
> To associate yourself with them was a big crime
> If your sister only talk to a steelband man
> The family want to break she hand
> Put she out,
> lick out every teeth in she mouth
> Pass you outcast!

As noted, this sentiment was shared by middle- and upper-middle-class blacks who had internalized all the class prejudices of their former colonial masters. Yet it was at this time, as Trinidad and Tobago was moving in the direction of independence, that the steelband and steelbandsmen became objects to be used for political ends, and were officially incorporated into the political culture of the country. Under the leadership of Dr Eric Williams, the African-dominated People's National Movement (PNM) party made quick and skilful use of the situation and moulded its agenda of nationalist and populist identity politics around the class and race attributes of the steelbandsmen: "The PNM . . . made a number of overtures to them as the bearers of the Afro-creole cultural traditions who had created the steelband" (Lee 1997, 73).

In a country where the ethnic divide roughly paralleled the urban-rural divide, the PNM found in this urban constituency a ready-made source of votes and an opportunity for powerful symbolic politics. As steelbands became identified with specific politicians, they rallied to the sides of the latter, playing at their political functions and physically assuming the role of defenders of those politicians. Today the steelband movement is still overwhelmingly black and working class. But the steelpan having been elevated to the status of national musical instrument, being a "pan man" has also come to be seen in less stigmatized terms.

Sponsorships, advertisements, big prize money, recording contracts, opportunity for travel abroad and the general internationalization of steelband music have all combined to give players a fair measure of respectability. Still, however, its class and racial origins are difficult to shake off entirely. These are direct carry-overs from the period of colonial rule when such things as class, race and colour markers and ethnic distinctions were used to divide and control the subordinate populations. And although formal colonialism in many countries has ended, the scars of colonialism endure and can clearly be seen in the racialization of political consciousness in several Caribbean countries. Trinidad and Tobago is one such country where questions of citizenship and belonging are still racially framed.

Racialization of Political Consciousness

The racialization of political consciousness in Trinidad and Tobago (Allahar 1999) speaks to the tendency for racial differences to be perceived as crucial in determining political actions, economic opportunities, social standing and even national belonging, cultural legitimacy or authenticity. With racialization "race" is invoked as the prime cause and explanation of behaviour behind something as public as political-party allegiance or as private as the choice of a marriage partner. Race is also assumed to be biologically fixed and immutable so that any attempt to treat it as a social construction is resisted vigorously by those who have a great deal of political and emotional investment in notions of racial purity and the associated concept of cultural superiority (Allahar 1996). Although many are unwilling to publicly acknowledge it, lighter skin colour is seen as more socially acceptable across all colour segments of the Caribbean population and can influence class and economic mobility. For "belonging" is both class- and colour-coded, and those blacks who are seeking economic and occupational mobility will go to great lengths to escape their racialization as they attempt to emulate behaviour that is associated with those racial groups deemed more socially acceptable.

Owing to the very highly developed racialized consciousness that exists in Trinidad and Tobago (and no doubt in other Caribbean countries too), among the politically ambitious one finds a general tendency to minimize the importance of class as a political or even an analytical category. But this is the distraction of which I spoke earlier, and while it is in many respects a residue of the colonial past, I certainly do not want to give the impression that rivalry and hostility between and among different ethnic, tribal and national groupings was an invention of the colonial rulers. Such group and territorial differences long predated colonialism and the appearance of Europeans in Africa, India and the Caribbean (Allahar 1993). But in the present context of political opportunism, the complex dialectic of race and class inequality sees upwardly mobile members of the so-called coloured groups as opportunists who are prepared to play the race card as it suits their purposes.

The racialization of political consciousness in Trinidad and Tobago is linked to the country's history, the times and conditions under which the various waves of forced or voluntary immigrants arrived and those immigrants' relationship to capital and their differential access to and use of power. But in the context of the present argument, and with specific reference to the East Indians, Kelvin Singh commented that from the outset Indians were not given a warm reception and that, along with being assigned to the lowest-paid jobs, "they were also placed by the other social groups in the lowest position in the system of social stratification" (1974, 48–49). By the middle of the twentieth century, when Indians pressed for the construction of schools of their own cultural and religious persuasions, it was firmly resisted by the "still dominant planter and commercial classes" and certainly did not "meet the approval of the westernized Negro and coloured middle-class professionals whose dislike of the Indians was an already established tradition in the society" (59).

In the case of the African-Indian encounter, while there was ample evidence of amicable and cooperative living arrangements, length of stay in the new society and the different material circumstances that attended each community's daily social transactions were such that separation and xenophobia were more the order of the day: "The two races did not mix: they lived in uneasy but mainly non-violent, coexistence", owing to the fact that "neither felt that their existence was threatened by the other, or that the other way of living was dangerous or oppressive to their own" (Brereton 1974, 37). Yet much recent politicized historiography seeks to paint a picture of conflict and "competitive victimhood", claiming to measure which of the two groups suffered most under slavery and indentureship and whose "competitive claims of ancestral agonies" (Brereton 2011, 58) are most valid.

After emancipation the African former slaves opted for moving to the towns in search of non-plantation jobs, while the terms of indentureship that bound the Indians to the land confined the latter largely to the rural way of life and continue to carry serious implications for their claims to belonging. Thus, as late as the 1950s mutual feelings of xenophobia persisted, and since the Africans were there longer and boasted greater numbers, the logic of "first-come first-served" made some of them feel they were more rightfully entitled than the Indians to be the inheritors of the land (Deosaran 1987, 17; Warner 1993, 288).

Calypso and the Politics of Racial Belonging

In 1961, on the eve of independence, calypsonian Mighty Dougla sang "Split Me in Two", reflecting the ethnic apprehensions of the population. His calypso sobriquet of "dougla" indicates a person of mixed (black and East Indian) ancestry, and in this song he wonders what will happen to him in the post-independence period, if the country is partitioned between the blacks and Indians:

> Ah hear dey sending Indians to India
> And Negroes back to Africa,
> Will somebody please just tell me,
> Where dey sending poor me.
> I am neither one nor the other,
> Six of one half a dozen of the other,
> So if dey serious 'bout sending back people for true,
> They have to split me in two.

The Mighty Dougla's fear is that of a person with a fluid ethnic or racial identity who lives among a majority of other douglas and assorted creoles who choose to embrace fixed ethnic or racial identities and claims of belonging – and the fifty years since have done nothing to allay that fear expressed just before independence. Using the calypso as insight into Trinidad's political culture is most revealing, for it shows a clear picture of a classed and raced reality that is quite consistent with the argument that has been developed above. In this context, however, time and space limitations only permit me to touch the surface of this question.

No appreciation of the richly textured political culture of Trinidadian society can afford to ignore the role played by the calypsonians. In Gramscian terms they are true traditional intellectuals who in recent times have been called upon to act as organic intellectuals, giving ideological direction to the interests of the political classes and other social groups to which they belong and which they represent (Gramsci 1971, 5–8). For whether the theme is of unity and identity, as in Black Stalin's "Caribbean Unity", Drupatee's "Indian Soca", the Lord Kitchener's "National Band" and Brother Marvin's "Jahaaji Bhai"; racial divisions, as captured in Sugar Aloes's[7] "Ah Ready to Go" and Cro Cro's "They Look for Dat"; gender divisions, as with Denise Plummer's "Woman Is Boss"; class divisions, as lyricized in the Mighty Chalkdust's "Grandfather Back Pay"; or regional conflicts, as expressed in Sparrow's "Federation" or Dave Martins's "Not a Blade of Grass", these producers and performers of lived culture are not politically neutral. Whether they are deliberately employed by the classes whose interests they serve or whether they accidentally happen to serve those interests, calypsonians will continue to define and reflect social and political agreements and disagreements on key issues of social concern.

I choose to focus on this aspect of popular culture because it speaks directly to the politics of identity and belonging; as a source of political information and a shaper of national or regional identity, it is far more immediate than literary culture when defining insiders and outsiders. In other words, a popular singer and song will reach many more people and far more quickly than a popular author and book. The political uses of popular culture are therefore not to be casually dismissed. And it is with this in mind I want to direct attention to recent political developments in Trinidad and Tobago, where, following the 1995 election of the United National Congress government, the country had its first ever East Indian prime minister, Basdeo Panday, and its largest-ever number of East Indian members of parliament.[8] This development occurred in the context of a highly racialized consciousness in the population at large and again brought the issues of citizenship, identity and belonging to the forefront of public consciousness.

Take, for instance, the song "Caribbean Unity" (1979) in which Black Stalin appears to see only the African-descended people of the Caribbean and calls for racial unity in the region by invoking the common origins of all Caribbean people in Africa:

> Dem is one race – de Caribbean Man
> From de same place – de Caribbean Man
> Dat make de same trip – de Caribbean Man
> On de same ship – de Caribbean Man.

Reacting to the historical distortion and apparent erasure of the unique Indian experience in the Caribbean and in Trinidad in particular, Ramesh Deosaran branded the calypso racist (and sexist) and insulting to "the vast number of people from other races here who have come in different ships and from different places and who are also struggling to make this unity thing work" (1987, 114). At the surface level of the calypso, one might defend Black Stalin's attempt as non-malicious or well-intentioned; however, this was not to be the case, for in a subsequent interview he stated publicly that the calypso was really only about men of African descent, "that Africans were the ones who developed the Caribbean, and that they were the only ones concerned with Caribbean unity" (Deosaran 1987, 81). And the matter was not to rest there, owing to the intervention of commentators such as Selwyn Ryan, who came to Stalin's assistance when he noted that "one of the reasons why blacks believe that they are more integrally Caribbean than any other group is that they alone have completely severed primordial ties with their Motherland" (*Sunday Express*, 11 March 1979). In time, however, Ryan revised his position and declared:

> My own judgement at the time was that Stalin was using poetic licence to remind Caribbean blacks that they had a great deal in common, which could be used positively for their women and their children. It was seen as a pro-black and not an anti-Indian discourse. But Stalin subsequently made clear that his Caribbean Man was of African descent, and that Africans were the ones who had developed the Caribbean and the only ones who were concerned with African unity. In sum, he was unambiguously claiming the Caribbean for the African. ("Caribbean Man Revisited", *Trinidad Express*, 8 February 2011)

Stalin's point was clear: Trinidad and Tobago is a black country, and in this context one must also remember that the calypso art form was always identified as an African thing, a unique black contribution to the formation of Trinidad's culture. So it is not unusual to find that it was the (black) calypsonians who would reflect the above-mentioned angst. Thus, Keith Warner avers that from its very earliest days "calypso had a certain 'Africanness,' a certain 'blackness' about it. . . . calypso is seen by the Trinidad and Tobago public as first and foremost 'a black man's thing' " (1993, 277). And Earl Lovelace is unequivocal in tying the question of calypso as a black medium to the matter of national identity and cultural ownership: "it is the Africans who have laid the groundwork of a Caribbean culture – those Africans who struggled against enslavement and continued their struggle against colonialism – and the reason they do so is that they had to. They had no choice but to become Caribbean and address the Caribbean landscape and reality. No other group had to" (1988, 340).

But the tone for racial politics was set in the years leading up to the 1962 independence of Trinidad and Tobago, when the volatile ideas concerning decolonization, freedom, black self-rule and race filled the political air and was mixed in with talk of a West Indian federation that would take precedence over a series of independent states.

Under the leadership of Eric Williams, in the 1956 general elections of Trinidad's African-dominated, populist PNM successfully used clear ethno-racial appeals in reaching out to black voters in the more economically depressed areas. By 1958, however, the PNM's rival, the Indian-dominated Democratic Labour Party (DLP), was seen to favour West Indian federation over Trinidad's independence.

The Indians reasoned that, instead of putting themselves at the mercy of the black majority in Trinidad, their fortunes would be more certain in a wider federation with Indians from all over the Caribbean. As Kirk Meighoo would affirm, "In this environment accusations of racism flew all around" (2003, 39), and Eric Williams did little to temper them. He viewed the DLP as a political spoiler, and when the DLP defeated the PNM in those elections Williams felt betrayed and was led to utter that infamous indictment of Indians as "a hostile and recalcitrant minority" (*PNM Weekly*, 21 April 1958) – an indictment that has served to condition the ethnic dimension of Trinidad and Tobago's political evolution ever since. Will Kymlicka captures the mood very well when he says that "People talk about 'troublesome minorities,' but behind every minority that is causing trouble for the state, we are likely to find a state that is putting pressure on minorities" (2001, 2). But the racial insults were not one-sided. DLP leader Rudranath Capildeo, fearing that the Indians would be completely overrun in an independent Trinidad and Tobago, was racist and dismissive when he referred to the PNM as the "People's Nigger Movement" (Oxaal 1968, 179).

Thus, returning to the question of identity and belonging during the period of decolonization and transition from Crown Colony, and to the rise of nationalist politics, it is clear that those not defined as black were seen as not quite belonging and felt out of place. For example, David Trotman writes of the mood during the independence celebrations and the somewhat transparent attempt to create the image of Trinidad and Tobago as a racial paradise. But in that attempt he notes there was emphasis on black cultural contributions (such as steelband, calypso and carnival) to the definition of the national culture, "with no mention of any Indian cultural contribution. In this portrait the Indian is painted out" (1991, 394).[9]

Eric Williams's African-dominated PNM party, which held uninterrupted political power for almost four decades, did a great deal to condition the climate of racial consciousness and belonging in Trinidad and Tobago, where "the political battleground seemed irrevocably drawn along racial lines" (Trotman 1991, 386). This is an argument with which Kelvin Singh would agree, having already written that in the lead up to independence the existence of a "numerically larger" and more united "Negro and Coloured population . . . allowed the PNM to be organised on an essentially Negro basis, and to use race as a basis for winning power by electoral means" (Singh 1974, 64). For their part, the Indians (Hindu, Muslim and Presbyterian), who were no less given to seeing their worlds in racial terms, were far too divided among themselves to enable their Peoples' Democratic Party to mount a credible challenge to the PNM. The politics of race served directly to condition the sense of citizenship and belonging, again trumping the development of class consciousness.

By the close of the twentieth century the major economic gains made by the East Indians (Ryan 1991a and 1991b) contributed to the mood of Afro-Trinibagonian apprehension, and, when the political victory of 1995 registered itself in the African consciousness, the Indians appeared more threatening, and this was definitely reflected in calypsos by singers like Sugar Aloes ("Ah Ready to Go"), Cro Cro ("They Look for Dat") and Mystic Prowler ("A Vision of T&T-2010") (Allahar 1998). These and several other songs sounded a note of alarm as Indians were said to be poised to take over and seek revenge on blacks. In the process the 1995 election victory also served to alter the latter's sense of national belonging. As a consequence, a tone of alarm or angst seemed to have overtaken the Afro-Trinibagonians, which conditioned a climate of personal and economic insecurity among them and provoked a political and cultural defensiveness. On this score Rhoda Reddock tells us that "the Afro-Caribbean majority has constantly *to assert its cultural validity* in a situation of continued economic subordination. It is this economic *insecurity* which provides the major source of *tension* for the Afro-Caribbean population" (1996, 6; my emphasis).

Conclusion

The question of citizenship and belonging in the today's English-speaking Caribbean is multidimensional. The countries of the region are all unique in their ethno-racial compositions, and those compositions can exert a decisive influence on how people feel about their "home" that extends beyond the legal definition of citizenship. Of course they are also dependent capitalist economies that boast capitalist democracies, but what this means above all else is that they are not countries in which social and class equality are known to exist. These countries are multiethnic and increasingly multicultural, and in time multiculturalism will lead to assimilation, but assimilation is not a synonym for equality. Furthermore, as long as the actions of leading entrepreneurs of one ethnicity are permitted to flourish, the distraction of ethnic and racial divisions that have attended cricket disputes and carnival participation rates in the recent past will be likely to persist while the deeply entrenched class divisions will tend to be relegated to the margins of peoples' consciousness. But even if assimilation or creolization is able to mollify the socio-emotional aspects of citizenship and belonging, those class divisions will continue to simmer until the objective conditions of misery come together with the subjective moment of consciousness to provoke a class-based revolutionary upheaval.

In the dependent capitalist formations that comprise the Caribbean, the contentiousness of identity differences and regional or national belonging will depend on the resolve of governments and political, economic, educational, social and cultural leaders.

At the biological level the mixing of population groups has already yielded the dougla category that is common in Trinidad and Tobago and Guyana, among others, while at the sociocultural level mixing and blending is also afoot. To this extent the countries of the Caribbean could take the example of Canada, which is also a class-stratified capitalist society, yet was the first country in the world to have had a multiculturalism act as part of its constitution. This led Will Kymlicka to embrace the promotion of "[p]articipation in a common societal culture" as a means to generating "a sense of common identity and membership" (2001, 26). For him this is "essential to social equality and political cohesion in modern states" (26). The point is, however, that whether in Canada or in the Caribbean "social equality" must not be confused with "class equality", for we could all be citizens of a given country who feel a strong sense of belonging to that country while leading very materially unequal lives, wielding vastly different amounts of power and possessing varying degrees of legitimacy.

Finally, for those who are committed to the idea that there are no alternatives to the capitalist world order and who seek to work within the parameters of the latter, there is one solution that leads beyond the petty politics of national citizenship and identity. I am referring to the phenomenon of globalization and the associated notion of "global citizenship". As a concept, global citizenship defies the equation of citizenship with place of birth, and, because the Caribbean is not a country, one cannot be a Caribbean citizen except in the metaphorical sense. To better comprehend the metaphor here we may consider the concern today with global warming and environmental collapse that threaten the entire planet, out of which the idea of the "global citizen" was born (Lechner 2009, 262). This idea transcends the notion that citizenship should be tied to a discrete country and leads some people to suggest that, rather than waiting for corporate-dominated states and governments to do the right thing, a "bottom up" approach should be taken, in which ordinary citizens could take the initiative to safeguard the environment and act as if "the world is my country" (Lipschutz 2004, 224). In the process a "strong sense of global citizenship" (Bryner 2004, 97) would be secured, which is especially relevant in light of Alex Dupuy's observation that, while "modern capitalism gave rise to an inclusive liberal democracy", the universalization of the concept of citizenship has "disempowered the citizenry" (1996, 567). In the global age there is no doubt that the contemporary Caribbean is part of modern capitalism, albeit dependent, and it is to the citizens of the region and its discrete countries that one must look for the safeguarding of the greater good of all.

Notes

1. *Free Dictionary by Farlex* (online), s.v. "citizen", accessed 5 February 2015, http://legal-dictionary.thefreedictionary.com/citizen.
2. It is worth noting, however, that "it is not 'race' that gives rise to inequality but inequality that gives rise to 'race' " (Malik 1996, 39). Or, in the words of Eric Williams, "[s]lavery was not born of racism", but "rather, racism was the consequence of slavery" (1966, 7).
3. The Euro-Creoles were the local whites and "high browns", who played the role of junior partner of international capital. They were the leading local businessmen for whom colour was currency, and they were accepted by the foreign business classes as long as they knew their place. They also occupied elevated positions in the social hierarchy and belonged to exclusive clubs and associations. It is very well documented in the case of Barbados in the documentary *Fire in Babylon* (see Vallance and Woolridge 1986).
4. This was the refrain in the calypso "Victory Test Match" written and performed by Lord Beginner in 1950, the year of the West Indies cricket victory over England at Lord's Cricket Ground, the world headquarters of cricket at that time. In the chorus Beginner was moved simply to declare that it was a case of "Cricket, lovely cricket!" Also included as collaborators were Lord Kitchener, Roaring Lion, Invader and Terror, all of whom were based in the United Kingdom at the time.
5. The apparent absence of knighthoods for outstanding recent players (for example, Brian Lara) from countries such as Jamaica and Trinidad is due to the fact that, following independence, these former colonies became republics and their citizens are no longer eligible for knighthoods.
6. The term "Indian" here is taken in the context of everyday parlance and refers to those who either self-identify as East Indian or are identified by others as such – I am not using it as a biological concept or to designate geographical origins in India. In these terms, the representation of Indians on the West Indies team was not significant in the decades of the 1950s, 1960s and 1970s. The few Indian regulars on the team included the legendary Sonny Ramadin and Rohan Kanhai and a somewhat less outstanding Joe Solomon. (Although he might have appeared Indian, Deryck Murray's father was a white Englishman and his mother was a dark-skinned Indian; I am not sure how he self-identified ethnically). From the mid-1970s to the mid-1990s, however, when the West Indies were seemingly invincible, Alvin Kallicharran was probably the only regular player to be identified as Indian.
7. Aloes's recent opportunistic turn to sing in praise of Prime Minister Kamla Persaud-Bissessar ("She's Royal") is widely recognized as motivated by money and not his personal politics. He has said as much in his 2013 calypso "My Response" (on the album of the same name).
8. The current prime minister, Kamla Persaud-Bissessar, is also of East Indian descent and is the first woman to hold that post.
9. If the national culture is centred on steelband, calypso and carnival, one implication is those Indians who are devout Muslims or Hindus and who refuse to participate on religious grounds are seen as somehow less Trinibagonian, and their claims to citizenship

and belonging are less strong. At the same time, because Trinidad and Tobago is defined as a Christian nation, those Christians who refuse to participate on religious grounds are not seen in the same way.

References

Allahar, Anton L. 1993. "Unity and Diversity in Caribbean Ethnicity and Culture". *Canadian Ethnic Studies* 25 (1): 70–84.

———. 1994. "More than an Oxymoron: Ethnicity and the Social Construction of Primordial Attachment". *Canadian Ethnic Studies* 26 (3): 18–33.

———. 1996. "Primordialism and Ethnic Political Mobilization in Modern Society". *New Community* 22 (1): 5–21.

———. 1998. "Popular Culture and the Racialisation of Political Consciousness in Trinidad". *Wadabagei: Journal of the Caribbean and Its Diaspora* 1 (2): 1–41.

———. 1999. "Popular Culture and Racialisation of Political Consciousness in Trinidad and Tobago". In *Identity, Ethnicity and Culture in the Caribbean*, edited by Ralph Premdas, 246–81. St Augustine, Trinidad and Tobago: School of Continuing Studies, University of the West Indies.

———, ed. 2001. *Caribbean Charisma: Reflections on Leadership, Legitimacy and Populist Politics*. Boulder: Lynne Rienner.

———. 2004. "Ethnic Entrepreneurship and Nationalism in Trinidad: Afrocentrism and Hindutva". *Social and Economic Studies* 53 (2): 117–54.

Anderson, Benedict. 1983. *Imagined Communities: Reflections on the Origin and Spread of Nationalism*. London: Verso.

Angelou, Maya. 1986. *All God's Children Need Traveling Shoes*. New York: Random House.

Atzmon, Gilad. 2011. *The Wandering Who? A Study of Jewish Identity Politics*. Washington, DC: Zero.

Beckles, Hilary, ed. 1994. *An Area of Conquest: Popular Democracy and West Indies Cricket Supremacy*. Kingston: Ian Randle.

Bergson, Henri. 1959. *Oeuvres*. Paris: Presses Universitaires de France.

Black Stalin. 1979. Vocal performance of "Caribbean Unity". Recorded on *To the Caribbean Man*, Makossa International Records, 33⅓ rpm.

Brereton, Bridget. 1974. "The Experience of Indentureship, 1845–1917". *In Calcutta to Caroni: The East Indians of Trinidad*, edited by John La Guerre, 25–38. London: Longman.

———. 2011. "Ethnic Histories: The Indocentric Narrative of Trinidad's History". *Arts Journal* 7 (1–2): 55–70.

Bryner, Gary C. 2004. "Global Interdependence". In *Environmental Governance Reconsidered: Challenges, Choices and Opportunities*, edited by Robert F. Durant, Daniel J. Fiorino and Rosemary O'Leary, 69–104. Cambridge: Massachusetts Institute of Technology Press.

Burton, Richard D.E. 1985. "Cricket, Carnival and Street Culture in the Caribbean". *British Journal of Sports History* 2 (2): 179–97.

Cummings, Christine. 1990. "The Ideology of West Indian Cricket". *Arena Review* 14 (1): 25–32.

Deosaran, Ramesh. 1987. "The 'Caribbean Man': A Study of the Psychology of Perception and the Media". In *India in the Caribbean*, edited by David Dabydeen and Brinsley Samaroo, 81–118. London: Hansib/University of Warwick.

Dupuy, Alex. 1996. A review of *Democracy against Capitalism: Renewing Historical Materialism* by Ellen Meiksins Wood. *Contemporary Sociology: A Journal of Reviews*. 25 (4): 567–69.

Durkheim, Emile. 1984. *The Division of Labour in Society*. New York: Free Press.

Geertz, Clifford. 1973. *The Interpretation of Cultures*. New York: Basic.

Gergen, Kenneth J. 1968. "The Significance of Skin Color in Human Relations". In *Color and Race*, edited by John Hope Franklin, 112–28. Boston: Houghton Mifflin.

Giddings, Franklin Henry. 1896. *The Principles of Sociology: An Analysis of the Phenomena of Association and of Social Organization*. New York: Macmillan.

Gramsci, Antonio. 1971. *Selections from the Prison Notebooks*. New York: International.

Hector, Tim. 1994. "West Indian Nationhood, Integration, and Cricket Politics". In *An Area of Conquest: Popular Democracy and West Indies Cricket Supremacy*, edited by Hilary Beckles, 113–26. Kingston: Ian Randle.

Isaacs, Harold R. 1975. *Idols of the Tribe: Group Identity and Political Change*. New York: Harper Colophon.

James, C.L.R. 1963. *Beyond a Boundary*. London: Hutchinson.

Kymlicka, Will. 2001. *Politics in the Vernacular: Nationalism, Multiculturalism and Citizenship*. Oxford: Oxford University Press.

Lechner, Frank J. 2009. *Globalization: The Making of World Society*. Malden: Wiley-Blackwell.

Lee, Ann. 1997. "The Steelband Movement and Community Politics in Laventille". In *Behind the Bridge: Poverty, Politics and Patronage in Laventille, Trinidad*, edited by Selwyn Ryan, Roy McCree and Godfrey St Bernard, 69–90. St Augustine, Trinidad and Tobago: Institute of Social and Economic Research, University of the West Indies.

Lipschutz, Ronnie D. 2004. *Global Environmental Politics: Power, Perspectives and Practice*. Washington, DC: CQ Press.

Lovelace, Earl. 1988. "The On-going Value of Our Indigenous Traditions". In *The Independence Tradition* edited by Selwyn Ryan. St Augustine, Trinidad and Tobago: Institute of Social and Economic Research, University of the West Indies.

Malik, Kenan. 1996. *The Meaning of Race*. New York: New York University Press.

Meighoo, Kirk. 2003. *Politics in a Half-Made Society: Trinidad and Tobago 1925–2001*. Kingston: Ian Randle.

Mighty Dougla. 1961. Vocal performance of "Split Me in Two". Recorded on *Jump Up*, Island Records Limited, 45 rpm.

Mighty Sparrow. 1963. Vocal performance of "The Outcast". Recorded on *The Outcast*, National Recording Company NLP 4199, 33⅓ rpm.

Miles, Robert. 1989. *Racism*. London: Routledge and Kegan Paul.

O'Brien Thompson, L. 1983. "How Cricket Is West Indian Cricket? Class, Racial, and Color Conflict". *Caribbean Review* 12 (2): 23–25 and 50–53.

Oxaal, Ivor. 1968. *Black Intellectuals Come to Power: The Rise of Creole Nationalism in Trinidad and Tobago*. Cambridge, MA: Schenkman.

Purcell, Mark. 2003. "Citizenship and the Right to the Global City: Reimagining the Capitalist World Order". *International Journal of Urban and Regional Research* 27 (3): 564–90.

Reddock, Rhoda, ed. 1996. *Ethnic Minorities in Caribbean Society*. St Augustine, Trinidad and Tobago: Institute of Social and Economic Research, University of the West Indies.

———. 1999. "Jahaji Bhai: The Emergence of a Dougla Poetics in Contemporary Trinidad and Tobago". In *Identity, Ethnicity and Culture in the Caribbean*, edited by Ralph Premdas, 185–210. St Augustine, Trinidad and Tobago: School of Continuing Studies, University of the West Indies.

Richards, Vivian. 1992. *Hitting across the Line: An Autobiography*. Sydney: Pan Macmillan.

Riley, Stevan. 2011. *Fire in Babylon*. DVD documentary. London: Revolver Entertainment.

Rohlehr, Gordon. 1994. "Music, Literature and West Indian Cricket Values". In *An Area of Conquest: Popular Democracy and West Indies Cricket Supremacy*, edited by Hilary Beckles, 55–102. Kingston: Ian Randle.

Ryan, Selwyn. 1979. "Trinidad and Tobago: The General Elections of 1976". *Caribbean Studies* 19 (1–2): 5–32.

———. 1991a. "Social Stratification in Trinidad and Tobago: Lloyd Brathwaite Revisited". In *Social and Occupational Stratification in Contemporary Trinidad and Tobago*, edited by Selwyn Ryan, 58–79. St Augustine, Trinidad and Tobago: Institute of Social and Economic Research, University of the West Indies.

———. 1991b. "Race and Occupational Stratification in Trinidad and Tobago". In *Social and Occupational Stratification in Contemporary Trinidad and Tobago*, edited by Selwyn Ryan, 166–90. St Augustine, Trinidad and Tobago: Institute of Social and Economic Research, University of the West Indies.

Searle, Chris. 1990. "Race before Wicket: Cricket, Empire and the White Rose". *Race and Class* 31 (3): 5–32.

Shils, Edward. 1957. "Primordial, Personal, Sacred and Civil Ties." *British Journal of Sociology* 8 (2): 130–45.

———. 1968. "Color, the Universal Intellectual Community, and the Afro-Asian Intellectual". In *Color and Race*, edited by John Hope Franklin, 1–17. Boston: Houghton Mifflin.

Singh, Kelvin. 1974. "East Indians and the Larger Society". In *Calcutta to Caroni: The East Indians of Trinidad*, edited by John La Guerre, 39–58. London: Longman.

Snow, Nancy. 2003. *Information War: American Propaganda, Free Speech and Opinion Control since 9/11*. New York: Seven Stories.

Steckles, Garry. 2009. "The Triumph of Calypso Cricket". *Caribbean Beat*, no. 100. http://caribbean-beat.com/issue-100/triumph-calypso-cricket#axzz3YY6R3WBy.

St Pierre, Maurice. 1990. "West Indian Cricket: A Cultural Contradiction?" *Arena Review* 14 (1): 13–24.

Sugar Aloes. 2013a. Vocal performance of "My Response". Recorded on *My Response*. Philgaton Recording Studios, compact disc.

———. 2013b. Vocal performance of "She's Royal" recorded on *My Response*. Philgaton Recording Studios, compact disc.

Tarradath, Selwyn. 1991. "Race, Class, Politics and Gender in the Steelband Movement". In *Social and Occupational Stratification in Contemporary Trinidad and Tobago*, edited by Selwyn Ryan, 377–84. St Augustine, Trinidad and Tobago: Institute of Social and Economic Research, University of the West Indies.

Thomas, W.I., and Dorothy S. Thomas. 1928. *The Child in America*. New York: Alfred Knopf.

Trotman, David V. 1991. "The Image of Indians in Calypso: Trinidad 1946–1986". In *Social and Occupational Stratification in Contemporary Trinidad and Tobago*, edited by Selwyn Ryan, 385–98. St Augustine, Trinidad and Tobago: Institute of Social and Economic Research, University of the West Indies.

Vallance, Clem, and Ian Woolridge. 1986. *Calypso Cricket*. BBC Worldwide Television.

Warner, Keith Q. 1993. "Ethnicity and the Contemporary Calypso". In *Trinidad Ethnicity*, edited by Kevin Yelvington, 275–91. London: Macmillan.

Willey, Nancy Boyd, and Malcolm Willey. 1924. "The Conditioned Response and the Consciousness of Kind". *American Journal of Sociology* 30: 22–28.

Williams, Eric. 1966. *Capitalism and Slavery*. New York: G.P. Putnam's Sons.

Yelvington, Kevin A. 1990. "Ethnicity 'Not Out': The Indian Cricket Tour of the West Indies and the 1976 Elections in Trinidad and Tobago". *Arena Review* 14 (1): 1–12.

6 Identity Politics in the Territorial Fringe

Citizenship and Belonging in Puerto Rico and the Netherlands Antilles

Aarón Gamaliel Ramos

My aim in this chapter is to explore the contemporary conflict over citizenship and belonging in Puerto Rico and the Dutch Antilles, with special reference to Aruba, Curaçao and Sint Maarten. After World War II the United States and the Netherlands restructured the governmental system in their territorial possessions in the Caribbean. In contrast with the French policy of incorporating their colonial possessions into their political system and the British plan for self-government and decolonization, the United States and the Netherlands opted to create what I have chosen to call here a "territorial fringe", inhabited by people with the citizenship of their metropolis, but separated from their political system through special political arrangements. The United States and the Netherlands exploited Cold War tensions and redoubled their efforts to control Caribbean territories, effectively limiting the scope of the decolonization process and the formation of new sovereign states in the region. The United States maintained the traditional colonial structure in the Virgin Islands; however, it ended the practice of direct colonial rule over Puerto Rico by expanding the authority of local ruling groups over the government of the territory through the creation of an autonomous political arrangement in 1952 that was named, in English, the Commonwealth of Puerto Rico and, in Spanish, Estado Libre Asociado (Free Associated State).[1] In 1954 the Netherlands approved the Charter for the Kingdom of the Netherlands (in Dutch, Statuut voor het Koninkrijk; see Ministry of Foreign Affairs 2002), based on a new constitutional order, which created a federation of its Caribbean territories with internal self-government and political power exercised by ruling indigenous elites.[2]

Both the United States and the Netherlands adopted a restricted form of autonomy for their territories that permitted them to overcome the dilemmas they faced in that historical setting: on the one hand, the impetus towards decolonization and, on the other, their fears that creating independent states under nationalist leadership would upset the geopolitical hegemony of the United States and its allies in the Caribbean during the Cold War. In contrast with the United States, which strengthened its hegemony in the region in the aftermath of World War II, a decisive factor in the establishment of autonomous political structures in the Dutch Caribbean possessions was the weak condition of the Netherlands in the world during and after the war. Moreover, a limited form of internal self-government helped to defuse some of the tensions that were typical of traditional colonial rule, notably those that resulted from the presence of metropolitan agents in the highest echelons of the territorial governments.

The post-war policies of the United States and the Netherlands favoured and cultivated the emergence of indigenous business and political elites that mediated relations between the local society, the metropolitan state and foreign capital. These elites derived their legitimacy from their ability to mobilize internal political support through the celebration of the elements associated with belonging to a local society and cultural community and the promotion of allegiance to the metropolitan state through the bonds of citizenship.

However, since the inauguration of the two different political arrangements, the operation of local autonomy and common citizenship became a major source of debate and tension. There are two facets of the contemporary functioning of territorial autonomy that I discuss in this chapter. One is the waning role of the territorial state in the Caribbean, through the centralization of economic policymaking in the metropolitan states, the expansion of corporate control of economic processes worldwide and global regulation and integration via the multilateral institutions. I will argue that these political and economic developments diminished the roles of local elites and weakened the cultural appeals that marked the beginning years of the Commonwealth of Puerto Rico and the Charter for the Kingdom of the Netherlands. As a result there is a current trend towards an enlarged intervention from metropolitan governments in what are officially conceived as their "internal affairs". The other facet I am concerned with is the particular way in which right-wing movements in the United States and the Netherlands have gained visibility and notoriety by championing exclusionary nationalism in ways that emphasize and exploit race and language as well as fear and loathing towards immigrants. In this chapter I will explore current qualms in the United States over the issue of the full-fledged annexation of Puerto Rico and the ways in which racialized conceptions of homeland are reshaping the debate about common citizenship and local belonging in the Caribbean possessions of the United States and the Netherlands.

Puerto Rico and the Dutch Territories

The establishment of the Commonwealth of Puerto Rico and the Charter for the Kingdom of the Netherlands was the result of the way the two metropolises confronted the crisis of colonial rule during the 1930s and the challenges of capitalist expansionism after World War II. The war was a turning point for Caribbean territories. The economic crisis of the 1930s had devastating effects on European metropolises and their overseas possessions, uncovering the inability of the colonial powers to maintain a firm grip on the lands and peoples under their dominion. Beyond the more visible political crisis in the colonial systems there also existed a major strain in the capitalist world economy marked by the tension between the preservation of the historical barriers erected by old imperialist powers to the free movement of capital and the uncontainable movement towards US hegemony in the Caribbean. The post-war "decolonization era" was, from this perspective, a major shift in the international political economy as well as an end to traditional patterns in the international division of labour that imperialism had produced.

Global economic restructuring during the middle of the twentieth century led to the repositioning of Caribbean territories in the international economy. Taking advantage of the capitalist expansion during the beginning of that century, the colonial government of Puerto Rico encouraged corporate investment by agrarian interests to facilitate the production and export of raw sugar and tobacco to the US market. However, as a consequence of the widespread poverty and the economic depression of the 1930s, the US government drew on the New Deal to rethink its economic policy towards its territory. Following the end of the war, the US colonial administration in Puerto Rico supported the creation of an urban economy with an industrial manufacturing base out of the ruins of the sugar-dominated economy that prevailed during the first half of the century. While connected to the old landed and commercial classes that served a subordinate role during historical colonialism, the new ruling elites – grouped in the Popular Democratic Party (Partido Popular Democrático) of Puerto Rico – shifted their pro-independence posture towards an autonomous status with reformed capitalism.

Similarly, the Dutch territories became increasingly connected to ventures that were undertaken by US capitalist interests during the first half of the twentieth century, even when they retained their political link to the Netherlands. Just as had occurred in the British Caribbean colonies in the context of both world wars, American capitalist enterprises expanded their presence in the Dutch territories through the introduction of oil-refining activities and activated new linkages between local political and entrepreneurial sectors and foreign capital. The Dutch territories located in the southern Caribbean near South America, with a maritime frontier with Venezuela, became important refiners of crude oil. During the war, those territories supplied the allied European nations that were caught in the conflict with exports of goods and other resources, in addition to shoring up the Dutch treasury during the war. The importance of oil increased when the ties between the Netherlands and its colonies weakened, with the geopolitical significance of the territories increasing out of proportion to their size. This cleared the way for the entry of capital from various areas within the American economy, among them the Standard Oil Company in 1932.[3] This was also the moment when the first political parties were formed, such as the Democratic Party of Curaçao that became the main political organization to emerge during the process of capitalist expansion after World War II.

Territorial Fringes

For the United States, the establishment of the commonwealth was based on the doctrine of the non-incorporation of the former Spanish territories (Puerto Rico, the Philippines and Guam) in the federal system of states during the early part of the twentieth century. The idea of possessing overseas lands, inhabited by citizens of the metropolis with limited rights, began early in the twentieth century, when the US Supreme Court declared Puerto Rico to be a "non-incorporated territory", belonging to, but not being part of, the United States.[4] Thus, the various decisions taken by the US Supreme Court during the discussion of "the Indian question" in the nineteenth century allowed the metropolis to institute and sustain a differential treatment of Puerto Rico.[5] However, the non-incorporated status of Puerto Rico notwithstanding, the United States extended a statutory form of citizenship to the inhabitants of the territory under the provisions of the Jones Act in 1917.[6] Although the United States had flirted with the possibility of independence for Puerto Rico in the early 1940s, during the Cold War it adopted a stance against Caribbean nationalism. It feared the leaders of the new nations that were set to embark on decolonization would open the door to Soviet interference in the region and implied thereby that the inhabitants lacked agency to determine the appropriate course to self-government and sovereign autonomy.[7] After World War II the US Congress initiated the deconstruction of the traditional colonial structure by passing a law, in 1947, to allow Puerto Ricans, starting in 1948, to elect the governor of the territory and authorizing Puerto Rico, in 1950, to form a constitutional convention in order to draft a constitution for the territory. When the US Congress approved the constitution of the Commonwealth of Puerto Rico in 1952, the new territorial arrangement was inaugurated.

Although the establishment of the commonwealth expanded the authority of persons from internal political classes to exercise state power, it did not fundamentally change the status of the island as a US possession that operates under the plenary powers of the US Congress. The Commonwealth Constitution invested Puerto

Rico with the powers over certain internal administrative matters – for example, the island was given control over a broad spectrum of internal affairs such as taxation and culture, including the right to use Spanish as the language of government and public education. Other major areas such as the citizenship and naturalization, customs, defence and external affairs were reserved for the jurisdiction of the United States and administered by federal courts. The commonwealth maintained the post of a non-voting resident commissioner in the US House of Representatives. The structure of the commonwealth also included provisions that separated it from US states; however, the territory exercised fiscal autonomy with the US dollar as legal tender. Moreover, the industrialization process under Operation Bootstrap, which was the economic platform of the new political arrangement, operated with a governmental Minimum Wage Board, which guaranteed that salaries of island workers would remain below US standards, as a means of attracting labour-intensive corporate investment to the island.

The enactment in 1954 of the Charter for the Kingdom of the Netherlands set in motion a process for synthesizing a series of changes that the Dutch had introduced during the early decades of the twentieth century. The revisions to the Constitution of the Netherlands in 1922 reflected two important alterations. One significant modification was of a semantic nature, as the Netherlands replaced the phrase "colonies and possessions in other parts of the world" with "overseas territories of the Kingdom" (Wilhelmina, ca. 1943, 26–27; Oostindie and Klinkers 2003, 61). The second one was political: although maintaining their traditional colonial institutions, Dutch Guiana (Suriname) and Curaçao (which at the time also administered Aruba, Bonaire, Sint Maarten, Sint Eustatius and Saba) would henceforth be formally considered integral parts of the Kingdom of the Netherlands. The constitutional modifications in the charter of 1954 regarding overseas possessions introduced internal self-government in the territories.

The proposal for the creation of an autonomous structure for the Dutch territories was laid out by the besieged Dutch queen, in a speech she delivered from London on 6 December 1941, in which she outlined the principles that would guide the post-war relationship between the Netherlands and its Caribbean territories. The queen's speech emphasized political autonomy, an egalitarian relationship between the Netherlands and the Antilles and the principle of solidarity, based on "the voluntarily accepted aegis of the Netherlands Kingdom, of which the Indies are not colonies but a component part, just as the Netherlands in Europe" (Wilhelmina circa 1943, 9).

Beginning in 1954, the Kingdom of the Netherlands consisted of formally autonomous countries that included the Netherlands, Suriname and the Netherlands Antilles, each with autonomy over its internal affairs. However, this entity underwent various changes. After Suriname became an independent country in 1975, the Dutch Caribbean was reduced to "the Netherlands Antilles", a grouping of the six Dutch islands with the administrative seat in Curaçao. Moreover, in 1986, Aruba became a separate country within the kingdom, which was henceforth called "the Netherlands Antilles and Aruba". In 2010, when the federation was dissolved, Aruba, Curaçao, and Sint Maarten became separate *countries* within the kingdom, while Bonaire, Saba and Sint Eustatius were converted into *municipalities* of the Netherlands in the Caribbean. Under the current charter, each country has the power to manage their financial affairs and organize local life with minimal formal intervention from The Hague. They have their own legislative bodies, ministers plenipotentiary representing the interests of the territories in the Netherlands and a prime minister in charge of the local government. Over and above these countries is the kingdom, currently represented by the queen, who acts as a unifying agent with binding legal powers over the constituent units. The kingdom enjoys authority over matters such as nationality, external relations, good government and human rights.[8] However, as Steven Hillebrink has observed, the idea that the Dutch kingdom is a federation of autonomous countries is largely rhetorical, since there is no real distinction made between "the Kingdom of the Netherlands" and "the country of the Netherlands". Therefore, Aruba, Curaçao and Sint Maarten must abide by Dutch law enacted in The Hague and verified by its Supreme Court, which takes precedence over local consensus and legislation. Moreover, the kingdom cannot appropriately be considered as a federation, since there is no division of power between the kingdom organs and the organs of the country of the Netherlands (Hillebrink 2007, 169; see also Van Aller 1994, 8).

Both the US and the Netherlands conceived of a territorial periphery, run by local governments in the name of local communities, subject to the laws enacted in these two metropolises and inhabited by American and Dutch citizens, who were not eligible for certain services that were available to citizens residing in their respective metropolises (Hillebrink 2007, 194). In fact, the United States and the Netherlands each instituted a dual system of citizenship, which created a disjuncture between civil and political rights, especially for citizens inhabiting the overseas territories. American and Dutch citizens could exercise their full rights in the metropolis; however, they were denied certain rights when residing in the overseas territories, which were not, strictly speaking, an integral part of the metropolitan political systems.

The categories of citizenship that were created for the peoples of the territories reflected circumscriptions regarding membership in metropolitan societies. Since becoming a colonial power during the early twentieth century, the United States privileged the requisite of proximity to Anglo-Saxon culture in its treatment of the inhabitants of the newly acquired territories, creating a subordinate status that was inferior to US citizenship. As Rogers M. Smith has argued, "Puerto Rican citizenship was a category Congress created for a certain subset of its nationals. And Congress created that category expressly as another subordinate status, inferior to

US citizenship, and inferior explicitly because America's political and intellectual leaders regarded Puerto Ricans as not just separate but as yet another unequal race, incapable of self-governance" (2001, 380).

The debates that preceded the approval of the legislation that granted citizenship to the inhabitants of Puerto Rico in 1917 highlighted the belief that the territory was "whiter" and more European than the Philippines – and hence better positioned for assimilation. However, the endorsement of the Taft administration of the Jones bill cautioned that it would be "entirely disassociated from any thought of statehood" (Torruella 1988, 89).

The Netherlands conceived citizenship in analogous terms, favouring proximity to Dutch culture as a requisite of citizenship. Historically, the Netherlands operated under the principle of jus sanguinis whereby Dutch citizenship was inherited through kinship – for example, the sons and daughters of Dutch citizens automatically acquired the citizenship of their parents regardless of where they were born, and Dutch descendants born in the colonies also acquired Dutch citizenship and the rights that pertained thereto. In contrast, however, the natives of the overseas territories were categorized and classified as belonging to an inferior community that was considered separate and distinct from the Dutch people (Anderson 2006, 122).

However, while under this scheme Dutch citizenship was intimately and substantively connected to membership in the Dutch nation and culture, it was possible for some of the native inhabitants of the territories to become citizens of the Netherlands. Thus, when the Charter for the Kingdom was approved, a sizeable number of the natives of the Netherlands Antilles had already acquired Dutch citizenship. Still, the new system preserved the ambiguities and uncertainties that surrounded citizenship by making it a common and defining characteristic of membership in the Kingdom of the Netherlands, while locating the Antillean islands on the borders of its political system.

The idea that Dutch territories are autonomous "countries" of the Kingdom of the Netherlands contrasts sharply with the limitations that are imposed by The Hague on the ability of the Caribbean units to exercise authority at the local territorial level. This inequity remains a source of disagreement dating back to the creation and implementation of this structure. The Netherlands declared that it reserved the right to exercise authority over the internal affairs of Suriname and the Dutch Antilles, including the right to overturn legislation enacted by local governments that the metropolis considered to be in contradiction with international law or with the general interest of the Netherlands (Oostindie and Klinkers 2003, 77). In addition, it was not prepared to tolerate or accept the intervention by these territories in certain areas of their own internal affairs. Arguing from the Dutch perspective, Gert Oostindie and Inge Klinkers reasoned that it was inconceivable that the former colonies would interfere in matters considered exclusively Dutch. Furthermore, in creating a common frontier, the Maastricht Treaty of 1992 established voting rights for European citizens, irrespective of their place of residence in what became the European Union (CEC 1992). However, since the autonomous Dutch Caribbean territories are not an integral component of the Netherlands, as the French overseas departments and collectivities are of France, they do not participate in European Union elections, as the French citizens of the departments of Guadeloupe, Martinique and French Guiana and of the collectivities of Saint-Martin and Saint-Barthélemy do.

The tension over the unequal distribution of authority between the metropolitan and Antillean governments was at the centre of the debate during the initial years of the creation of this new constitutional arrangement. Such inequality in the distribution of political power between The Hague and the other constituent units of the kingdom was one of the reasons for the departure of Suriname in 1975 to become a sovereign state. The Charter for the Kingdom underwent various revisions as a result of the withdrawal of Aruba from the Federation of the Netherlands Antilles in 1986 to become a separate country within the kingdom and the dissolution of the federation in 2010. After the termination of the Federation of the Netherlands Antilles, Curaçao and Sint Maarten were created as two new unit members of the kingdom, and they acquired a status similar to that of Aruba. Furthermore, The Hague altered their historical policy towards its Caribbean territories by integrating Bonaire, Sint Eustatius and Saba – known as the BES Islands – into its political system as public entities (*openbare lichamen*) of the Netherlands, which are local government structures that are similar to a Dutch municipality.[9]

This new political status is seemingly a departure from earlier Dutch aversion to the incorporation of its overseas territories and peoples; however, it is clear that this arrangement fails to meet the requirements of full-fledged integration.[10] In establishing these public entities The Hague crafted a special arrangement that is in many ways a return to a form of direct metropolitan control. The Dutch did not create a new overseas province formed by the three islands, nor were they integrated as part of a Dutch province, such as Drenthe or Utrecht. Therefore, citizens of Bonaire, Sint Eustatius and Saba do not participate in provincial elections in the Netherlands. However, the Dutch citizens of these islands are entitled to vote to elect members to the House of Representatives of the Netherlands and to the European Parliament. At the same time, they lack adequate representation mechanisms in the Dutch political system to accommodate their needs. More specifically, while the autonomous islands of Aruba, Curaçao and Sint Maarten have a minister plenipotentiary representing their interests in the The Hague, Bonaire, Sint Eustatius and Saba do not have equivalent representation through an equivalent delegate. The absence of a representative of those islands in the Kingdom of the Netherlands is a matter of concern, considering that the Dutch electoral system is not organized on the basis of electoral districts or constituencies.

Individual members of the national legislature are selected from a list of political parties with national representation that are presented to electors during a general election. On this basis, Bonaire, Sint Eustatius and Saba end up without direct representation in the legislature of the Netherlands, as the political parties in the overseas municipalities face difficulties in contributing candidates to the political parties and the electoral lists.

Belonging and Citizenship

In establishing formally autonomous territorial states, the United States and the Netherlands also created political structures that served to redefine collective identities. Thus, beyond their role as managers of the colonial state apparatuses, those who assumed control of the Commonwealth of Puerto Rico and the Federation of the Netherlands Antilles became powerful agents for consolidating an imaginary of the homeland. However, beyond the formal act by each metropolitan power of converting their colonies into autonomous territories under their sovereignty, the visions about belonging and citizenship in Puerto Rico and in the Dutch Caribbean are very dissimilar. Autonomy under the Commonwealth of Puerto Rico was conceived as a way to reconcile the two positions that had dominated the political arena during the crisis of colonialism in the interwar period – the call for independence on the one hand and the request for full-fledged integration into the United States on the other. In keeping with what tends to be normative in the rest of the Hispanic Caribbean, nationalists in Puerto Rico privileged the vision of a European-derived white community, largely oblivious of slavery and the post-emancipation black experience and with language and customs as the central ingredients that comprise the relational connectedness of a national community. Annexationists introduced citizenship, as a symbol of a proposal for the construction of a civilized and democratic community arising out of the ruins of Spanish absolutism.

Within the first decade of its inauguration, the supporters of the commonwealth project began to draw attention to the distinction between homeland and citizenship. In the search for legitimation, the governing Popular Democratic Party intensely worked in the sphere of cultural interpretation to portray the commonwealth as constructing a Puerto Rican homeland (*patria*), as a distinct nation within the US political system. The main political actors during the early 1950s, when this political arrangement was launched, represented the island as a Latin American nation associated with the United States. The cultural ideals underlying the commonwealth political vision privileged the historical visions of the old landed classes and marginalized the cultural identities of many citizens, notably blacks and the urban poor. A distinction was made between the Puerto Rican cultural community and US citizenship shorn of its cultural and patriotic referents (Ramos 2003–4,

66–70). Indeed, in the opening speech Luis Muñoz Marín, the territorial governor, delivered in January 1953, he summed up the core of the identity aspect of the new arrangement as follows: "Puerto Ricans are now a Spanish-American country composed of good citizens of the United States" (Wells 1969, 240).

The Netherlands Antilles followed a different historical path. In contrast with Puerto Rico, where the population shared common cultural attributes, the Dutch Antilles was a kaleidoscope of cultural ingredients, fostered by waves of immigrants from different geographical locations. In addition, Dutch colonial policies did not emphasize the cultural assimilation of the inhabitants residing in their colonies; it was only in 1936 that Dutch became the official language of formal education in the colonies.

Historically, English became the language of economic and social intercourse in the Leeward Islands of Sint Maarten, Sint Eustatius and Saba that formed part of a trade belt that was dominated by British commercial interests. Papiamento – a creole language spoken in Aruba, Bonaire and Curaçao – became a shared language of both the dominant elites and the broad mass of the people of the colonies. The situation was also complicated by intricate internal inequalities in each territory that reflected social class and race differences, which were manifested during the May 1969 labour uprising in Curaçao.

The Dutch intention to construct a confederal operational entity was not successful. After the creation of the charter, the Dutch failed in their attempt to construct a "country" composed of their six territories. The relational ties between the territories were not sufficiently strong to secure and solidify the arrangement in the face of their differences in size and population, disparities in political representation and distribution and allocation of resources. Sint Eustatius and Saba, located in the northern section of the eastern Caribbean, objected to the limitations of political representation for the smaller islands, voicing their aspiration for direct relations with the metropolis. In addition, Aruba and Curaçao competed in the same economic arena (their economies having been jointly integrated into the oil industry of Venezuela and the United States throughout the twentieth century) and they pursued similar strategies for participating in the tourism and financial sectors of the international economy. The economic crisis that occurred during the 1970s exacerbated the tensions between the two islands, and, during the first part of the 1980s, Aruba made a final push towards becoming a separate country within the kingdom.

After Aruba became a country within the kingdom, its government redoubled its efforts to foster discursive frameworks, with narratives of identity and belonging through which the distinctive traits of the islands were officially recognized as basic ingredients for building each territorial unit into a separate cultural community. Flags were designed, hymns were written and a new era of governmental sponsorship of culture emerged. Significantly, the pro-independence political parties that had fought for full-fledged sovereignty during the early post-war period, replaced their goal with the proposal for a limited form of autonomy within the framework of direct relations with the metropolis. The Netherlands considered the separate-country status – or *status aparte* – in 1986 as a first step in a ten-year programme designed to lead to independence. However, the proposal was put on the back-burner of the two main political organizations, the Movimentu Electoral di Pueblo (the Electoral Movement of the People, in Curaçao) and the Arubaanse Volkspartij (Aruban People's Party, in Aruba), which from this time opted to work within the limitations established in the charter.

The Waning of Autonomy

Globalization and economic crisis enervated the territorial states, reducing their ability to impose a homogeneous vision of a people on their societies. The increase in the flow of capital, technology, people and ideas unsettled many of the cultural assumptions that had guided political life in Puerto Rico and the Dutch territories since the middle of the twentieth century. The territorial state in Puerto Rico managed to achieve a certain degree of legitimacy during the first years of the commonwealth. For all the ambiguity surrounding the autonomy project, Puerto Rico benefited from post-war economic growth and the social and welfare policies of the United States during the early 1950s. The post-war economic strategy of attracting light-manufacturing industry under Operation Bootstrap intensified the integration of the rural and urban population into an increasingly urbanized industrial economy. Economic growth during the first years of the commonwealth favoured the government's attempt to portray Puerto Rico as an autonomous entity in association with the United States and created institutes and fostered cultural programmes to promote the nation as a cultural community within the limitations imposed by the island's colonial status (Dávila 1997, 14).

Various factors contributed to the demise of the commonwealth project in Puerto Rico. The collapse of the industrial project during the early period of the commonwealth weakened the autonomist ideal advanced by the Popular Democratic Party. If the quest for autonomy during the 1950s was associated with the inflow of US capital, the economic crisis during two subsequent decades shook its bases. In addition, the capital-intensive investment in the electronics-assembly and pharmaceutical sectors further diminished labour participation and drastically increased unemployment and poverty on the island. The collapse of the industrial project during the recession of 1973–75 contributed to the transformation of the island's political arena. Paradoxically, the autonomist political elite attempted to sustain the commonwealth by forging an alliance between the territorial government and US corporate interests to convince the US Congress to include Puerto

Rico under section 936 provisions of the US Internal Revenue Code, which exempts American corporations doing business in territories from having to pay federal income tax on profits earned from their foreign operations.

To a large extent, the dramatic increase in support for the pro-annexationist New Progressive Party (NPP/Partido Nuevo Progresista) during the 1970s is related to its mobilization of the urban poor and its portrayal of statehood as a status with the potential to benefit the so-called underclass. In their quest for equal treatment, NPP administrations petitioned and obtained from the US Congress equal treatment with US states in the allocation of federal funding for social programmes. Federal funds to the island soared, increasing from $1,550 million in 1975 to $4,300 million in 1990, which represented almost half of the commonwealth's annual budget. This was the beginning of a period of massive industrial and social dependence on US federal funding that eventually transformed the NPP into the largest political party in Puerto Rico.

During the mid-1970s, the NPP parted ways with the traditional idea of statehood understood as integration into the United States through assimilation. Earlier annexationist ideas on this subject emphasized universal cultural values that equated ethnicity to a lingering primordial or at best primitive sentiment that would in time be absorbed within world-scale pluralism. In contrast with the commonwealth conception of belonging, which conceived of Puerto Rico as an autonomous country in association with the United States, the NPP embraced the idea of Puerto Ricans as an ethnic group within the United States. This NPP perspective not only addressed the prevailing cultural-nationalist mood on the island, it was also attentive to the public debate in the United States on civil rights and to the receptiveness of the Carter administration to issues of race and ethnicity in the United States and in American foreign policy. Nonetheless, despite the overtures from the annexationist white elite to the Black Caucus in the US Congress, the African component in Puerto Rican society remained largely hidden in the rhetoric for the incorporation of Puerto Rico into the United States.

Isar Godreau suggests that there is conflation of blackness with poverty that limits the politicization of a black identity in Puerto Rico, arguing that the rejection of the emphasis on racialized black cultural expressions in pro-statehood politics "could be understood as a promotion of whitening that is achieved by moving up the social-class ladder laid by US capitalism" (Godreau 2015, 153).

Even when advocacy for Puerto Rican statehood with the United States stressed citizenship affinity with the metropolis, the NPP did not fully abandon the cultural ideology of the commonwealth. Significantly, the modern annexationist notion of a creole form of statehood manifested its intellectual ties with commonwealth beliefs on the nature of belonging in the US political system, as it laid out its double claim to an allegiance to a local community, through its commitment to "the preservation of our identity as a people" and the economic value of US citizenship (Ramos 2003–4,

72). Both ideological camps held to the idea of preserving a local community, distinguishable from the metropolis through language and customs. While the dominant elites of the island share views with respect to culture, there are differences when it comes to their idea of the location of the island in the US political system. By representing Puerto Ricans as an ethnic group within the population of the United States, the NPP managed to align itself with the discourse on cultural nationalism, while maintaining its commitment to the ideal of equality within the US political system. The influence of commonwealth ideology on the pro-annexationist programme is most pronounced in the arguments in favour of full-fledged incorporation that were laid out under the thesis of a creole state. Carlos Romero Barceló, a former governor and one of the main leaders of this movement, persistently argued that the United States is a "nation of nations", that Puerto Ricans cannot be easily assimilated and that Puerto Rico would eventually become the first Spanish-speaking state in the US federal system (Alegría-Ortega 2001, 35).

A cultural offensive on autonomy coupled with a new discourse on identity was initiated when the Popular Democratic Party regained control of the government in 1984. The push towards autonomy began during the 1990s, when Spanish investment capital expanded throughout Latin America, coincidental with the celebration of five hundred years since the arrival of the Spanish in the Americas. These two factors provided the ideological and cultural stimulus for a revival of identity politics in Puerto Rico. The pro-autonomist government of Rafael Hernández Colón inserted Puerto Rico in the festivities, in which the emphasis on Puerto Rico's historical and sociological connection to Spain was intended as a background for expanding the autonomous powers of the territory. The identification with Spain also alerted the policymaking circles of Washington about the cultural identity of Puerto Rico, as the economic failures of the island and the increasing dependency on federal funding promoted the expansion of the movement for the incorporation of Puerto Rico as a state within the United States. A major step in that process was the approval of a law that made Spanish the sole official language of Puerto Rico. As a consequence, in 1991 Puerto Rico was awarded the prestigious Principe de Asturias (Prince of Asturias) Award for Letters to the People of Puerto Rico, "whose representative authorities, with exemplary decisiveness, have declared Spanish to be the only official language of their country". In his acceptance speech, Governor Hernández Colón explained his decision to convert to Spanish as the only language of the Commonwealth of Puerto Rico: "English is a very efficient tool for us, that we appreciate. But our mother tongue is what represents us as a people, with which we express our most intimate feelings and beliefs, our thoughts and deepest values" (my translation).

Even as language was presented as a common element of Puerto Rican identity, the political debate over the question of belonging did not address the issue of the diversity of the language experience in contemporary Puerto Rico, considering that a significant portion of Puerto Ricans living in the United States use English as their main means of communication. Despite the warm reception in Spain of Puerto Rico's embrace of Spanish as its only official language, the debate on language this time around took place in a society in which English, while not spoken by a majority of the population, was recognized by the population as an important secondary language.

In contrast with Puerto Rico, where the rhetoric of culture in autonomist politics seeks a special type of accommodation in the metropolitan state, in the Netherlands Antilles the promotion of autonomist and pro-independence ideals in the three remaining Dutch Caribbean countries of Aruba, Curaçao and Sint Maarten is associated with problems that are related to the exercise of authority by the metropolitan power over territories in which it has very little economic presence or social influence. While the authority granted to these Dutch territories in the international sphere is larger than what Puerto Rico is permitted to exercise,[11] they lack sufficient autonomy to manage economic affairs.

There is an increasing economic and social connection between these islands and North and South America. The main trading partners of Aruba and Curaçao are the United States, Venezuela, Colombia and Panama; visitors from the United States and Venezuela principally sustain the tourist sector of the economy. There has also been a contemporary trend towards migration to Aruba and Curaçao from the Dominican Republic, Colombia and Venezuela.

The tensions between the Netherlands and its Caribbean territories have also been fuelled by a pattern of Dutch intervention in formally local governmental affairs related to finances, justice and human rights. While having historically favoured a strong economic presence in their territories by American interests, the Netherlands has been concerned with the type of relationship that has developed between the territorial governments and corporate agents. The trend towards increased supervision of the finances of the territories by the Kingdom of the Netherlands began in Sint Maarten during the early 1990s. The government of this island, controlled by Claude Wathey and the Democratic Party, had been successful in transforming the island into a tourist and real-estate paradise for foreigners. The Hague initiated an audit of the finances of the territory and triggered a prosecutorial investigation into the allegation of corrupt practices by public servants. The Dutch government also became concerned with administrative corruption and money laundering in Aruba during the economic boom the island experienced in the 1990s, and investigated its finances in 1996, when the separate-country status of the island became permanent. Subsequently, the Dutch government voiced its concern about the possibility of good government and the application of justice in small-island contexts inhabited by communities intimately related through family ties. While these were occasional interventions, the supervision of internal finances of Curaçao and Sint Maarten became a permanent feature when they became autonomous countries within the Dutch kingdom in 2010.

To support the proposal to create a new constitutional order in Curaçao and Sint Maarten the Dutch government set several conditions, among them the need for the countries of Aruba, Curaçao and Sint Maarten and the municipalities of Bonaire, Sint Eustatius and Saba to operate within the Dutch policy of good governance, to cooperate with the programmes against corruption and drug trafficking signed by the Netherlands and the United States, and to support the mission of the US Coast Guard in this sphere (see Government of the Netherlands 2015).

Various authors have referred to the notion of "recolonization" to describe the reduction of the autonomous powers of the territories through the expansion of metropolitan intervention in certain key areas – notably regional security, internal finances and human rights issues. There is a significant contrast between the policies of the United States and the Netherlands in the breadth of autonomy in these spheres. While in the US constitutional order it is clear that both the states and the territories are compelled to follow federal law, under the terms of the Charter for the Kingdom of the Netherlands it was understood that internal autonomy extended to the authority of the Dutch Caribbean territories to overrule the applicability of Dutch laws in certain areas. Nevertheless, in justifying its persistent intrusion into the internal affairs of the territories after 2010, The Hague increasingly invokes article 43 of the Charter for the Kingdom of the Netherlands of 1954, which establishes that while "the countries shall see to the realization of fundamental human rights and freedoms, legal certainty and good governance", the safeguarding of these areas shall be a kingdom affair (Ministry of Foreign Affairs 2002).

As with Puerto Rico, the local customs and language are centrepieces of political discourse, which calls attention to the cultural differences between the metropolis and the territory. Lacking effective political power, the political elites contest Dutch interference in the internal management of the territories by performing rituals of the demarcation of authority that emphasize cultural difference. The conflict over common citizenship and belonging resurfaced in 2001, when a same-sex couple that had been married in the Netherlands requested recognition of their legal relationship in Aruba. When the Aruban Registrar rejected the petition, the case was moved to the Joint Court of Appeals of the Netherlands Antilles and Aruba, which ruled that the territory was required to recognize the marriage under the terms of article 40 of the charter.[12] Although the Aruban prime minister, Nelson O. Oduber, contested the ruling, declaring that same-sex relations "go against Aruba's way of life" the Supreme Court of the Netherlands upheld the decision in 2005, establishing that "[t]he Dutch marriage can be inscribed in the register. Since Aruba is part of the Kingdom of the Netherlands, it must comply with demands of the Kingdom" (Curry-Sumner 2006, 161).

Language plays an authenticating role in the political life of the islands of Aruba, Bonaire and Curaçao. The use of the creole language of Papiamento in these three islands was encouraged during the latter half of the twentieth century through various processes, including government promotion of the language as a means of reinforcing cultural differences with the metropolis.

As with other language scenarios in the Caribbean, the broadening of social and economic inequalities is associated with the emergence of political struggles involving language and other markers of identity. Moreover, there has been a sustained decline of Dutch speakers in these islands as a result of the confinement of Dutch language to the public sphere coupled with a tourist economy that attracts English speakers from North American countries and Spanish-speaking workers from Colombia, Venezuela and the Dominican Republic. As a consequence, the importance of the language theme in political discourse has grown.

The role of Papiamento in the politics of belonging in Curaçaoan politics was manifested in 2003, when the prime minister of the Netherlands Antilles, Mirna Louisa Godett, planned her first official visit to the Netherlands. Declaring that Papiamento was the language of the people of this island, she was accompanied on her official visit to the metropolis by an entourage of interpreters who were responsible for translating her official speeches and other talks. The prime minister made it clear that while she would speak with Dutch government officials through interpreters, she would speak in Dutch with the queen, who represented the kingdom as a whole. This symbolic act was meant to underscore the autonomy of the unit countries of the kingdom: while Dutch is spoken with the monarch, each unit country reserves the right to use its own language in official communication with one another. However, there is ambiguity in the use of the local language as a marker of identity since – as Rose Mary Allen warns in reference to Curaçao – Dutch still holds a position of relative advantage for its role as a language of social mobility (Allen 2010, 120).

The discourse of autonomy in the Dutch Caribbean territories and claims for the expansion of authority to deal with dominant domestic as well as foreign economic actors require paying close attention to how the contradictory process of global capitalist integration is affecting the ways societies understand their position in the global arena.

One of the major concerns being debated in the Dutch territories today is related to the effects of large-scale immigration from Europe on small island societies, including concerns over ownership of land and businesses by foreigners and the displacement of local landowners and entrepreneurs. While European Dutch citizens face certain restrictions when applying for residence in the Caribbean territories, common citizenship in the Netherlands has contributed to an influx of Dutch citizens to Aruba and Curaçao.

Three main themes in the discourse of authenticity have taken root in the Netherlands Antilles with the emergence of organizations like pro-independence Pueblo Soberano (Sovereign People), Movimentu Futuro Kòrsou (Movement for the Future of Curaçao) and Movimentu Antia Nobo (Movement for a New Antilles), which lean towards a more radical form of autonomy. The victory of an alliance of the three political parties in the Curaçao elections in 2010 reignited the debate on belonging with issues related to foreign control of the economy, the widening of the gap between the social classes and the need for the integration of immigrants into Curaçaoan society. In addition, under the leadership of Helmin Wiels, who was assassinated in 2013, Pueblo Soberano voiced concern over Dutch control of land and key economic sectors in this island, as well as the current obstacles to establish closer relations with Venezuela as a result of the US-Dutch security alliance in the southern Caribbean.

As with Puerto Rico, there is a wide-ranging ideological spectrum that reflects deep-seated divisions in different sectors of these societies with respect to the issues surrounding the tension between local belonging and metropolitan citizenship. The debate has not ended in Aruba, despite the electoral victory of the Aruban People's Party (Partido di Pueblo Arubano/Arubaanse Volkspartij), which represented a turn away from the autonomist route taken by the People's Electoral Movement (Movimiento Electoral di Pueblo). If voices from MEP had proposed revisions to the relationship with the Netherlands with an orientation towards a form of free-association, the AVP leader Mike Eman moved early in his tenure to restructure and strengthen ties with the Netherlands and Europe.

Metropolitan Anxieties

Globalization has played a major role in the expansion of right-wing ideology in Europe and the United States, drawing attention to what Hans-Georg Betz calls "a nativist agenda of exclusion" concerned with the sociocultural integrity of European societies (2003, 74–93). Some of the major driving forces behind this right-wing tendency have been the intensification of movement of peoples as immigrants, refugees and asylum seekers on a world scale and the widening of social inequalities.

Thus, a simultaneous upsurge of racism and anti-immigrant sentiment by rightist political parties, movements and other ideological currents concerned with national identity has occurred in the United States and Europe. These movements have revived old imperial nationalist claims that celebrate the existence of a privileged cultural community and react with hostility to the presence in their midst of people from certain other parts of the world.

Generally, the political discourses of these movements revolve around the promotion of policies that favour indigenous inhabitants and exaggerated claims about the failure or inability of new immigrants to adapt to the society. The problem has been complicated by the propagation of the beliefs that those immigrants who are disinclined to abandon ties with their cultures of origin pose a mortal threat to the survival of national identity in European and American societies. At the heart of these ideas is the ideological notion of an organic citizenship that connects membership in the body politic with cultural belonging. This ideology is present in the political arenas of most European countries and is deeply entrenched in the Tea Party Movement in the United States. Moreover the contemporary nativist agenda has reached beyond civil society and into the structures of the state in Europe and the United States, where it has promoted the enactment of legislation requiring the integration of immigrants into the receiving society through the knowledge of its language and affinity with its customs.

The "Kingdom Fellows"

The Netherlands represents an interesting case of a country in which the anti-immigrant ideology has played an influential role in shaping government policy. Known for its cultural liberalism, Dutch society has made notable changes in its views on immigration during recent decades. The Dutch government initially confronted the problem in 1979, when it commissioned its Scientific Council for Government Policy to compile a comprehensive survey of government policy with respect to ethnic minorities in the Netherlands (Penninx 2006, 58). The report, titled *The Ethnic Minorities*, conceived immigrant integration from a multicultural perspective, underlining that "migrants had become permanent minorities of an open and multi-ethnic society" (Scholten 2011, 92–95). Nonetheless, two decades later in 1998, the Dutch government set forth a legislative trend with the objective of assimilating immigrants, including those coming from the Dutch Caribbean. The Newcomers Integration Act (Wet Inburgering Nieuwkomers), was ostensibly designed to integrate newcomers into society while eliminating their dependence on public welfare. The promoters of this controversial legislation argued that the aim was to avoid the formation of marginalized ghetto communities of foreigners in the society. The law required foreigners residing in the Netherlands to take courses in Dutch in order to strengthen their knowledge of the metropolitan language, familiarize themselves with Dutch culture and take advantage of vocational counselling within the broader context of social orientation.

Moreover, in 2004, the Dutch parliament commissioned a report on immigration policy that led to the introduction of certain changes while preserving other provisions that were contained in the old legislation. The report, which called for a new-style integration policy, rejected the idea of the Netherlands becoming a multicultural society and reiterated the requirement that immigrants "master the Dutch language, become aware of Dutch values, and deepen his or her knowledge of Dutch society" (PPLH 2002–3, 14, quoted in HRW 2008, 10).

Caribbean immigration into the Netherlands is a major topic of debate in the political life of contemporary Dutch society. Immigration from Suriname became a central theme after the declaration of independence by Dutch Guiana in 1975 contributed to an influx of Surinamese Dutch citizens to the metropolis. The public debate also gathered momentum when the Antillean governments encouraged the movement of young people from the Antilles to the metropolis as a way to temper youth unemployment in their Caribbean territories.

A major turn occurred in 2004 when Rita Verdonk, minister for aliens' affairs and integration in the government of Prime Minister Jan Peter Balkenende, submitted a proposal to deal with what she termed the "problematic character" of the Antilleans living in the Netherlands. The minister outlined separate entry procedures, on the one hand, to apply to the native population and certain residents from other European countries and, on the other, to subject Dutch citizens from the Netherlands Antilles to the same entry requirements that apply to foreigners. According to María Bruquetas-Callejo et al., "The fact that the Netherlands did not see itself as an immigration country is manifested in the various ways the nation went about naming factual immigrants. People from the Dutch East Indies were labeled 'repatriates'; from Suriname and the Netherlands Antilles, 'Kingdom fellows' (rijksgenoten in Dutch); and from Southern Europe, Morocco and Turkey, 'guest workers' " (2011, 132).

The Dutch minister for immigration and integration issued a proposal in 2006 to legislate in matters of "civic integration of Dutch citizens of Antillean origin" who had difficulty speaking Dutch and integrating effectively into the local society (see Besselink 2006). Ironically, the policy that was directed at integrating Dutch citizens from the Antilles was not any different than that which applied to other foreigners of West Indian background who entered the Netherlands. This point is borne out by the declaration that immigrants from both groups were to be deported if they did not fulfil the linguistic and related cultural provisions and requirements established by the immigration law. According to the policy on Dutch citizenship, the "Kingdom fellows" – or fellow citizens of the Kingdom of the Netherlands (*rijksgenoten*) – could immigrate under certain conditions to countries that comprise the kingdom, provided that they demonstrated their ability to speak Dutch.

In many ways, the nativist reaction of the Dutch government contradicts its historical practices that are traceable to the colonial period when the Dutch opened their colonial territories to immigrants from different parts of the world, a strategy that led to the creation of new societies in their colonies.

Moreover, since the Dutch colonial policy did not require the teaching of the Dutch language, only a few members of the colonial elite were able to speak the language of the colonizer. Gert Oostindie and Inge Klinkers point out that Dutch never became the language of communication beyond the ruling classes and other highly privileged groups inhabiting the colonies, especially in Indonesia and in the Caribbean (2003, 201–2), where Papiamento, English and Spanish became the main spoken languages. Although official government documents published in the Netherlands Antilles are published in Dutch, the authorities allowed the use of local languages for publishing certain public documents pertaining to areas of governmental affairs. Thus, these linguistic peculiarities of the Dutch Caribbean were already known in 1954, when the Netherlands decided to include citizenship as a common element in the constitution of its kingdom.

The immigration debate in the Netherlands had an impact on relations between the territories and The Hague. For example, the disagreement between The Hague and the Antillean governments on the question of culture ended with Aruba and the Netherlands Antilles rejecting the Dutch policy of assimilation. Largely, the debate between The Hague and the Antilles territories emphasized the moral aspects of the Dutch proposal with reference to the unequal application of the law within the kingdom, and it exposed the inability of the Netherlands government to interpret Dutch citizenship outside its narrowly defined cultural parameters. In response to a request made by the Dutch minister of immigration and integration to the governments of the Dutch Antilles to comment on the draft of the proposed law, Emily de Jongh-Elhage, prime minister of the Netherlands Antilles, reiterated the vision of autonomy that is a defining aspect of the Charter for the Kingdom of the Netherlands. Prime Minister Jongh-Elhage emphasized the complexities built into the structure of the kingdom, in which citizenship is shared by people from different ethnic backgrounds, and reminded the minister that failure to take this fact into account at the level of policy and practice might lay the basis for dispensing "substantial differential treatment" to different groups of Dutch citizens. The prime minister also drew attention to the ambiguity and confusion that the kingdom's arcane legal system fostered.

Prime Minister Jongh-Elhage reiterated the argument contained in the Charter for the Kingdom and in Dutch public discourse, declaring that although the subjects of the Dutch sovereign are all Dutch nationals they do not constitute one Dutch nation in the sense of being "the Dutch people". She argued that Her Majesty's subjects comprise several "peoples" as acknowledged by the Kingdom Act, at the time of the inauguration of the king in 1992, which clearly mentions "the peoples of the Kingdom". Antilleans and Arubans are Dutch by nationality, but they are neither considered to be a part of the Dutch "people" nor considered to otherwise exude "Dutchness", just as people from the former British West Indies who have acquired United Kingdom citizenship are considered black British but they are not considered to be English. The confusion arising from the distinction made by The Hague between Dutch nationals and Dutch people should be kept in mind when reflecting on the position of the Dutch government about what it means to be Dutch.[13]

The position adopted by The Hague towards Antillean immigrants highlights the deep division and separation that inform relations between the Dutch and their former colonies, historically and contemporarily. There is no evidence that the cultural differences separating the two parts of the Netherlands are about to fade away, considering also that the anti-immigration stance of the right-wing forces in the

Netherlands applies equally to the West Indian communities in Dutch society and the political class in the Netherlands Antilles. A number of conservative organizations in the Dutch political arena, such as the Party for Freedom and Democracy (Partij voor de Vrijheid, PVV), the Independent Citizens Party (Onafhankelijke Burger Partij, OBP) and the Democratic Political Turning Point (Democratisch Politiek Keerpunt, DPK), have taken their nativist views further, in calling for a break in the relationship between the Netherlands and the overseas territories. While racist discourse in the contemporary Netherlands is generally oriented towards immigrants from the Muslim world, it also extends to migrants from the Netherlands Antilles. In 2009, Hero Brinkman, who was a member of the Dutch parliamentary delegation that explored alternative political futures for these islands, called the governments of the West Indies a "burden of corrupt thieves".[14] Such disparaging rhetoric is designed less to hurt the feelings of Antillean political elites than it is to reinforce anti-immigrant emotions in the Netherlands and to pressure the Dutch government to adopt a more restrictve immigration policy, including the control of incoming population flows from the Caribbean.

The Hispanic State

The history of the US domination of Puerto Rico has been marked by political conflict over culture and citizenship in the colony. Looking at Puerto Rico's history through the lens of the long term allows us to discern and account for major shifts in US attitudes towards the territory. Nationalism emerged and remained a matter of serious concern in Puerto Rico from the start of the twentieth century to the Cold War. However, a major shift occurred with the growth of a massive movement that petitioned for the integration of Puerto Rico into the US system as a state during the second half of the century, and thereby generated new concerns over the question of belonging.

Today, half a century after the commonwealth project was implemented, the vision and strategy for an autonomous polity and a society capable of maintaining its own cultural institutions and practices as part of the sovereign state of the United States has come to an end. The current political reality is that of a territory inhabited largely by a majority of impoverished US citizens, petitioning for full incorporation into the United States. The debate over the admission of Puerto Rico as a Spanish-speaking state into the Union has been addressed by various commissions and remains a major theme on the agenda of those groups in the United States that aspire to make English the official and only language of the United States. The US Congress has historically emphasized the importance of English in the functioning of the American order as a whole; however, it is the conservative demand to make English the official language of the United States that has intensified the recent debate over language. The language question in the United Sates has affected Puerto Rican politics, as representatives of the two governing ideologies on the island understand it as an important issue that affects their relationship with the United States.

The political actors in contemporary Puerto Rico draw on their respective ideologies and political support bases to defend, protect and preserve at all costs the cultural heritage and features of the island. In Puerto Rico, local state actors – government officials and political parties – validate their political roles through the promotion of a conception of autonomy that involves the reconciliation between belonging to a local cultural community and allegiance to the metropolis through citizenship. The two parties that have dominated the political arena for the past four decades – the Popular Democratic Party and the New Progressive Party – have promoted and supported two different proposals around autonomy. On the one hand, the commonwealth advocates made the case for Puerto Rico as a distinct cultural community operating with special rules under the US flag. In their minds, autonomy meant the exercise of authority over the internal affairs of the territory in areas that were not within the jurisdiction of states within the American federal system, such as the control over the entry of aliens into the territory, the ability of the local government to determine the allocation of federal funds and the right of the commonwealth to repeal certain federal laws. On the other hand, the modern annexation perspective that emerged during the 1970s held to the vision of a territory administered as a US state, with limited authority over cultural affairs, including the maintenance of Spanish as a language of Puerto Rico.

While the pro-commonwealth sector thought of Puerto Rico as a nation, the pro-statehood promoters conceived of Puerto Ricans as an ethnic group within a culturally diverse United States of America (Ramos 1987, 47). Within the annexationist imagination Puerto Ricans approximated a huge national minority in the United States inhabiting or even possessing their own territory.

The victory of the pro-annexationist NPP in the 1968 elections represented the final blow to the divide between citizenship and homeland in the commonwealth conception. Determined to proceed with statehood for the Puerto Rican territory, the NPP promoted policies during the 1970s that launched a trend of increased dependency on federal funding for the operation of the government and to support the largely impoverished population. The NPP also initiated a new proposal and drive that favoured the full-fledged incorporation of Puerto Rico as a US state, while maintaining its own cultural traits. In contrast with the notion of Puerto Rico as a distinct nation associated with the United States, the pro-statehood forces view Puerto Ricans as an ethnic group within the US society, in possession of its own territory. The contemporary annexationist position is that the island territory of Puerto Rico, with its people, symbols, cultural identity, language and other peculiarities, is also an integral part of the United States, which it views as a larger creole state. Puerto Rico is by extension entitled to participate in and represent itself internationally by sending its own delegations and participants to represent the country in international sports and cultural fora, such as the Olympics.

Among the factors framing the new linguistic scenario is the movement of Puerto Ricans between the territory and the US mainland that led to the formation of a Puerto Rican community in the United States for whom English is the first language. Significantly, Spanish remains the main language of Puerto Ricans because the Spanish language is an integral part of a deeply rooted sociocultural reality. Undeniably, the majority of the Puerto Rican population on the island does not speak English. That English has not become a second language commonly spoken in Puerto Rico is surprising, considering its relation to the media and its significance for education (Torres-González 2002, 265–306). This fact has attracted the attention of persons in the US state agencies and in civil society organizations that are seeking to make English the official language and the exclusive language of educational instruction to be used in that country.

The movement to make Puerto Rico a US state has by its very logic drawn attention to the fact that a US territory inhabited by mostly monolingual Spanish speakers produced electoral majorities that favour statehood within the federal system. US-based organizations that seek to make English the official language of that nation, such as US English, have made the Puerto Rican case a high priority on their political agenda. In 2012, Mauro Mujica, chairman of US English, released a statement warning that "[i]n order to ensure that Puerto Rico would work seamlessly with the other 50 states, the territory should prepare to function as an English-speaking state. The United States cannot, and should not, accept a state in which a majority of citizens are unable to speak the common language in this country: English" (US English 2012; see also US English Foundation 2011).

The idea that the incorporation of Puerto Rico with its particular cultural traits could subvert the basic cultural fabric of American society has become firmly entrenched in the US Congress. The various congressional committees, which have examined the future political status of Puerto Rico since the commonwealth was created, have concluded that English would be the official language in the relationship between the federal government and Puerto Rico. A statehood proposal in 2005 underscored the current situation with respect to language, namely that "the provisions of the Federal law on the use of the English language in the agencies and courts of the Federal Government in the fifty states of the Union shall apply equally in the State of Puerto Rico, as at present" (PTF 2007). Furthermore, while the 2011 Presidential Task Force Report on the Status of Puerto Rico advised the president and Congress to ensure that an integrated Puerto Rico will control its own cultural and linguistic identity, it also recognized that, if Puerto Rico were admitted as a state, "the English language would need to play – as it does today – a central role in the daily life of the Island" (PTF 2011).

Thus, while the proposal to create a creole state within the United States enjoys widespread support in Puerto Rico, it has the opposite effect in decision-making centres in Washington, where the claim for American cultural uniqueness is reinforced by the vision of a nation that is linguistically homogeneous – arguments that resonate with the ideology of American exceptionalism.

While strongly criticizing the commonwealth arrangement as a colonial status, and championing full-fledged annexation, NPP intellectuals and strategists did little to transform the terms of the debate. In the NPP's vision of the road to full integration in the US political system as a state, US recognition of the Spanish language as a marker of Puerto Rican identity was crucial. The NPP considers language to be a legitimate patrimony reserved to the states and to the people under the Tenth Amendment of the US Constitution that deals with the Rights of States. In stressing the issue of belonging to a cultural community, albeit in a "minority" role, the NPP succeeded in upholding and sustaining the value of cultural identity and solidarity in its political project. Conversely, there is a conservative consensus in policymaking circles of the metropolis with respect to English as a binding element of US society.

In political life in modern Puerto Rico the capacity of the local government to contribute effectively to the construction, interpretation and reproduction of social reality through long-term representations of symbolic, social and material practices has been compromised and impaired by its limited resources in ways that highlight its relative powerlessness to act independently. The construction and performance of identities in current political life in Puerto Rico reveal a double intention that is marked, on the one hand, by a political discourse for an internal audience and, on the other, a set of discourses and practices geared to a metropolitan audience. The concern seems to have less to do with establishing a universal standpoint on identity, as used to be the case, and much more to do with demonstrating a greater eagerness to "perform" in representational ways in contemporary times.

Conclusion

The foregoing is, admittedly, a broad review of the trajectory and current issues on citizenship and cultural identity in Puerto Rico and the Dutch Caribbean. Their contemporary political settings have brought to the fore new actors as well as new issues linked to the old subject of exclusion and incorporation on the border of the relationships the United States and the Netherlands have with their Caribbean territories. However, having compared and contrasted the politics of citizenship and belonging in Puerto Rico and the Netherlands Antilles, I wish now to draw out three major conclusions.

My first is that the political arrangements that were put in place by the United States and the Netherlands as ways to manage and control the trajectory of the decolonization process failed to deliver the anticipated outcomes. Thus, the complexities of their relationship pose real political questions that must be carefully considered when examining their current dilemmas and the proposals that have been continuously debated in their political arenas over time. One question concerns the ambiguous political location of the territories with respect to the political systems of their metropolises and the constraints that limit their ability to express their interests on their own behalf, internally and in the new global arena. The commonwealth arrangement failed to deliver on the promise of autonomy and to meet popular expectations about development, which was subsumed under national security considerations in US post-war strategy. Similarly, a Dutch kingdom comprising the metropolitan state and its overseas territories as equals has not withstood the test of time.

Not only did the American and the Dutch political arrangements for incorporating their overseas territories fail to satisfy the complex array of material and symbolic needs of the local societies, they also proved problematic at the metropolitan level. The crisis of neo-Keynesianism, which framed political liberalism and ordered the institutional and substantive economic and social arrangements of the welfare state after World War II, paved the way for the transition to neo-liberal globalization and its neoconservative ideology that gained ascendancy in the United States and in Dutch society. Furthermore, the contemporary debates on culture, language and belonging in the Netherlands Antilles and in Puerto Rico are also conditioned by their ambiguous location within the political system of their metropolises, a situation that imposes certain constraints on how they manage to express their interests and assert their identities in the global arena.

My second conclusion is that cultural difference is not in itself the source of the lack of recognition or hostility between people from different cultures. Rather, the contemporary debates and tensions around culture, language and belonging in the Netherlands Antilles and in Puerto Rico help to uncover important areas of conflict related to the way in which political actors in the metropolises and the territories view their internal problems and the challenges of belonging in the contemporary world. Thus, analysing the conflict over identity issues requires going beyond a notion of culture conceived as an organic or unalterable trait of societies.

Third and finally, the capacity of the local territorial governments to contribute effectively to the construction, interpretation and reproduction of social reality through long-term representations of symbolic, social and material practices has been compromised and impaired by their limited resources and external interference that also highlight their relative powerlessness to act independently. The construction and performance of identities in political life in contemporary Puerto

Rico, as well as in the Netherlands Antilles, reveal a double intention: the mobilization of political forces and the construction of difference as a resource for holding on to their limited internal authority.

Notes

1. The United States has two territories in the Caribbean: Puerto Rico and the (US) Virgin Islands (the latter bought from Denmark in 1917). In contrast with Puerto Rico, the US Virgin Islands remain a colony ruled from Washington through the Bureau of Insular Affairs. While US citizenship was extended to the inhabitants of the Virgin Islands in 1927, the historical efforts to authorize the creation of a Constitutional Convention to draft a constitution for this territory have been persistently rejected by the US Congress.
2. The Charter for the Kingdom of the Netherlands of 1954 included Suriname and the Netherlands Antilles (formed by Curaçao, Aruba, Bonaire, Sint Maarten, Sint Eustatius and Saba). However, when Suriname – the former Dutch Guiana – became independent in 1975, the composition of the kingdom was reduced to the Netherlands and the Netherlands Antilles.
3. Because of the proximity of Aruba, Bonaire and Curaçao (the so-called ABC Islands) to Venezuela, political and social relations with the South American country have historically been close. By virtue of the fact that Venezuela lacked good ports for its oil trade during the long century between 1820 and 1920, the Dutch Antilles in the southern Caribbean witnessed a lessening of direct linkages with the Venezuelan economy and an increase in the inflow of foreign capital. The Dutch oil company Royal Dutch Shell took advantage of the proximity of Aruba and Curaçao to oil resources in Venezuela's Lake Maracaibo and established an oil refinery in Curaçao in 1928. From that moment, the economy of Curaçao began to undergo reorganization by gradually replacing the old plantation order with the oil-refining industry. The expansion of economic activity also stimulated labour immigration from other Caribbean islands into Aruba and Curaçao, which altered the social structure and ethnic composition of these islands (see Mitchell 1963, 128–37).
4. This juridical provision has its roots in the debate over the location and status of the indigenous nations and populations in the US political system, which created the system of reservations in the continental United States and allowed for the existence of distinct cultural communities in the continental United States. Priscilla Wald and others suggest that the legal thinking over the creation of the tribal homelands inside the United States may have spilled over into the discussion of the legal status of Puerto Rico that took place during the initial decades of the twentieth century. In rejecting the notion of "foreign" in reference to the Indian nations, Priscilla Wald quotes Justice Marshall in his argument that "the Indian territory is admitted to compose a part of the United States [and] it may well be doubted whether those tribes that reside within the acknowledged boundaries of the United States can, with strict accuracy, be denominated foreign nations" (Wald 1993, 62; see also Levinson 2001, 132–33).

5. Thomas Aleinkoff argues that, although "Indian tribes, being within the territorial limits of the United States, were not, strictly speaking, foreign states", "they were alien nations, distinct political communities", with whom the United States dealt with through treaties and acts of Congress (2002, 19).
6. As outlined in a Congress Research Service Report to Congress: "In 1917 the Congress extended citizenship to 'citizens' of Puerto Rico who were not citizens of foreign countries. Persons born in Puerto Rico after 1941 are citizens of the United States at birth, again through federal statute. Such 'statutory' citizenship differs from 'constitutional' citizenship that automatically confers upon persons born in the United States (as opposed to the areas subject to the territories clause)" (Bea and Garrett 2010, 26).
7. While the Congress of the United States approved a law in 1934 activating the itinerary for the independence of the Philippines, the US Congress turned down two similar bills, presented in 1936 and in 1943, to lead Puerto Rico in the same direction.
8. Article 3 of the charter stipulates that kingdom affairs shall include: maintenance of the independence and defence of the kingdom, foreign relations, Netherlands nationality, regulation of the orders of knighthood, the flag and the coat of arms of the kingdom, regulation of the nationality of vessels and naval standards, supervision of the rules governing the admission and expulsion of Netherlands nationals and aliens, and deportation.
9. In 2010, the Netherlands declared it would name a kingdom representative with the power to approve island ordinances and "impose an order subject to administrative coercion" (Minister of Justice 2010). However, the three islands are not an integral part of any Dutch province, nor do they constitute a province of the Netherlands in the Caribbean.
10. In the United Nations Resolution 1541/15, principle 8 clearly states that integration should be on the basis of complete equality between the peoples of the integrated territory and those of the metropolis, where "both should have equal rights and opportunities for representation and effective participation at all levels in the executive, legislative and judicial organs of government" (UNR 1541/15).
11. While the external relations of Puerto Rico fall exclusively under the US Department of State, the Charter for the Kingdom of the Netherlands states that the autonomous countries "shall be involved in the preparation and implementation of agreements with other Powers which affect them" (Ministry of Foreign Affairs 2002, art. 27) and that "in accordance with international agreements entered into by the Kingdom, they may, if they so desire, accede to membership in international organizations" (art. 28).
12. The same-sex marriage was recognized in the Population Register, but not in the Register of Civil Status, since the Aruban Civil Code only allows the inclusion in the Register of marriages celebrated on the island (JCJ 2005).
13. See the comments by a judge of the Caribbean Court of Justice, Jacob Wit, to the Honourable Emily de Jongh-Elhage, prime minister of the Netherlands Antilles, on the draft bill circulated by the Dutch minister of alien affairs and integration (Wit 2006, 4).
14. This particular legislator also proposed that the Netherlands should get rid of their Caribbean possessions by selling them over the Internet for the prince of one euro. See "The Antilles: A Mafia within the Kingdom", https://sxmpolitico.wordpress.com/tag/brinkman-report-on-corruption-in-st-maarten-english-translation/page/18/.

References

Alegría-Ortega, Idsa E. 2001. "Culture, Politics, and Self-Determination in Puerto Rico". In *Islands at the Crossroads: Politics in the Non-Independent Caribbean*, edited by Aarón Gamaliel Ramos and Ángel Israel Rivera, 28–44. Kingston: Ian Randle.

Aleinikoff, Thomas Alexander. 2002. *Semblances of Sovereignty: The Constitution, the State, and American Citizenship*. Cambridge: Harvard University Press.

Allen, Rose Mary. 2010. "The Complexity of National Identity Construction in Curaçao, Dutch Caribbean". *European Review of Latin American and Caribbean Studies* 89 (October): 117–25.

Anderson, Benedict. 2006. *Imagined Communities: Reflections on the Origins and Spread of Nationalism*. London: Verso.

Bea, Keith, and R. Sam Garrett. 2010. *Political Status of Puerto Rico: Options for Congress*. Congress Research Service Report RL32933. 23 April.

Besselink, Leonard F.M. 2006. "Expulsion and Integration: Erecting Internal Borders within the Kingdom of the Netherlands". *CHALLENGE Liberty and Security* (website). 12 September. http://libertysecurity.org/article1096.html.

Betz, Hans-Georg. 2003. "The Growing Threat of the Radical Right". In *Right-Wing Extremism in the Twenty-First Century*, edited by Peter H. Merkl and Leonard Weinberg, 74–96. London: Frank Cass.

Bruquetas-Callejo, María, Blanca Garcés-Mascareñas, Rinus Penninx and Peter Scholten. 2011. "The Case of the Netherlands". In *Migration Policymaking in Europe: The Dynamics of Actors and Contexts in Past and Present*, edited by Giovana Zioncone, Rinus Penninx and Maren Borkert, 129–64. Amsterdam: Amsterdam University Press.

CEC (Council of the European Communities). 1992. "Citizenship of the Union", part 2, art. 8, 8a, 8b. In "Provisions Amending the Treaty Establishing the European Economic Community with a View to Establishing the European Community", Title 2. In *Treaty on European Union*. 7 February.

Curry-Sumner, Ian. 2006. "Private International Law Aspects of Homosexual Couples: the Netherlands Report". In *Netherlands Reports to the Seventeenth International Congress of Comparative Law*, edited by J.H.M van Erp and L.P.W van Vliet, 147–76. Antwerp and Oxford: Intersentia.

Dávila, Arlene M. 1997. *Sponsored Identities: Cultural Politics in Puerto Rico*. Philadelphia: Temple University Press.

Godreau, Isar P. 2015. *Scripts of Blackness: Race, Cultural Nationalism, and US Colonialism in Puerto Rico*. Urbana, Chicago and Springfield: University of Illinois Press.

Government of the Netherlands. 2015. "The Role of the Netherlands". Government of the Netherlands website. http://www.government.nl/issues/caribbean-parts-of-the-kingdom/role-of-the-netherlands.

Hillebrink, Steven. 2007. *The Right to Self-Determination and Post-Colonial Governance: The Case of the Netherlands Antilles and Aruba*. The Hague: T.M.C. Asser.

HRW (Human Rights Watch). 2008. "The Netherlands: Discrimination in the Name of Integration, Migrants' Rights Under the Integration Abroad Act". Briefing paper. May. http://www.hrw.org/en/reports/2008/05/13/netherlands-discrimination-name-integration.

JCJ (Joint Court of Justice for the Netherlands Antilles and Aruba). 2005. Case no. EJ 2101/04–H.12/05, 23 August.

Levinson, Sanford. 2001. "Installing the Insular Cases into the Canon of Constitutional Law". In *Foreign in a Domestic Sense: Puerto Rico, American Expansion, and the Constitution*, edited by Christina Duffy Burnett and Burke Marshall, 121–39. Durham: Duke University Press.

Minister of Justice, The Hague. 2010. "Act of May 17, 2010, Providing Rules with Regard to the Public Entities Bonaire, St Eustatius and Saba". In *Bulletin of Acts and Decrees of the Kingdom of the Netherlands 2010*, no. 345.

Ministry of Foreign Affairs, The Hague. 2002. "Charter for the Kingdom of the Netherlands (Act of 28 October 1954, containing Acceptance of a Charter for the Kingdom of the Netherlands)". In *Bulletin of Acts and Decrees 1954*, no. 503.

Mitchell, Harold. 1963. *Europe in the Caribbean: The Policies of Great Britain, France and the Netherlands towards Their West Indian Territories in the Twentieth Century*. Stanford: Hispanic American Society.

Oostindie, Gert, and Inge Klinkers. 2003. *Decolonizing the Caribbean: Dutch Policies in a Comparative Perspective*. Amsterdam: Amsterdam University Press.

Penninx, Rinus. 2006. "The Vicissitudes of Dutch Integration Policies". *Canadian Diversity/Diversité canadienne* 5 (1): 57–62.

PPLH (Parliamentary Papers of the [Dutch] Lower House). 2002–3. 28 627, no. 91.

PTF (President's Task Force on Puerto Rico's Status). 2007. *Report by the President's Task Force on Puerto Rico's Status*. December.

———. 2011. *Report by the President's Task Force on Puerto Rico's Status*. March.

Ramos, Aarón Gamaliel. 1987. *Las ideas anexionistas en Puerto Rico bajo la dominación norteamericana*. Río Piedras: Ediciones Huracán.

———. 2003–4. "Performing Identity: The Politics of Culture in Contemporary Puerto Rico". *Pouvoirs dans la caraïbe, la revue du CRPLC* (Dossier thématique: Identité et politique dans la caraïbe insulaire) 14: 63–79.

Scholten, Peter. 2011. *Framing Immigrant Integration: Dutch Research-Policy Dialogues in Comparative Perspective*. Amsterdam: Amsterdam University Press.

Scientific Council for Government Policy. 1979. *Ethnic Minorities*. The Hague: SDU.

Smith, Rogers M. 2001. "The Bitter Roots of Puerto Rican Citizenship". In *Foreign in a Domestic Sense: Puerto Rico, American Expansion, and the Constitution*, edited by Christina Duffy Burnett and Burke Marshall, 373–88. Durham: Duke University Press.

Torres-González, Roamé. 2002. *Idioma, bilingüismo y nacionalidad: La presencia del inglés en Puerto Rico*. San Juan: Editorial de la Universidad de Puerto Rico.

Torruella, Juan R. 1988. *The Supreme Court and Puerto Rico: The Doctrine of Separate and Unequal*. Río Piedras: Editorial Universidad de Puerto Rico.

UNR (United Nations Resolution) 1541/15. 1960. http://daccess-dds-ny.un.org/doc/RESOLUTION/GEN/NR0/153/15/IMG/NR015315.pdf?OpenElement.

US English. 2012. "US English to Puerto Rico: English Is Next Step Toward Statehood". 12 November. http://www.us-english.org/view/924.

US English Foundation. 2011. "A Clash of Cultures: The Future of Puerto Rico and the United States". Washington, DC: US English Foundation.

Van Aller, H.B. 1994. "Dutch Decolonization: A Qualified Failure?" In *The Future Status of Aruba and the Netherlands Antilles*, edited by Armando Lampe, 11–35. Oranjestad: Fundini.

Wald, Priscilla. 1993. "Terms of Assimilation: Legislating Subjectivity in the Emerging Nations". In *Cultures of United States Imperialism*, edited by Amy Kaplan and Donald E. Pease, 59–84. Durham: Duke University Press.

Wells, Henry. 1969. *The Modernization of Puerto Rico: A Political Study of Changing Values and Institutions*. Cambridge: Harvard University Press.

Wilhelmina, H.M. Queen. ca. 1943. "Problems of War and Peace". In *The Queen Looks at the Future: Important Statements of H.M. Queen Wilhelmina on War and Peace Aims*, 8–10. New York: The Netherlands Information Bureau.

Wit, Jacob. 2006. Correspondence addressed to the Hon. Emily de Jongh-Elhage. 11 April. http://vorige.nrc.nl/redactie/binnenland/BobWit.pdf.

7 Disillusioned Citizens

The Experience of French Territories in the Caribbean

JUSTIN DANIEL

Guadeloupe, Martinique, French Guiana and Réunion (this last an island located in the Indian Ocean), make up the four "old French colonies" – in contrast with the more recent French territories – which were colonized during the nineteenth century. French Guiana, which does not border the Caribbean Sea, is linked geographically to Amazonia and shares with Guadeloupe and Martinique the experience of colonial habitation – or plantations – and proceeds from the same social-historical matrix as they do, which explains why it is classified with Caribbean societies. These three "old" colonies also belong to the generic category of non-independent territories of the Caribbean, a rather obvious category which yet seems difficult to grasp, because it does not fully account for the great range and variety of political situations it encompasses. By subsuming very distinctive cases, this category also tends to gloss over the specificity and historical concreteness of each territory. In reality, the so-called non-independent territories approximate a misleading residual category, incorporating a number of more or less distinct range of territories, the common denominator of which is defined negatively with respect to the idea of independence. Nonetheless, the concept of a non-independent territory has the advantage of partially avoiding the teleological debate around the dilemma of colonization and decolonization that controversies surrounding post-colonialism have hitherto failed to resolve (Bayart 2010).

In many respects, the experience of non-independent territories in the world is polarized around two scenarios: on the one hand, a vision of "instant" decolonization, which would be immediately achieved through the attainment of sovereignty and, on the other, a reality of persistent colonialism in endless pursuit of its historical destiny within the prevailing international conjuncture. Historian Frederick Cooper discusses the limitations of postcolonial theories and argues that while the prefix "post" emphasizes the importance of the colonial past for the determination of future possibilities and current constraints, these factors cannot be reduced to a colonial effect, any more than a colonial or postcolonial period can be perceived as a coherent whole, as if the multiple efforts and struggles in which peoples were engaged in various situations were always settled in the same way (Cooper 2005). In reality, the process has followed relatively heterodox and multidimensional paths that dispute the notion of a supposedly one-dimensional trajectory to decolonization, as well as traditional categorizations of decolonization, self-determination and others that fall under the United Nations classification and provisions.

This situation is particularly relevant to the case of the three French territories of the Caribbean mentioned above. France's colonial settlement in the Caribbean region followed a specific modality that was based on the imposition of a political-administrative model, which was founded on a fourfold principle of assimilation, centralization, universalism and standardization that greatly affected the fate of the three territories. The Haitian Revolution resulted in the sovereign Republic of Haiti in 1804; the Dominican Republic attained independence in 1844; Cuba achieved formal sovereignty in 1899; and the Federation of the West Indies lasted from 1958 to 1962, opening up the path to independence for the British West Indian colonies. However, the three French territories remain in the bosom of France as an external and far-away power. For the Caribbean region as a whole, the process of political transformation may be considered incomplete, even if the populations of a number of territories seem to have renounced any interest in the possibility of independence (the exception would be Bermuda). Fully integrated into the Franco-European unit, French Guiana, Guadeloupe and Martinique thus share a unique relationship with Paris, having been made overseas departments (*départements d'outre mer*) in 1946. In effect individuals from the territories, when they travel to France, share the same institutions as their counterparts in France, are governed by the same laws and regulations and formally enjoy the same rights as any other French citizen.

The three French Caribbean territories have clung to the dream of becoming communities of full-fledged citizens as an ultimate goal; however, they are managed on the basis of a political status chosen in 1946, well before the United Nations Special Committee on Decolonization took up the question of decolonization with a view to self-determination and sovereign autonomy for colonized people. When we re-examine the situation it becomes apparent that the political status currently enjoyed by the three territories is rooted in politically accepted conditions of economic dependence (Daniel 2001; McElroy and Sanborn 2005), a characteristic that they share with other non-independent territories of the Caribbean attached, in different ways, to other external powers (Daniel 2011).

The rather peculiar political status of the non-independent French territories is also shored up by a conception of citizenship and cultural identity that was forged by a specific juridical political tradition, in a historical relationship based on subjugation that was progressively modified to accommodate certain constraints that were rendered acceptable, thereby making these territories unique in historical terms.

Their current situation is therefore ambiguous, full of contradictions and marked by a long-lasting restrictive citizenship, despite claims made by the French of a transparent adherence to the principle of republican equality. This restrictive approach to citizenship has almost always underpinned the public policies implemented in these former French colonies in the Caribbean, and it explains the current state of local disenchantment with the implementation of departmentalization. This has given rise to a quest for new approaches to governing the relationship with Paris, simultaneously reconciling enhanced political autonomy and the achievement of full citizenship for local populations and their representatives.

This chapter is organized around three hypotheses. The first is that departmentalization rests on and reveals a series of contradictions and paradoxes that are rooted in the French Republic, which compromises and restricts the ability to exercise citizenship in the three French territories of the Caribbean. The second is that, far from having lessened the contradictions and paradoxes, departmentalization has actually intensified them, in effect complicating and rendering more explosive the struggle for equality and recognition. The third is that there has emerged in the current period a new policy, which attempts to reconcile equality of opportunity and recognition of diversity with republican universalism, in response to local demands that seem to be ambiguously formulated. Thus the ambiguous legacy of French republicanism in the French Caribbean territories can be discerned in the social limits to equality that inhere in the republican experiment as it exists in France and in the Caribbean colonies.

The Difficult Reconciliation of the Republican Project with the Colonial Context

The difficult experience of citizenship in the French territories of the Caribbean initially stems from contradictions that are inherent in the "colonial republic" (Bancel, Blanchard and Vergès 2003; see also Blanchard and Bancel, 2005). From the outset the "colonial republic" proclaims its assimilationist designs and intentions with respect to political-administrative institutions; however, it seems uninterested in any ambition to extend or broaden the field, scope and content of individual rights. Thus, during the national convention, François-Antoine de Boissy d'Anglas (the reporter of the Constitution of Year 3 of the Convention) stated: "The colonies will be subject to the same administrative norms as France. There can only be one good form of administration; and if we have found it for European lands, why should those of the Americas be disinherited" (Boissy d'Anglas 1795). In other words, according to Boissy d'Anglas's expectations, the slaves' preservation of their recently acquired liberty would necessitate the assimilation of the French Caribbean colonies in the Americas "by other parts of the Republic" (ibid.) and the abolition of administrative differences between France and its colonies. The republican spirit that arose since the convention clearly feeds on the dual principles of uniqueness and universality of the French administrative model; however, we already know that the universalist claims of the republic were not simply thwarted by the return to the colonial order that was reinstituted under Napoleon. In fact, those same universalist claims were subsequently reaffirmed with special attention to contingencies arising from the specific nature of the colonial experience. The tensions between frequently denounced centralization and repeatedly emphasized local particularities erupt in ways that transcended the application of supposedly universal norms, adaptation and flexibility in the functioning of institutions and, in certain cases, the elaboration of specific rules governing institutional organizations.

At the level of the individual citizen, the universalist claims of the state were designed to reduce and otherwise limit and control the scope and extent of struggles and collective resistance for the protection especially of local languages and cultures. The aim of the state was to create a collective loyalty and allegiance of citizens to the state, a project that immediately comes up against obstacles and resistance arising from the local cultural and political terrain. The first abolition of slavery at the outbreak of the French Revolution forced the revolutionaries to deal with local demands by colonists for autonomy and to combat their hostile opposition to the application of republican law – a development that found the revolutionaries imposing on colonies the "violation of principles and ideals which form the basis of modern sovereignty – liberty and equality, the notions of a people and of a nation" (Bancel, Blanchard and Vergès 2003, 30). The second abolition, in 1848, proclaimed French citizenship and the principle of universal suffrage for all those who were freed, as well as the representation of colonies in the National Assembly. However, it did not signify the end of the struggle by former slaves who were obviously anxious and eager to play an active role in political life. Indeed, it became very difficult to establish a new civic and legal framework, given the reluctance of the former masters to provide mayors with the necessary information for drawing up electoral lists or to authorize their former slaves, often still tied to plantation work, to travel to city hall to be registered (Périna 2005, 517).

Substantively, the civic and political component of citizenship that was taken for granted since 1848 has been the site of a struggle by former slaves who were forced to confront a restructured colonial order from which they had just ostensibly acquired juridical (that is to say, deontological) freedom. As Mikaëlla Périna points out, certainly,

> from a legal perspective, it was still extremely difficult to find instruments which would have allowed new citizens to exercise their full rights . . . [while] at the same time, the colonies kept their statutory particularities as well as their legislative system. In other words, the "universal" quality of being a member of the state, accorded to new citizens from the colonies, did not exclude the characteristic of being a member of a specific local group and, even more, the continued links to the local government, in particular, minimized the sense of belonging to the state. (2005, 521)

Therefore, while the general law was introduced as a mechanism for regulating social relationships following the abolition of slavery, the republic did not manage to abolish the forms of domination, or even erase the servile features remaining in the legal and social identity of more than half of the population (Cottias 2007). Moreover, the transition from the status of slave labourers to wage workers, small farmers or peasant producers was marked by a burning desire for autonomy (Chivallon 1998) and rights, which had remained elusive and inaccessible, because the proclamation of liberty did not lead to any diminution of inequalities in the racially polarized class societies.

This situation continued in the Second Republic, under which – despite institutional and political declarations of civic and political equality and deliberate proclamations that political rights and universal suffrage would be exercised and universally respected – deliberate measures of social control were introduced and implemented from the onset of the proclamation of the abolition of slavery. These measures confined former slaves, as "new citizens", within a very restrictive and narrow system of obligations at the hands of the former social-legal state. Thus, post-emancipation citizenship was shorn of its social content from the outset (Sainton 2003).

The situation did not improve under the Third Republic (or beyond, to a certain degree) when the endlessly reiterated proclamation of a civil equality was fundamentally and paradoxically compromised by the incontestable and undeniable exclusion of newly freed citizens from certain civil and political rights. The general law therefore remains patently deficient and defective in its application to the "new citizens", as can be seen in the very nature of the complex relationships between the republic and the three "old" colonies. The evidence is discernible via an examination of the treatment that has been meted out to the latter, who are forever reminded of their condition as "citizens entirely apart instead of full citizens", according to the famous formula attributed to Aimé Césaire in relation to other circumstances that highlight an undeniable historical continuity that extends beyond the various political-institutional iterations and incarnations of the republic (Larcher 2014).

In the midst of such difficult and harrowing conditions it is to be expected that the newly emancipated citizens, perpetually confronted with an alienating colonial system undergoing transformation, would turn to the state – perceived as a sort of miracle-worker – to provide and even protect. Yet it would be misleading to consider this desire for equality exclusively in terms of the acquisition of a collection of rights inherent in citizenship; it is also a broader wish for recognition. These two hopes are inextricably intertwined. Such is the meaning of the demand for assimilation which ended, almost a century after the abolition of slavery, in the departmentalization of 1946. In the face of the ever-delayed and protracted promise of assimilation, there emerged little more than the promise of a dreamed-of republic, largely incapable of guaranteeing either the acquisition and exercise of one's rights or provision for the enjoyment of full and complete recognition within the republic.

From a historical perspective, the departmentalization of 1946 represented the synthesis envisaged by Boissy d'Anglas of three questions. First, is it necessary to establish in the "former colonies" a system of administration – an assimilation of institutions – that is identical to that of the metropolis, regardless of the wishes and desires of the local population? Second, should an identical system of administration that is disconnected from locally expressed desires, based on what obtains and works in mainland France, be established in the "old" colonies? Third, should a system of values and legal standards reflecting the desires and expectations of the entire population in mainland France be established in those same colonies, in essence broadening the effective scope and reach of the motherland (that is, should there be an assimilation of individuals) (Sablé 1955)? Substantively, departmentalization was achieved in the name of a postulated cultural assimilation, upholding the illusion of complete acculturation (Daniel 1999) ostensibly produced by the long history of participation by these colonial entities in the national history of France. This notion falls within the framework of a historic development, condensing over a relatively short period the phases of citizenship as interpreted by sociologist Thomas Marshall (1977).[1]

While the second abolition of slavery in 1848 seems to have corresponded to the formal universalization of civil and political rights, the 1946 departmentalization inaugurated the process of acquisition of social rights. Again, it is necessary to add that the process was very gradual and punctuated by numerous battles for social equality (François-Lubin 1997; Michalon 2005). The reality, according to the experience of a long and restricted citizenship in the French Antilles and French Guiana, does not corroborate the linear vision of a definitive evolution as suggested by Marshall's approach.

Furthermore, it reveals that the figure of the citizen was always confronted by forms of concurrent identification with the official allegiance due largely to the deficiencies of the republic, which fail to uphold and live up to its own values and ideals, and the endlessly repeated, but always deferred, promise of assimilation.

The conjuncture of these different elements explains the importance of the struggle for equality and recognition within the departmental framework, as well as the disenchantment and the frustrations born of the establishment of the law that tend to encourage particularistic claims.

The Struggle for Citizenship, Equality and Recognition

Undeniably, the process of becoming a full-fledged French department coincided with a demand for allegiance to a community of people provided with the means and resources to exercise full citizenship. The former slaves, as newly enfranchised people, in the Antilles and French Guiana sought to expand and enrich emancipation, which they experienced as a state of incompleteness. They imagined that emancipation meant an escape from a colonial order that was based on perpetuating social and racial discrimination against them and their descendants. The reality, however, is that the slow pace of the extension of social rights – as witnessed in the reluctance of the central government to implement the principle of legislative identity and in the restrictive interpretation of texts (in particular article 73 of the constitution of 1958) – made the departmental framework an arena for incessant battles designed to compel the recalcitrant central authority to recognize and uphold the social composition and content of citizenship.

The persistence of an explosive economic and social situation, the perpetuation of inequality in practice, despite proclamations of equality in principle, and the more or less deliberate slowness of the extension of rights have contributed to disenchantment and the exacerbation of tensions. The general malaise associated with this situation contributed to tensions that sometimes lead to major crises, the best known of which broke out in December 1959 in Martinique and in May 1967 in Guadeloupe. The Martinique and Guadeloupe crises were part of larger centrifugal tendencies that developed in overseas departments, which not only contested their status but also heightened their demands for autonomy within the context of the worldwide processes of decolonization (Dumont 2010). Departmentalization is thus, to a certain extent, experienced as hope betrayed, bearing in mind that social equality was proclaimed in 1996, fifty years after the law of 19 March 1946 that transformed the four former colonies into overseas departments.

The contradictions arising from departmentalization led to the rise and assertiveness of the autonomist movement in the 1960s and 1970s in the Antilles and in French Guiana. This movement, which argues for political autonomy and a model of development more geared and sympathetic to local particularities, reached its peak with the Convention for Autonomy (Convention pour l'autonomie) of Morne Rouge.[2] The autonomist movement clearly reflects a growing dissatisfaction with the conditions of the implementation of departmentalization; however, it has not managed to make headway at the polls, due to an inherent paradox associated with the republican model itself:

> [T]he gap between the real and the ideal, the Republic contradicted by its own actions had never, to date, been an obstacle to its force of uniting, producing and reproducing a common political culture rooted in its founding moments and driven toward the future. From the Marianne symbol to the social elements, the path was always possible. The defects of the real Republic could . . . be traced back to its own incompleteness. (Bertho 2005, 15–16)

For all practical purposes, the social mobilization of the autonomist movement in conjunction with the broader struggle for equal rights opportunistically exploited the gap between the ideal world proclaimed by departmentalization and the actual experience and has contributed to a certain extent to reinforcing citizens' attachment to the republican model, the cruel deficiencies of which they continue to endure.

The political attachment to the local populations to the republican model as expressed in departmentalization can hardly be explained as accommodation on purely instrumental grounds defined in terms of an alienated or false colonial consciousness. The struggle for social equality is indeed part of the larger struggle for the recognition of our universal humanity, considering that a contradictory relationship connects the two notions, depending on the prevailing circumstances within a given historical context and considering that republicanism has consistently set limits to social equality. This observation is implicit in Aimé Césaire's framework in which he establishes that the conquest of the social equality said to inhere in citizenship could be achieved solely by claiming cultural specificity (see Suvélor 1983); it was later confirmed through the unambiguous rejection of cultural assimilation. Similarly, the social struggles which punctuated the post-abolition period and permeated the lives of all West Indian societies during the twentieth century reveal, according to classical mechanisms highlighted by historians, that the social experience of injustice and the struggle for equality largely fed the persistent claims expressed in and through collective representations of "honour", "respect" and "dignity" (Thompson 1988).

The same claims, beyond strong ethnic polarization and staging of identities forged by various contradictorily situated dominant and dominated groups within the characteristically non-egalitarian colonial order, are also directed at the state: by emphasizing universal rights, they also reaffirm rallying behind the republican banner as well as appealing against the degrading status experienced by the social and ethnic classes through their inheritance from colonialism (Daniel 2000). As suggested by Axel Honneth (2003), a relationship of equivalence is hence established between social injustice and institutional procedures, the latter having been deemed inadequate and inappropriate for meeting the demands of social recognition to resolve problems stemming from social injustice. Beyond institutional reforms and the search for new modes of governance, this tendency also can be seen through the demands made via the republican framework, for specific rights for citizens of overseas communities and, correlatively, the implementation of rather ambiguous public policies, geared to the promotion of diversity.

An Ambiguous Policy: Equality of Opportunity and Promotion of Diversity versus Republican Universalism

For a long time the theme of diversity was absent from the toolbox of French public policies and from the discourses of decision makers. In the 1990s, in the face of the crisis of legitimacy and acknowledgement of the loss of impetus in assimilating immigrant populations, the French model introduced diversity first in the field of human resources, through the recognition and promotion of "differences" from a threefold social, cultural and ethnic perspective (Yazid and Méhaignerie 2004). Progressively established as a legitimate subject for informing public policy targeting populations that are victims of discrimination and demonstrating the will to assume responsibility for the representation of minorities (Masclet 2012; Sénac 2012), the rhetoric and discourse of diversity now pervade political debate throughout France, including the overseas territories. In the latter case, this evolution assumes two forms. On one hand, this paradigm shift is revealed in the ritual affirmation of the extraordinary diversity and the great cultural wealth possessed by humanity that inhabits the overseas territories, such that we now speak of "overseas areas" in the plural. On the other, it is also blossoming in the institutional and statutory reforms implemented overseas that are spurred by the re-emergence, since the 1990s, of the critique of the linear French model of local government and of the uniform application of legal systems throughout the national territory, without respect to any distinctive local particularities. Substantively, this is a discourse that is echoed and amplified in the French Caribbean territories where the possibilities of adaptation or of special dispensation have long been judged insufficient or inefficient, with respect to national law. This is especially the case because identity claims are superimposed on institutional demands, which are difficult to reconcile with the constitution or, more precisely, with the largely restrictive jurisprudence of the Constitutional Council. In general, French overseas territorial communities and especially the French Caribbean territories are thus forced to re-evaluate their relationships with an external and far-removed centre, which is motivated by standardization and is sometimes blind to local particularities and imperatives.

Paris's strategy has been to deepen the integration of local autonomous bodies into the unitary state, hoping thereby to defuse the tensions that are associated with a republican model that confronts the weakening of its normative, abstract (deontological) and universal principles, which explains why it stressed granting, acknowledging and taking into consideration institutional diversity as the only way to guarantee the existence of the system in the medium term. Far from constituting a threat to unity, diversity is then represented as a condition of its preservation, which explains the introduction of institutional reforms in the French Caribbean since 2003, and the paradigm of diversity that increasingly conditions the symbolic and material approach to public policies in the struggle against discrimination. More specifically, these policies target citizens from "overseas areas", whether they live overseas or on metropolitan soil, where they encounter twin discrimination mostly in the areas of housing and employment.

It is worth remembering that official recognition of discriminatory practices on French soil has been slow in coming. Indeed, the persistence of discrimination seems to be a defeat for a model whose capacity to assimilate victims of discrimination is often vaunted by the state, which leaves the problem unresolved by approaching the issues on an individual case-by-case basis at the expense of exchanges with established communities to rectify the problem. In addition, assimilation in overseas territories yields mitigated outcomes because the policies that are implemented are inadequate to eliminate injustices, reduce persistent inequalities or challenge and confront the discriminatory attitudes that immigrants encounter in mainland France. In effect, the so-called assimilationist policies, long considered by France to be the solution to the protracted problems that immigrants encounter, prove illusory for those who have relied on them and approached them with high expectations. In fact, the same assimilationist policies collide with a sort of obdurate otherness, tending to perpetuate an unequal social order, which, ultimately, is what the population concerned experiences every day, in effect living with the social limits to equality, which the liberal republican state imposes on certain social strata and other forces that are deemed racially different or other.

The strategic struggle against discrimination, adopted in the 1980s as an initial means of claiming the right to be different, was combined with the policy of equality of treatment. Nonetheless, since 2004, a subtle paradigm shift took place. A policy of "diversity" through the intervention of the consensual notion of "equality of opportunity" has replaced the policy of equal treatment, which underscores the assimilation approach and the fight against discrimination (Noël 2006, 5). Now, in the name of a modern conception of citizenship that takes into account not only inequalities and equity, diversity is supposed to be part of a policy encouraging equality of opportunity. According to this liberal move, it does not matter that discrimination and inequality prevail; rather, what matters is that deontological equal opportunity is said to level the unequal playing field – which is exactly what characterizes the American model with its durable substantive inequality. Largely, a persistent problem with liberalism is that it reduces complex social relations between humans to technical relations between things. In this context individual rights, individual autonomy and other forms assumed by the alienated social subject assume primacy, with the burden routinely put on the victim to show due cause: the underlying notion is that the sum of the parts (individuals) always seems greater than the whole (society). In other words, the victims who happen to be racialized and deemed second-class citizens are always at a disadvantage when having to seek redress for legitimate grievances. This signals that rights in the liberal schema are mainly deontological – which means they are hardly demandable.

The French model of diversity or affirmative action seduced many actors and decision makers, including in the overseas departments and especially in the Antilles and French Guiana. It was principally put forward by then-president Sarkozy who, in the name of diversity, implemented it in January 2010 for Martinique and French Guiana through statutory reform, former president Chirac having cleared the way in 2003 through a constitutional revision, which specified the institutional differentiation of the overseas territories that provided for the transformation of Saint-Martin and Saint-Barthélemy into juridical-institutional entities distinct from Guadeloupe. After organized consultation with their populations on 10 and 24 January 2010, French Guiana and Martinique (unlike Guadeloupe and Réunion, both of which avoided the need for such a procedure by choosing to remain within a framework governed by ordinary law) opted to create a single authority as a substitute for the department and for the region beginning in 2015. Above all, beyond territorial reforms and with attention to the particular condition of the original inhabitants of the overseas territories absorbed by France, Sarkozy appointed a cross-ministerial delegate with responsibility for equality of opportunity for overseas French citizens. The delegate's mission is to "prevent specific difficulties that overseas French citizens encounter in metropolitan France and to facilitate their relations with their native land."[3] In addition, at the cross-ministerial council meeting of 6 November 2009, which was devoted to matters pertaining to and affecting the overseas territories, Sarkozy symbolically promoted Marie-Luce Penchard, a native-born Guadeloupean, to full ministerial rank as minister of overseas territories.

More recently, President François Hollande and his prime minister also stressed diversity at the time they were forming a new government, in 2012. Representatives of "visible minorities" symbolizing and representing this diversity have significant representation with four immigrant members, including three from Guadeloupe and French Guiana, in the socialist government of Jean-Marc Ayrault. In effect, and in a configuration never before seen in French history, three ministers (including two women) from the French territories of the Caribbean, are now members of the French government.

Similarly, former president Sarkozy was proud of having initiated the promotion of diversity in the public service operating in overseas territories,[4] thus responding to local officials' demand to favour local employees in appointment and promotion. It is true that resolutions numbers 5 and 6 adopted by the Congress of Departmental and Regional Elected Officials of Martinique (Congrès des élus départementaux et régionaux de la Martinique) on 18 June 2009 include two series of measures which are clearly oriented in the same direction. One makes provisions for the local authorities of Martinique to share with the state "competence in the area of training, recruitment and assignment of teaching personnel coming from the state public service" (Congrès des élus 2009a). The other states that "the local authorities of Martinique may take measures favoring access to salaried positions in the private sector to benefit individuals demonstrating a sufficient period of residence in Martinique or those demonstrating that they have been married to, or have been cohabiting or in a civil union with, a Martiniquan for a sufficient period" and that, "for those with equal merit, such measures be applied under the same conditions for access to positions in the public service of the Community of Martinique and its communes" (Congrès des élus 2009b).

This type of demand is indicative of the malaise that persists in the French territories of the Caribbean. It also characterizes the different nationalist parties that have not abandoned their goal of sovereignty and differentiates among the local citizens, drawing distinctions between "native-born citizens" and "non–native born citizens". This strategy serves principally as a foundation stone and reference point for dealing with competition for access to limited resources. Directed in particular against the category of "metropolitans" – white citizens from mainland France – it is part of a symbolic struggle that seeks to overturn the enduring relationship of domination that presents a constant obstacle to an endlessly deferred emancipation and springs from a somewhat ambivalent nationalist ideology, iterations of which have already been tried in other social-historical contexts. This nationalist ideology is founded on a twofold rejection – on the one hand, the rejection of the domineering intruder who must be surpassed according to his own criteria and, on the other, the rejection of ancestral ways of doing things, which are considered obstacles to progress even as they are still cherished as markers of identity (Berlin 1990).

In the context of nationalist ideology as expressed in the Antilles and French Guiana we find all the ambiguous positions around the perpetually debated issue of slavery – abhorred and rejected, yet simultaneously considered by some as the core marker of the identity of the people of the Antilles and French Guiana, that supposedly miraculously shapes their character and behaviour – their ways of being and thinking as well as their intersubjectivity – in contemporary society. Such a logic and strategy, however, serves as support for the demand (if not for the independence mostly rejected by the local populations) for specific and preferential treatment compatible with the republican framework – in other words, for locally rooted citizenship, which partially legitimizes the discourse of diversity. Thus, it confirms that the frame of reference of diversity is increasingly at the centre of public action in metropolitan France as well as in the former colonies.

Conclusion

Is the shift to diversity as the frame of reference such that it is likely to dissipate the feeling, strongly anchored in the French territories of the Caribbean, of a citizenship which has not yet been fully achieved? When examined more closely, even if the stress on diversity provides for what appears to be a less ambiguous relation between the populations of these territories and socially disadvantaged categories, nothing seems less certain, in light of the following supporting considerations. The policies promoting diversity approximate little more than symbolic actions, rather than being designed to initiate significant and sustainable change. They draw public attention to the minorities facing discriminatory practices and are also a reminder of the deficiencies of the republic in the former colonies. They are far from sufficient to solve the problems of inequality, which is an integral part of the former colonies' experience. In addition, diversity policies fail to address the territorial imbalances which, when compared with mainland France, are precisely what reinforces the sense of second-class citizenship.

Moreover, a number of recent studies emphasize the scale of these persistent and enduring imbalances and remind us of the degree to which individuals from the overseas territories and their descendants have confronted economic, social and civic obstacles to their integration, especially as victims of discrimination in the area of employment (Temporal, Marie and Bernard 2011; Mazuy, Prioux and Barbieri, 2011; Breton et al. 2009) . When all is said and done, notwithstanding the special demands made by elected officials more than by the populations at large, the citizens of the French territories of the Caribbean, following the model of their counterparts in Réunion, remain largely committed to the principle of republican equality.

In other words, the "social question" remains at the core of citizen concerns. Significantly, the social movements in February and March 2009 in Guadeloupe and Martinique bear witness to a history that seems circular, because it was not completely settled with regard to the question of slavery and the persistence of inherited inequalities. This situation has been the subject of many debates that have saturated the public spaces for a number of years, to the point of being appropriated by metropolitan public authorities with the symbolic adoption in 1998 of the law making slavery a crime against humanity. Regardless of the novelty, rarity and intensity of their form, these movements remain largely shaped by the history of these territories (Daniel 2009; Larcher 2009). Certainly, they signal the return of the social question, if somewhat modified[5] and even a bit obscured during recent years by exacerbated identity claims that add to the mix of locally expressed demands (Daniel 2009).

At the same time, however, the movements draw a contrast between the poverty among blacks and the discriminatory treatment they have historically endured in the eyes of the principles of the republic, in contrast with the pre-eminence of whites from the local bourgeoisie. This contrast is sometimes drawn at the risk of neglecting the complexity of the societies of the Antilles and French Guiana when approached from the threefold perspective of the development model at work, the complex social structure and the social hierarchies. This has resulted in a severe ethnic polarization, exacerbated by the documentary bearing the significant title *Les derniers maîtres de la Martinique* (*The Last Masters of Martinique*), produced by the French journalist Romain Bolzinger and broadcast on 30 January 2009 on French television. This polarization was also intensified by the reactivation of plans allowing socially disadvantaged groups to mobilize and acquire a strong identity, permitting them to acquire a voice in the public arena and by the manipulation of historic symbols, also with a great mobilizing potential, in societies that still bear the scars of the period of slavery.

Notes

1. Marshall identifies three elements in the acquisition of citizenship, from "civil rights in the eighteenth century, political in the nineteenth, and social in the twentieth" (1977).
2. This convention was held at Morne Rouge, Martinique, 16–18 August 1971. It brought together the Guadeloupean General Confederation of Workers (Confédération générale des travailleurs guadeloupéens), the Women's Union of Guadeloupe (l'Union des femmes de la Guadeloupe), the Guadeloupean Communist Party (Parti communiste guadeloupéen), the Martiniquan Communist Party (Parti communiste martiniquais), the Martiniquan General Workers' Confederation (Confédération générale des travailleurs martiniquais), the Friends of Elected Officials in the South of Martinique (l'Amicale des élus du sud de la Martinique) and a few organizations coming from Réunion, including the Communist Party (Parti communiste réunionnais).
3. See Decree no. 2007–1062 (2007), establishing an interministerial delegate for equality of opportunity for French citizens living overseas.
4. Some measures recommended in the context of the cross-ministerial council that met at the Elysée on 6 November 2009 were as follows: "The objective is to favour, in respect of republican principles, the assignment of overseas citizens to their department and to favour promotions on the spot, in softening certain statutory measures. Furthermore, some measures have been taken to encourage the emergence of overseas managers in French state services, through a policy of tracking profiles and establishing a pool [of managers]. For the nominations of Heads of Service, the counter-signature of the

minister in charge of the overseas territories will now be required" (Meeting of Cross-Ministerial Council, 2009).

5. This is a formula derived from the title of a work by Robert Castel (1995).

References

Bancel, Nicolas, Pascal Blanchard and Françoise Vergès. 2003. *La république coloniale: Essai sur une utopie*. Paris: Albin Michel.

Bayart, Jean-François. 2010. *Les études postcoloniales: Un carnaval académique*. Paris: Karthala.

Berlin, Isaiah. 1990. "The Bent Twig". In *The Crooked Timber of Humanity: Chapters in the History of Ideas*, edited by Henry Hardy, 238–62. London: John Murray.

Bertho, Alain. 2005. "Malaise dans la république". *Mouvements* (38): 14–18.

Blanchard, Pascal, and Nicolas Bancel. 2005. "La fondation du républicanisme colonial: Retour sur une généalogie politique". *Mouvements* (38): 26–33.

Boissy d'Anglas, François-Antoine de. 1795. "Rapport et projet d'articles constitutionnels relatifs aux colonies", presented by Boissy d'Anglas to the Convention Nationale, meeting of the 17 Thermidor, Year III. 22 August.

Breton, Didier, Stéphanie Condon, Claude-Valentin Marie and Franck Temporal. 2009. "Les départements d'outre-mer face aux défis du vieillissement démographique et des migrations". *Population et sociétés* (460): 2–4.

Castel, Robert. 1995. *Les métamorphoses de la question sociale: Une chronique du salariat*. Paris: Fayard.

Chivallon, Christine. 1998. *Éspace et identité à la Martinique: Paysannerie des mornes et reconquête collective (1840–1960)*. Paris: CNRS.

Congrès des élus départementaux et régionaux de la Martinique. 2009a. *Resolution no. 5*. 18 juin. Conseil général, Fort-de-France.

———. 2009b. *Resolution no. 6*. 18 juin. Conseil général, Fort-de-France.

Cooper, Frederick. 2005. *Colonialism in Question: Theory, Knowledge, History*. Berkeley and Los Angeles: University of California Press.

Cottias, Myriam. 2007. "Esclavage, assimilation et dépendance". *Les cahiers du Centre de recherches historiques* 40: 143–61.

Daniel, Justin. 1999. "Identidad cultural e identidad política en Martinica y Puerto Rico: Mitos y realidades". *Revista de ciencias sociales* (7): 33–65.

———. 2000. "Conflits sociaux et construction identitaire à la Martinique". In *Au visiteur lumineux: Des îles créoles aux sociétés plurielles (Mélanges offerts à Jean Benoist)*, edited by Jean Bernabé, Jean-Luc Bonniol, Raphaël Confiant and Gerry L'Etang, 85–102. Petit-Bourg: Ibis Rouge Editions/Presses Universitaires Créoles.

———. 2001. "The Construction of Dependency: Economy and Politics in the French Antilles". In *Islands at the Crossroads: Politics in the Non-Independent Caribbean*, edited by Aarón Gamaliel Ramos and Ángel Israel Rivera Ortiz, 61–79. Kingston: Ian Randle.

———. 2009. "La crise sociale aux Antilles françaises". *EchoGéo*. 30 March. http://echogeo.revues.org/index11117.html.

———. 2011"Regards croisés sur les réformes institutionnelles dans les départements français d'Amérique et les territoires non-indépendants de la caraïbe". In *Les outre-mer à l'épreuve du changement: Réalités et perspectives des réformes territoriales*, edited by Justin Daniel, 31–64. Paris: L'Harmattan.

Decree no. 2007-1062 de 5 juillet 2007. *Journal officiel de la République française*, 6 juillet 2007.

Dumont, Jacques. 2010. *L'Amère patrie: Histoire des Antilles françaises au 20e siècle*. Paris: Fayard.

François-Lubin, Bertrand. 1997. "Les méandres de la politique sociale outre-mer". In *1946–1996: Cinquante ans de départementalisation outre mer*, edited by Fred Constant et Justin Daniel, 73–95. Paris: L'Harmattan.

Honneth, Axel. 2003. "La reconnaissance: Une piste pour la théorie sociale contemporaine". In *Identités et démocratie. Diversité culturelle et mondialisation: Repenser la démocratie. Rencontres internationales de Rennes*, edited by Ronan Le Coadic and Christian Demeuré-Vallée, 205–21. Rennes: Presses universitaires de Rennes.

Larcher, Silyane. 2009. "Les Antilles françaises ou les vestiges de l'empire? Les aléas d'une citoyenneté sociale outre-mers". *La Vie Des Idées*. 20 février. http://www.laviedesidees.fr/Les-Antilles-francaises-ou-les.html.

———. 2014. *L'Autre citoyen*. Paris: Armand Colin.

Marshall, Thomas H. 1977. *Class, Citizenship, and Social Development: Essays*. Chicago: University of Chicago Press.

Masclet, Olivier. 2012. *Sociologie de la diversité et des discriminations*. Paris: Armand Colin.

McElroy, Jerome L., and Katherine Sanborn. 2005. "The Propensity for Dependence in Small Caribbean and Pacific Islands". *Bank of Valetta Review* (31): 1–16.

Mazuy, Magali, France Prioux and Magali Barbieri. 2011. "L'évolution démographique récente en France: Quelques différences entre les départements d'outre-mer et la France métropolitaine". *Population-F* 66 (3–4): 503–54

Meeting of Cross-Ministerial Council of Overseas Territories. 2009. Presidency of the French Republic. 6 November.

Michalon, Thierry. 2005. "Les départements français d'Amérique entre rêve caraïbe et attaches européennes". In *Géopolitique, intégration régionale, enjeux économiques*, vol. 2, 149–65, of *Le monde caraïbe: défis et dynamiques*, edited by Christian Lera. 2 vols. Pessac: Maison des Sciences de l'Homme d'Aquitaine.

Noël, Olivier. 2006. "Entre le modèle républicain de l'intégration et le modèle libéral de promotion de la diversité: La lutte contre les discriminations ethniques et raciales n'aura-t-elle été qu'une parenthèse dans la politique publique en France?" Paper presented at CASADIS, Confédération Générale du Travail, Montreuil, 8 November.

Périna, Mikaëlla. 2005. "Construire une identité politique à partir des vestiges de l'esclavage? Les départements français d'Amérique entre héritage et choix". In *L'Esclavage, la colonisation, et après . . .*, edited by Patrick Weil and Stéphane Dufoix, 509–31. Paris: PUF.

Sablé, Victor. 1955. *La transformation des isles d'Amérique en départements français*. Paris: Éditions Larose.

Sainton, Jean-Pierre. 2003. "Modalités du passage de l'esclavage à la citoyenneté aux Antilles françaises sous la Seconde République (1848–1850)". *Société française d'histoire d'outre-mer* 90 (36): 338–39.

Sénac, Régine. 2012. *L'Invention de la diversité*. Paris: PUF.

Suvélor, Roland. 1983. "Éléments historiques pour une approche socio-culturelle". *Les temps modernes* 39 (441–42): 2174–208.

Temporal, Franck, Claude-Valentin Marie and Stéphane Bernard. 2011. "Insertion professionnelle des jeunes ultramarins: DOM ou métropole?" *Population-F* 66 (3–4): 555–600.

Thompson, Edward Palmer. 1988. *La formation de la classe ouvrière anglaise*. Paris: Seuil.

Yazid, Sabeg, and Laurence Méhaignerie. 2004. *Les oubliés de l'égalité des chances*. Paris: Institut Montaigne.

8 Immigration, National Belonging and the Dilemma of Self-Determination in the Cayman Islands

SEAN GILL

> [Giving Jamaicans Cayman status is] like a blank cheque . . . They will bring an unknown number of children and their spouses over with them and that's the really scary part . . . What you [will] have is almost another country within a country . . . This is [*sic*] the facts of life . . . If we are going to have an open immigration policy, then eventually we are going to have a welfare state. (David Ritch, chairman of Work Permit Board of the Cayman Islands, quoted in Markoff 2006a)

During the latter half of the twentieth century, the tiny UK colony of the Cayman Islands experienced a level of economic growth unparalleled in the history of the Western Hemisphere. Between the 1960s and 1990s, with the establishment of a flourishing financial service and tourism industry, its gross national product increased a thousandfold, while its population multiplied five times (Craton 2003, 363). Access to migrant labour has been critical for the Cayman Islands' economic and demographic growth. Since 1995 foreigners holding work permits have typically composed more than 50 per cent of its workforce (ESO 2007). Workers from Jamaica have historically constituted a dramatic majority of these migrants. Under the looming threat of over ten thousand Jamaicans eventually becoming eligible for permanent residence and Caymanian status, in 2003 the Caymanian state passed a new immigration law, which for the first time gave clear legal grounding to the eviction of migrant workers from rights or access to political and economic belonging. In this chapter I examine discourses on belonging constructed and circulated through historical scholarship, the media and the law in the post-2003 period. More specifically, I analyse the multiple modes of regulation through which migrants – on the basis of race, class and nationality – are systematically marked for exclusion from rights to belonging in Caymanian society. I conclude the chapter with brief observations on the salience of the Cayman Islands' colonial relationship with the United Kingdom in interpreting the severity of its immigration regulations.

The Cayman Islands in the Caribbean Context

Much scholarly work has recently been done to map the material and discursive dimensions of migration, nationalisms and nation states in the Caribbean and its diaspora. This work responds to a series of historical assumptions, which generally hold true for the majority of Caribbean nations: (1) the existence of anti-colonial nationalist movements ultimately culminating in the end of direct political rule by European colonial powers by the 1960s and 1970s; (2) the experience of substantial, permanent immigration to North America and Europe from the 1950s onwards and (3) the contradictory socio-economic impact of the increasing economic dependency of the newly independent states on the United States and Europe, following the end of colonialism and continuing through to contemporary times. In the context of these premises, analyses of Caribbean nationalisms and nation states are generally framed by two dominant concerns: first, the political, cultural and socio-economic consequences resulting from the failure of anti- and postcolonial nationalist thought to break with the foundational assumptions about "modernity" and "progress" upon which colonial domination was based and, second, the issues surrounding Caribbean diasporas, the emergence of transnational cultural identities and their impacts on discursive constructions of "the nation". However, there are a number of Caribbean countries, such as the Cayman Islands, the historical dynamics of which diverge substantially from the premises identified above regarding nationalisms and the nation state.

The key divergences of the Caymanian context in particular relate to its continuing existence as a British colony without a history of anti-colonial struggle, as well as the radically different socio-economic dynamics that have shaped its historical trajectory. While the majority of the Caribbean region began to experience increasing levels of emigration starting in the period following the transition to formal independence – a consequence of programmes of "economic development" and post-1970 structural adjustment – the Cayman Islands began to experience an opposite trend: a booming territorial economy and a massive influx of migrants from all over the world. Commonalities can thus be seen between the Cayman Islands and other British Overseas Territories in the Caribbean, most predominantly in the cases of Bermuda, the British Virgin Islands, Turks and Caicos Islands, and Anguilla. However, the social science literature on migration, belonging and nationalism in these countries remains quite limited.[1] Studies of Bermuda, Turks and Caicos, and Anguilla in particular are either simply non-existent or remain unaccounted for in the major social science (sociological, political science and anthropological) databases.[2] The British Virgin Islands have received the greatest scholarly attention (Oakes 1992; Maurer 1995, 1997, 2000). Bill Maurer's insightful study, *Recharting the Caribbean* (1997), is the most comprehensive contribution to the study of these dynamics in the British Virgin Islands. Colleen Ballerino Cohen (1998, 2010) has also written on the British Virgin Islands, focusing on the articulation of discourses of belonging through cultural and artistic production and tourism. At the time this chapter was written, the Cayman Islands had been addressed in three previous publications that focus on issues of migration and nationalism (Amit-Talai 1997, 2001; Gill 2013). In what follows, I hope to offer an analytical contribution to closing the gap in scholarship on the dynamics of migration, belonging and nationalism in the British Overseas Territories of the Caribbean, and I hope that it will spark further discussion, debate and analysis of these under-studied islands.

Drawing on Maurer's work, with support from Amit-Talai's (1997) analysis of the Caymanian nation-building efforts of the 1990s, Eric Hobsbawm (2007) and Sunera Thobani (2007), I analyse discourses surrounding employment, residency and belonging from a number of sites, including the sole comprehensive history of the Cayman Islands, Michael Craton's 1993 *Founded upon the Seas*; statements from public officials in the *Cayman Compass* in 2006 and 2010;[3] post-2003 Caymanian immigration law; the Bill of Rights, Freedoms and Responsibilities contained in the 2009 Constitution of the Cayman Islands and local census information between 1995 and 2008.

Historicizing the Caymanian Nation: Craton's *Founded upon the Seas*

In *Recharting the Caribbean*, Maurer (1997) points to the crucial role of historical representation in the consolidation and legitimization of the relations of power that underpin the nationalist project in the British Virgin Islands. He identifies the "transition narrative" as a central component in British Virgin Islanders' constructions of their nation's history and their assessments of the place of immigrants within it. Essential to such narratives is the deployment of conceptions of continuity and change in a relationship of perpetual tension, both to each other and to nature. Maurer suggests that the central nexus of the transition narrative is that between "nature" and "choice", through which themes of "hierarchy and equality, inclusiveness and exclusiveness" (1997, 28) become expressed. Transition narratives are thus "reiterative technologies" which "presuppose as they produce the stable, real objects that are their subjects" (28): namely, "nature" and its simultaneous construction as both the ground of human choice and its constraining condition. In this section I employ Maurer's concept of the transition narrative in a reading of Craton's 2003 *Founded upon the Seas*. I provide a critical overview of Craton's account of the pre-1960 history of settlement and immigration in the Cayman Islands and trace his account of the discourse of nationhood to legitimate the post-1960 restriction of social, political and economic rights to those perceived and treated as not-national subjects.

The elements of Craton's narrative relevant for this inquiry are structured around three central themes of Caymanian identity, said to originate between the time of initial colonization of the Cayman Islands by European settlers, including their enslavement there of Africans, around 1700, and the mid-twentieth-century transformation of the islands. The first theme is the perseverance of Caymanians under both internal and external conditions of adversity through the simple values of a "rugged self-reliance" (Craton 2003, 124), premised on hard work, dedication and ingenuity. In a place where the land demanded strenuous labour to yield just the bare necessities of life, the historical experience of privation nurtured the "distinct character" of Caymanians and a prevailing "hope for an easier way of life" (205). All but ignored by the colonial administration for the majority of their history, Caymanians learned to take the initiative and independently explore the outside world in their quest for self-improvement. Nature here, as suggested by Maurer in the case of the British Virgin Islands, is portrayed as both "the enemy" and "the blessing" (1997, 23); it is the constraining condition, which at the same time enables the emergence of an ethic of self-reliance, with which natural constraints can in turn be attenuated or overcome.

The beginning of the twentieth century marked the onset of a particularly important episode in the history of Caymanian "self-reliance". During this period, in response to changing global conditions associated with "improvements in sea communications, World War One, and the worldwide boom in the early 1920s" (Craton 2003, 254), exceptionally large numbers of Caymanians travelled to Latin America and the United States, motivated by economic reasons. Craton estimates that between 1891 and 1931 (at which times the resident population totaled 4,322 and 5,930 respectively) around 3,500 Caymanians migrated in search of better opportunities elsewhere, two-thirds of whom likely headed to the United States (258, 259). With the exception of a brief period of stagnation in the 1930s, this trend continued with the employment of large numbers of Caymanians in the maritime industries both during and after World War II. This Caymanian diaspora would come to play a role of substantial historical significance: the broadened political, economic and intellectual experience of its members, in conjunction with their remittances-turned-capital, laid the cultural and economic foundation for the coming transformation of the Cayman Islands through the introduction of the tourist and financial services industries between the 1950s and 1970s (290, 301–2).

The second theme relates to the continuity of a unique Caymanian identity, even in the context of mass migration and the socio-economic and demographic upheavals of the mid to latter twentieth century. Craton argues that regardless of how far away they travelled or how long they were gone, the Caymanian migrants of the twentieth century resolutely retained both their identity and the conviction that the Cayman Islands was "their true home and heartland" (2003, 259–60). Furthermore, in a context where, as the twenty-first century approached, "the frenetic pace of modernisation, the pressure of external influences, and materialism threatened to submerge traditional values and Cayman's distinctive culture" (7), Caymanians acknowledged the need to both recognize and preserve their distinct culture. In the decade leading up to the year 2000 several institutions – many of them funded and directly run by the government – arose with the express intention to "preserve, promote and interpret Caymanian 'heritage' and 'identity'" (Amit-Talai 1997, 53; see also Craton 2003, 410).

The third theme concerns the willingness of Caymanians to come together across lines of race and class. Craton claims the degree of social cohesion apparent throughout Caymanian history to be unique in the wider Caribbean context. While small cotton plantations existed in the pre-emancipation period, until the 1950s the economy of the Cayman Islands remained predominantly based in small-scale farming, fishing, turtle hunting, boat building and seafaring. The absence of plantation slavery and its brutal conditions of labour for enslaved blacks, the presence of a much larger white population than has been typical in the Caribbean (approximately 50 per cent) and the simple material conditions shared by most, regardless of race, are all cited as factors in the formation of social divisions "much more subtle, and far less discordant" in comparison to "anywhere else in the British Caribbean" (Craton 2003, 3). This is a trend which continued in the post-emancipation period: rebellions and protests over political or socio-economic issues (for example, colonial oppression or discrimination on the basis of gender, race or class) have simply never been a significant part of the Caymanian sociocultural milieu. Furthermore, to the present day, Caymanians can take "well-deserved pride" in both the "long-standing tradition" among the wealthy of community support (377), and the perpetually expanding efforts of the government to meet community needs through the provision of social services.[4] In sum, Caymanian identity and society, from its inception onwards, is constructed in *Founded upon the Seas* as ruggedly self-reliant, hard-working and egalitarian.

Amit-Talai's observations from 1997 indicate a historical continuity between Craton's narrative and those that precede it. In her article "In Pursuit of Authenticity: Globalization and Nation Building in the Cayman Islands", Amit-Talai also identifies the first two of the above themes as operating in the historical chronicles produced by the Caymanian cultural industry in the 1990s. In both cases, "[t]he claims to authenticity of the national identity being constructed . . . derive from largely abandoned lifestyles that predate the economic development of the last 25 years" (Amit-Talai 1997, 59). Furthermore, while central significance is accorded to "the foreign maritime adventures" of bygone generations of Caymanian men, "the arrival and contributions of thousands of migrants over the last 25 years are almost always excluded" (59). The transition narratives encountered in both Craton's text and those analysed by Amit-Talai are thus concerned with the construction of a heritage and identity only for those said to possess long-standing ancestral connections to a long-dead way of life. In addition, imagining a Caymanian past characterized by the three themes detailed above – and attributing exclusive "cultural ownership" (59) of it to "authentic" Caymanians – enables Craton to construct what Sunera Thobani has, in relation to the Canadian context, referred to as a "myth of benign national origins and responsible citizenship" (2007, 87).[5] Echoing Amit-Talai, Thobani cautions that such myths are often deployed to render invisible the vital contributions of "foreign" workers to the development of the economy. This is typically achieved through the ideological representation of such workers as possessed of iniquitous motives to corrupt and exploit the nation. Craton's narrative is a clear example of such a myth.

In chapter 15, entitled "The Engineered Miracle: Economic Development, 1950–2000", Craton summarizes the creative process by which the foundations of the modern Caymanian economy – tourism and banking – were laid:[6]

> On one side of the table were American, Canadian, and British entrepreneurs eager for profitable investment; on the other, British officials wishing to place the Cayman Islands on a sound economic footing. In between, and most significant for the future of the islands, were Caymanians themselves. Among the most dynamic and astute were retired sea captains, returned migrants, and Cayman Brackers. But Caymanians as a whole were willing to embark on a new kind of voyage towards what promised to be a strong economic future. They sought advice, attracted capital, and welcomed reputable people seeking residence. At the same time, they guarded the right to Caymanian citizenship, strove to exclude undesirable elements, and made sure that Caymanians controlled the process of change and shared in the ultimate rewards. (2003, 331–32)

The use of language here is of particular salience. Agency, which would be seen as "foreign", is attributed only to "American, Canadian and British entrepreneurs" and "British officials", while the local agency that is given centre stage is that of the wealthiest of Caymanians. With the blankly homogenizing category of "Caymanians as a whole" Craton invokes a sense of national unity that transcends the class distinctions he indirectly hints at and positions the unified nation at the helm of the "new voyage" towards economic prosperity.

However, this is a kind of prosperity which – unsurprisingly as a transnational capitalist endeavor – is seen to require a careful balance between risk and reward. Entities useful in servicing the economy and the state are described as "sought", "attracted" and "welcomed", while potential threats to the nation necessitate the guarding of citizenship, practices of exclusion and the continuity of local control of both the process of change and its ultimate rewards. Craton bolsters this exclusionary rhetoric through the deployment of population statistics coupled with images of "foreigners" as a torrential force of nature against which both civilization and citizenship must be defended. The safeguarding of the privileges of the nation is seen as necessary given that after 1970 the "trickle" of newcomers to which Cayman had been historically accustomed became a "flood" (Craton 2003, 364). As evidence of this, Craton observes that between 1989 and 1999 alone the resident population born in Jamaica had more than doubled and at the turn of the century accounted for more than a quarter of the Cayman Islands' total population (366). This theme of risk versus reward finds continuity even in the titles and subtitles of the chapters of *Founded upon the Seas*. In chapter 15, the section titled "Welcoming the Outside World" does not, as one might presume, refer to Caymanian immigration policy and the massive growth in the foreign-born population; it highlights the introduction of tourism and finance as industries dependent on the mobility of transnational capital (346). Rather, the chapter on population growth through immigration is entitled "Change and Adjustment" and contains a section entitled "Rumblings of Discontent" (363, 372).

In sum, the transition narrative at work in Craton's account of Caymanian history operates according to a logic which strongly parallels that captured in Eric Hobsbawm's concept of "inventing tradition". According to Hobsbawm, the three major overlapping functions of invented traditions are: (1) the establishment or symbolization of social cohesion within communities, whether real or artificial; (2) the establishment or legitimization of institutions, social standing or relations of authority and (3) the work of socialization and indoctrination into systems of belief, values and behavioural conventions (2007, 9). The adjudication of claims to membership in the national community on the grounds of proximity to a historical culture, which has been all but rendered extinct by drastic socio-economic and demographic change, provides a powerful symbolization of social cohesion through exclusion. Furthermore, this strategy also legitimates the role of the state as the arbiter of the status of "foreigners".

Measured against the standard of this invented tradition, "foreigners" cannot escape their construction as a potential threat to both the continuity of local culture and the prosperity which has accompanied socio-economic change; as such, they are produced as legitimate objects of surveillance and regulation. Yet how does this discursive construction of history and identity within the Caymanian nationalist project relate to its legal regulation of boundaries of belonging? Given that *Founded upon the Seas* was sponsored and endorsed by the Caymanian government (see Craton 2003, foreword and preface), Maurer's observation that history and law operate as "complementary modes of knowledge production within modern narratives about the 'nation-state'" (1997, 228) rings true for the Caymanian context, and points towards the discursive mechanisms through which the three aforementioned overlapping functions of an invented tradition are performed. The analysis of Craton's account of Caymanian history thus provides an important point of reference for interpreting and analysing contemporary legal and media discourses on immigration and national belonging in the Cayman Islands.

No Home for You Here: Unmapping Economies of Belonging in Caymanian Law

In this part I chart the intersection of the legal mechanisms and discursive modes of representation through which non-status "foreigners" – Jamaicans, in particular – are marked for exclusion from a permanent presence within the Caymanian political, economic and social community. I begin by providing a brief summary of how the right to obtain residence in the Cayman Islands has been historically constituted, focusing primarily on the instruments of exclusion first given legal standing in 2003 (as well as the changes to immigration law proposed by the premier of the Cayman Islands in late 2010) and the Bill of Rights, Freedoms and Responsibilities contained in the Cayman Islands Constitution Order 2009. I then analyse a selection of newspaper articles featuring statements from Caymanian politicians and administrative officials on the Jamaican presence in the Cayman Islands and questions of immigration more generally.

Though an immigration law of one form or another has been in place in the Cayman Islands since 1916, the first legal definition of a "Caymanian" was given in the Regulation of Immigration Law of 1934: "a person born in the Cayman Islands or of parents born therein or of parents . . . [who are] British subjects and resident more than twelve months therein" (as quoted in Craton 2003, 369). It was not until 1961 – one year prior to the passing of the landmark Commonwealth Immigrants Act of 1962 in the United Kingdom – that immigration law began explicitly to concern itself with the question of labour, requiring "aliens" to possess employment permits issued by the local government (369–70). The historical context of the 1960s is crucial for understanding the development of Caymanian immigration policy since 1961, when concern over the Cayman Islands' relationship with Jamaica emerged as the focal point in local discourses of belonging.

The movement of Jamaica, of which the Cayman Islands had been a dependency since 1865, towards independence from British colonial rule in the early 1960s, stirred a significant amount of debate and concern in the Cayman Islands. Without an independent anti-colonial nationalist movement of its own, and in the context of a nascent economic boom, the Cayman Islands ultimately decided to separate from Jamaica, forego independence and remain a British colony. Craton credits this decision to "Caymanians' fear of being dominated by a Jamaica whose standard of living was rapidly falling behind that of the Cayman Islands, and whose population was a hundred times larger and overwhelmingly black" (2003, 316).[7] By the late 1960s, after the early "Jamaican dilemma" had been resolved (both through the choice to remain a British colony and to implement the Aliens Law in 1961), concerns had begun to emerge among Caymanians about the relative ease with which foreigners as a whole, steadily growing in numbers, were able to acquire and exercise the entitlements typically associated with citizenship (Amit-Talai 2001, 582). These anxieties led to the enactment of the Caymanian Protection Law of 1971, which created an administrative bureaucracy through which to monitor and regulate immigration and related matters, including the provision of work permits and rights to permanent residence. The most significant impact of the law in respect to employment was the establishment of preferential employment rights for persons possessing Caymanian status (Craton 2003, 371).

As Amit-Talai (2001) notes, this legislation was the starting point for the distinction between "citizenship" (a category of entitlement regulated by the British government) and "status" or "the right to be Caymanian" (regulated by the local legislature). British Overseas Territories Citizenship (BOTC) associated with the Cayman Islands confers the right – by virtue of birth, descent, naturalization or marriage to a Caymanian – to reside permanently in the islands but not the right to hold office, vote or work. Only the local government has the authority to confer those rights. The right to hold office is the exclusive domain of those who possess "Caymanian status" (a term that was in use until 2003, when it was replaced in immigration law by "the right to be Caymanian") and BOTC associated with the Cayman Islands. The right to vote is restricted to those possessing "the right to be Caymanian". The right to work without restriction is part of "the right to be Caymanian", but otherwise permission to be employed (with restriction) is tightly regulated by the local work permit board.

Between 1971 and 2003 the fundamental features of immigration law remained the same, with changes in 1992 aimed at drastically restricting grants of Caymanian status, and facilitating permanent residence for what Craton describes as "well-heeled foreigners" (2003, 371). In fact, as noted in a local newspaper, previous to 2003 the Caymanian government maintained a policy of allowing workers to reside continuously in the Cayman Islands for undetermined periods of time (with some cases of individual "foreign" workers approaching forty years of residence) while upholding a "moratorium on grants of Cayman status" (Fuller 2011). In 2001, however, a successful court challenge of this policy led to six thousand long-term residents (most of whom were Jamaican) becoming eligible to apply for Caymanian status. The fundamental changes made to Caymanian immigration policy in 2003 (all of which are preserved in the 2009 revision to the Immigration Law) were in part a response to the court's decision (ibid.).

The following are the key components of the 2009 revision to the Immigration Law. It seems logical to begin with a basic explanation of how the category of "Caymanian" is defined and regulated within immigration law. The law delineates five categories of Caymanians; the two most relevant to the current inquiry are "Caymanians as of right" and "Caymanians by grant". According to the law a "Caymanian as of right" is a child born inside or outside the Cayman Islands, "at the date of whose birth at least one of his parents was settled in the Islands and was Caymanian", or a child born outside of the Cayman Islands "at the date of whose birth at least one of his parents was Caymanian otherwise than by descent" (IL 2009, sec. 21). In addition, a person can receive the right to be Caymanian "by grant" in several ways: (1) if they are eighteen years of age or older, "legally and ordinarily resident in the Islands" and can satisfy the Caymanian Status and Permanent Residency Board that either a parent or grandparent was born in the Cayman Islands (sec. 22); (2) if they have had seven years of marriage to a Caymanian or (3) through the completion of five years of legal and continuous residence after receipt of a grant of BOTC associated with the Cayman Islands "by reason of a certificate of naturalization or registration issued under the British Nationality Act, 1981" (sec. 22[3]; BNA 1981, sec. 18[1]). A person becomes eligible for BOTC through naturalization after having resided in an overseas territory for a minimum of five years, without being "subject under the immigration laws to any restriction on the period for which he might remain in that territory" (BNA 1981, schedule 1, 5[2][c]). As I will elaborate shortly, under Caymanian immigration law, all persons in the Cayman Islands who are not Caymanian as of right or grant or who do not possess permanent-residence rights are subject to restrictions on the duration of their residence there. The Caymanian legislature maintains control over the terms by which non-Caymanians are able to access BOTC associated with the Cayman Islands. These individuals are the work permit holders and are the major focus of this chapter.

Prior to the authorization of permits for "foreign" workers, an employer in the Cayman Islands must demonstrate his or her "genuine need to engage the services of the prospective worker"; that he or she has, through advertising in a local newspaper, ascertained that (in order of precedence) no Caymanian, spouse of a Caymanian, or permanent resident who has employment rights is qualified and willing to fill the position and that he or she "has established adequate training or scholarship programmes for Caymanians" (IL 2009, sec. 44[2]). In considering an application for a permit, the work permit board must consider "the protection of local interests and in particular of Caymanians", "the requirements of the community as a whole" (sec. 44[3]) and the desirability of granting permits "to applicants with different backgrounds and from different geographical areas so that a suitable balance in the social and economic life of the Islands may be maintained" (sec. 24[j]). Work permits, as well as permanent-residence and status grants, can thus be denied on the basis of nationality. Immigration data on work permits granted between 1995 and 2008 indicate a significant trend in this regard, focused on persons of Jamaican nationality. With numbers remaining steady from 1995 until 2005, Jamaicans possessed over 50 per cent of the total work permits issued to foreigners; in 2006 this number had been reduced to 43 per cent – while overall work permits issued increased (ESO 2007) – where it has remained in the last-available statistics from 2008 (ESO 2008). During the same period work permits issued to migrants from Asia increased by 10 per cent, rising from 5.6 per cent in 1995 to 15.62 per cent in 2008 (ESO 2007; ESO 2008).[8] The presence of non-status Jamaican workers in Caymanian society and economy was thus systematically reduced (as we will see later) over a three-year period under the imperative of allaying local fears of a "Jamaican takeover".

For those of all nationalities who remain as foreigners holding work permits, the current immigration law is premised on four major tiers of exclusion. The first tier concerns the duration and renewal of work permits as well as the conditions of employment. Work permits in the Cayman Islands can be granted on a temporary (that is, less than six months) or annual basis for most positions (ID 2010), with certain exceptions enabling the duration to be extended up to three years (IL 2009, sec. 48[2]). Regardless of duration, all permits tie the employee to particular employers and occupations, preventing a change of employer unless the "Immigration Board, or the Chief Immigration Officer believes there are special circumstances", or under direction from the governor (sec. 50). This creates conditions of dependency and likely circumscribes the potential for collective mobilization by workers over conditions of employment, wages and issues of status. In addition, the conditions outlined in the previous paragraph concerning the search for qualified Caymanian candidates apply not only to the first work permit granted for a position but to every renewal that follows. Thus long-term job security is practically non-existent.

The second tier prevents migrant workers with regular work permits from ever becoming eligible for permanent residence by limiting the term of their employment to seven years – just one year under the eight required to apply for residency (IL 2009, sec. 52). This is commonly referred to in the media as "the rollover policy". A worker who has been "rolled over" must leave the islands for a period of no less than one year, after which he or she can return if granted another work permit (sec. 52). There are only two ways to move beyond the work permit limit: either to acquire, through marriage to a Caymanian, a permanent residency and employment rights certificate (sec. 31) and eventually "the right to be Caymanian" (sec. 22) or to be designated as a "key employee", which, by extending the term of employment, bestows eligibility for permanent residence – but not "the right to be Caymanian" (sec. 49).

However, the criteria for key-employee status are heavily weighted against "unskilled" workers (IL 2009, sec. 49). According to 2008 Business Staffing Plan Board chairman Andrew Reid, it is primarily applications "for managerial, professional and technically skilled employees" that "satisfy the relevant criteria" (as quoted in Fuller 2008). It is important to note that the majority of these "skilled" workers hail from North America and Europe.

The third tier of exclusion faced by migrant workers is the distinction between permanent residency and "the right to be Caymanian" (Caymanian status). Permanent residency does not confer Caymanian status – permanent residents can neither vote nor run for office; they only have the right to reside and work permanently without a permit. Furthermore, a residency and employment rights certificate restricts the holder "to working within the particular occupation or occupations specified by the [Caymanian Status and Permanent Residency] Board" (IL 2009, sec. 30). Under the current law, with the exception of immigrants present in the Cayman Islands for sufficient duration prior to 2004, eligibility for permanent residence is thus only attainable in two ways: through receiving a designation as a key employee or through marriage to a Caymanian. In addition, foreign-born individuals can only apply for Caymanian status after seven years of marriage to a Caymanian (sec. 22[4]).

The fourth tier of exclusion faced by migrants is the reality that none of the categories of belonging which are legally accessible to them are unalienable; both permanent residency and Caymanian status can be revoked by the state on grounds that include divorce, absence of five or more years from the islands and conviction of a serious crime (IL 2009, sec. 27, sec. 28).[9]

With respect to permanent-residence applications on a basis other than marriage to a Caymanian – at this point only possible with key-employee status – Jamaicans in particular face systematic discrimination. The points system "award[s] points to applicants from countries whose nationals hold less than twenty percent of the total number of work permits in effect at that time" (ID 2008). Given the 2008 level of 43.2 per cent (ESO 2008) it is unlikely to fall below 20 per cent any time in the foreseeable future; therefore, Jamaican applicants automatically score lower than every other group. As noted by Cayman Islands Honorary Consul for Jamaica Robert Hamaty, this would have significantly decreased the chances of being granted permanent residence for more than five thousand Jamaicans eligible by 2006 (Markoff 2006b). As of 2009 there were less than a thousand permanent-residence holders in Cayman entitled to work (we can assume the rest were listed as dependents or financially self-supporting individuals or retirees), nearly half of whom are Jamaican (Fuller 2009a). Given that there were only another 1,600 applications from individuals of all nationalities awaiting a decision, these numbers do not suggest a high rate of grants for Jamaican nationals (Fuller 2009a).

With regards to gender, Caymanian immigration law discriminates equally between non-Caymanian men and women in all but one respect. In the case that a child is born out of wedlock to a non-Caymanian mother, and "a Caymanian holds himself out to be the father . . . the status or domicile of the Caymanian shall not be taken into account" unless the man has been legally adjudged to be the father of the child, ordered to pay weekly child maintenance or is able to prove to the satisfaction of the Status and Permanent Residency Board that he is the child's father (IL 2009, sec. 20[5]). Cayman Islands immigration law itself makes no explicit provision for a scenario under which a non-Caymanian mother claims a Caymanian to be the father of the child. It does, however, stipulate that when a child born out of wedlock in the Cayman Islands is not granted the right to be Caymanian at birth, it shall "be subject to immigration control in a manner appropriate in all the circumstances and having regard to the immigration status of the . . . mother" (sec. 67[7]). Though I do not have specific knowledge of any actual cases in which the question has been disputed of whether a Caymanian man is or is not the father of a child born out of wedlock to a non-Caymanian woman, one could surmise that the law is designed to protect Caymanian men from paternity claims by non-Caymanian women.

Let us shift focus now from immigration law to the Cayman Islands Constitution Order 2009 and, more specifically, the Bill of Rights, Freedoms and Responsibilities.[10] The non-discrimination clause outlined in section 16(2) of the Bill of Rights does not apply to laws "with respect to the entry into or exclusion from, or the employment, engaging in any business or profession, movement or residence within, the Cayman Islands of persons who are not Caymanian" (CICO 2009, sec. 16[4][b]). Discrimination is defined as "affording different and unjustifiable treatment to different persons on any ground such as sex, race, colour, language, religion, political or other opinion, national or social origin, association with a national minority, age, mental or physical disability, property, birth or other status" (sec. 16[2]). The Bill of Rights also upholds the exclusion of non-Caymanians from holding public office or serving a corporate body in laws which require this (sec. 16[5]). Furthermore, non-Caymanians can be expelled from the islands "in a manner and on grounds prescribed by law" (sec. 13[3]) without recourse to legal representation, contestation, appeal or review "where the interests of defence, public safety or public order so require" (sec. 13[3]). As a result, non-status persons living and working in the Cayman Islands are exempted from the protection of the rights and freedoms bestowed upon those with the right to be Caymanian. Life for those without that right can thus be very precarious indeed.

"A Country within a Country": Political Discourse on Race, Nation and the Jamaican Dilemma

As might be expected the discourses on the nation and state articulated by Caymanian politicians and bureaucrats closely mirror those of the realms of history and law. These discourses are premised on the construction of what Maurer refers to as a modernist fiction of state and society as "sutured totalities" (1997, 75). Within this fiction, the state is metaphorically conceived of as a machine concerned with solving technical problems of governance, separate and apart from the national subjects imagined to interface with the state machine on equal terms. Discourses on national belonging thus construct an apparently seamless continuity between the political territory of the Cayman Islands and a pre-existing place and people. Evacuated from this narrative, however, are "the antagonisms and contradictions made evident by the absent presence of immigrants in the discourses creating state and society" (76).

In this section, drawing on Maurer's theoretical framework, I engage with three statements from government officials in the news media and consider how they construct this twofold modernist fiction: (1) of the state as an objective and impartial entity concerned primarily with administrative efficiency, not politics, and (2) of Caymanian society as a homogeneous, empty category defined principally through opposition to the threatening "other", which stands outside of it. As Hilbourne Watson would argue, the policy on labour and immigration in the Cayman Islands reflects a politics of exclusion, domination, insecurity and fear central to the propagation of loyalty in all states (personal communication 17 November 2012); this is quite clear in the following examples from the Caymanian news media.

In the October 2006 newspaper article from which the epigraph to this chapter is taken, former Work Permit Board chairman David Ritch is quoted as describing the issue of the Jamaican presence in Cayman as a "serious" one (as quoted in Markoff 2006a), threatening the very numerical predominance of Caymanians in their own society.[11] With large numbers of Jamaicans having already received Caymanian status – five thousand with sufficient duration of residence to allow eligibility for permanent residence and another six thousand working towards such eligibility – in the absence of legal mechanisms of discrimination Jamaicans could "[i]n a short time period . . . out-number established Caymanians" (ibid.). Furthermore, according to Ritch, this "country within a country" would constitute a grave threat to the governmental coffers; the "unknown number of children" which would accompany this "labourer class" would collapse the local school system, create massive unemployment and lead to the creation of a welfare state (ibid.). And Jamaicans were not the only concern: other groups, such as Filipinos, if allowed to rise to similar levels would pose the same threat. Ritch described these notions as "the facts of life" that, though uncomfortable, had to be talked about because they justified the 2003 legal changes placing limits on both the terms of work permits and the number of workers admitted from any one country (ibid.).

Later that year then–cabinet minister Charles Clifford thought that cooler heads should prevail and "set the record straight" (as quoted in Markoff 2006c): "Much has been said by irresponsible individuals and print media, which suggest that Caymanians don't want Jamaicans in their country or don't want this and that nationality in their country" (ibid.). Clifford denied this notion, suggesting that "the Government [and residents] welcomed all immigrants and visitors to the country" (ibid.). Nevertheless, he felt it necessary to clarify his position, saying,

"It is common sense for a country in this position to have policies in place which ensure that you have a good mix of nationalities in your expatriate work force and that no one nationality is allowed to dominate. . . . To take such a sensible policy position and spin that into an allegation that Caymanians don't like Jamaicans is reckless and provocative" (ibid.).

In Ritch's account we witness a palpably violent appeal to fear; in Clifford's, we hear an impartial invocation of the objectivity of reason. Nonetheless, these two statements in fact operate on identical epistemological and ontological foundations. Both interlocutors construct the Caymanian state as duly concerned only with the efficient management of circumstances supposedly external to its making, which it thus has no responsibility to change.

In the context of a status quo in which expatriates, and Jamaicans in particular, are excluded from belonging to the national community, the state's only responsibility is impartially to take heed of "the facts of life" and act in accordance with the dictates of "common sense". The only substantive difference between the two narratives is that Ritch, as an appointed official, perhaps feels he has the political leeway to spell out in uncompromising terms what Clifford, as an elected one, diplomatically sums up as "domination". Conjuring images of the racialized swarms of lower-class labourers' children descending on the helpless Caymanian state, Ritch's account paints the Jamaican family in broad strokes as a parasitic force which threatens to erode both the identity and the material foundations of "Caymanian" existence. In responding to such "irresponsible" remarks, the central concern for Clifford becomes dispelling the myth that "Caymanians don't like Jamaicans", rather than reflecting on whether or not the Caymanian state systematically discriminates against Jamaicans in terms of access to rights of residence, employment and status and what the long-term consequences of such discrimination might be. The assumption underpinning both statements is that legalized discrimination against racialized working-class migrants is functionally necessary for the preservation of the legitimate and apparently natural monopoly on rights and privileges claimed as the birthright of "Caymanians".

As Amit-Talai astutely suggests, the extremely uncertain nature of the Caymanian polity and economy – subordinate as they are to the UK Foreign and Commonwealth Office and the transnational flows of capital and labour upon which the local economy depends – has established restrictions on permanent residency and status as "one of the few levers available to Caymanians to ensure their share in the global economic bridgehead so tenuously perched on a territory that they officially still do not own" (2001, 586). It is important to stress that the vigour with which the Cayman Islands authorities regulate immigration substantially reflects the acute significance of symbols of political and social autonomy in the absence of sovereign autonomy. In asserting the full extent of Caymanian political autonomy permitted by UK oversight to formulate (or invent) an exclusive national identity, the Caymanian colonial state is able to create an image or sense of sovereignty with which to mask the fundamentally uncertain nature of local self-governance.

As one set of interlocutors in the discussions surrounding the non-independent Caribbean note, "political life in the [British Caribbean] colonies is thus determined by a deep-seated tension" (see Ramos 2001, xvii) between the safeguarding of the socio-economic gains perceived to be linked to the preservation of colonial ties to Britain and questions concerning the meaning of national identity (Connell 2001, 130). This tension is exacerbated by the inherent necessity of an ever-increasing number of expatriate workers for the reproduction and growth of the economies of the majority of these territories, most certainly of the economy of the Cayman Islands (Amit-Talai 2001, 575). Furthermore, the fact that, of all the six British Overseas Territories in the Caribbean, the Cayman Islands is the "most opposed to any movement towards independence" (Connell 2001, 120), these tensions pose a perennial dilemma for the Caymanian state, the management of which requires continually evolving strategies. Regarding the question of immigration, the immense significance of this dilemma in Caymanian political discourse and the need to devise new strategies with which to counter it are reiterated in the September 2010 address to the nation by then-premier of the Cayman Islands, McKeeva Bush. His speech reflects what Maurer has termed "the perennial ambiguity of . . . creolized colonial nationalism" (1997, 89) in its juggling act to balance its own demands with those of the global political economy.

In his speech Bush vociferously challenges many aspects of the current immigration law, highlighting the precarious nature of the Cayman Islands' existence in the global economy: "We have failed to implement our immigration policies in a manner which allows the continuation of growth in our major industry [financial services]. Our *unfriendly over-nationalistic policies* allow countries such as Canada, Ireland, Europe to encourage the movement of good jobs and economic activity created by our financial industry . . . to their countries" (Bush 2010a; my emphasis). He describes the implementation of Caymanian immigration policy as "a very serious and costly mistake" which "has caused severe suffering among our people and our businesses" in the context of the economic crisis of 2008 (ibid.). Caymanians have enjoyed the benefits of the financial and tourism industries based in their country; however, they should remember that these industries were created out of a joint effort with others. In order for Caymanians to continue to benefit from "the foresight and hard work of [their] ancestors" (ibid.), government policy must be amended to encourage the creation of new businesses in, and relocation of "foreign" businesses to, the Cayman Islands and promote the inclusion of wealthy "foreign" retirees to join Cayman's permanent-resident community.

Changes in immigration policy in particular should be implemented to "create fast, efficient, business-friendly services for our Caymanian and foreign businesses while ensuring that when our people are qualified and willing to work that they be given first opportunity and priority for jobs" (Bush 2010a) and to encourage money earned in the Cayman Islands by "highly skilled" migrants to remain there rather than being sent abroad. Bush also highlighted the extreme vulnerability of the Cayman Islands to fluctuations in population size. He foregrounds the combination of stringent immigration regulations and the weakening of the Caymanian economy in the wake of the global economic crisis as prime causes in the drastic decrease of the migrant worker population by more than 3,300 persons between 2008 and 2009 (Fuller 2009b):

> Working together and embracing the benefits of having guests and foreign workers . . . was one of our formulas for success . . . [W]hen we had a bigger population, we had no unemployment and our businesses were doing well. . . . Today, that has changed. Tomorrow, if we do not move quickly to implement intelligent and necessary measures, more businesses will fail, more of our people will become unemployed, our educated people will join the unemployed list, our children will not be able to receive an education to allow them to compete in a more globalized world, the Government will not have enough revenue to support our hardworking Civil Servants to pay their pensions and their medical expenses. (Bush 2010a)

The reduction of the "rollover" time to as brief a period as legally tenable (perhaps even thirty days – see Markoff 2010) without granting eligibility for Caymanian status is portrayed as critical to the prevention of this doomsday scenario. Doing so would encourage the migrant workers in the financial services industry to remain in the Cayman Islands and thus invest their money locally. In a follow-up speech given three months later, Bush presented further immigration reforms that would "make the Cayman Islands more attractive to our investors, make it easier to do business, and bring stability to business generally" (Bush 2010b); all of these focused on facilitating the eligibility for residence via investment in the Cayman Islands by "foreign investors and high net-worth individuals" (ibid.) as well as the unencumbered mobility of "legitimate business travelers and visitors from China [and Jamaica]" (ibid.).

Like Ritch and Clifford, Bush too is concerned with "sensible" immigration policy and the efficient management of the Caymanian economy. However, caught between the demands of Caymanian nationalism and those of the global economy, the source of his disquiet stems not from the excessive presence of migrant workers of one nationality or another but from their conspicuous absence from the local economy. Yet, echoing Maurer's observations on the British Virgin Islands, it is not without a touch of irony that these workers are themselves conspicuously absent from the premier's discourse on the Caymanian polity. His statement does not contain a single overt reference to the migrants employed in the domestic, service and construction industries who make up the vast majority of the "foreign" presence in the Cayman Islands (see ESO 2008, 31). Like "foreign investment" and "high-net-worth individuals", the category of "guest workers" is invoked as one among a number of variables which must be strategically managed by the state to produce a "formula for economic success"; yet in light of the lack of political influence and economic capital possessed by the most vulnerable of these migrants, their role and presence in the Cayman Islands becomes undeserving of anything more than a passing reference.

Neither the Caymanian state nor its leader holds any obligation to consider the precarious status – itself constructed through Caymanian historical narrative, law and media discourse – of these workers as "foreign" nationals, and on this basis, their social and economic vulnerability in the Cayman Islands remains obscured within the premier's speech. The language of inclusion in that speech is extended only to entities seen to be in shorter supply: foreign investment and individuals of "high net worth". Evidently, these transnationally mobile individuals and institutions are of far greater value than the most vulnerable group of migrants, the racialized labouring masses who raise the children of the nation, construct its buildings and provide the "unskilled" services required to make possible the realization of the value of its commodities. This is only logical given that any attempts to enfranchise these workers would deprive the Caymanian economy of one of its most attractive qualities for the financial services and tourism sectors: the "legal dispensability" of 55 per cent of the labour force, which allows the expedient adjustment of the proportions of the islands' labour force according to the exigencies of the global economy (Amit-Talai 2001, 587).[12]

Conclusion

Underlying the scholarly, legal and media discourses examined in this chapter is the notion that the prosperity of those hailed as "Caymanians" is intrinsically tied to two things: first, the ability of the local economy to attract and retain transnational capital and, second, the continued presence of an effective and readily adaptable regime of foreign labour exploitation. In the myth of the Caymanian nation encountered in Craton's *Founded upon the Seas*, in the legal exclusions upon which the presence of migrant workers – and Jamaican nationals in particular – are premised, and in statements from Caymanian public officials, we encounter the multiple discursive strategies through which social, political and economic rights are withheld from migrants. From the dry legalistic phrasing of immigration law to the lively tropes of race, gender and class encountered in media discourses, the presence of Jamaicans and all "unskilled" migrants is constructed as a threat to the prosperity and autonomy of "Caymanians". With the publication of Craton's *Founded upon the Seas* and the transformation of immigration law, the year 2003 must be recognized as a landmark moment in the history of the Caymanian nationalist project.

In closing this chapter I would like to offer some brief considerations concerning the connection between the acute emphasis on the restriction of rights to status and belonging apparent in Caymanian law, historical narrative and political discourse and the "structural vulnerability" (Amit-Talai 2001, 588) of the Caymanian political economy as a modern-day UK colony. It seems apparent that the vigorous legal and discursive attempts to centre the agency of the Caymanian state through the strategic management of immigration regulations cannot conceal the fundamental dilemma of the lack of sovereignty at the heart of the Caymanian polity. In the year and a half following the speeches of then-premier Bush discussed above, the Caymanian economy continued its economic decline. However, even the return of the economy to growth in 2012 did not bring resolution to the grave political and economic problems faced by the Caymanian state. In 2010 a severe budget crisis resulted in threats by the British Overseas Territories Department of the Foreign and Commonwealth Office to take a more direct role in the administration of Cayman Islands government finances. In the ordeal that continues to unfold, the Caymanian state (under the leadership of Bush until December 2012) was forced to temper its claims to internal political and economic autonomy.

In 2011 Bush, alongside then-minister of British Overseas Territories Henry Bellingham, signed a UK-drafted Framework for Fiscal Responsibility (FFR) with the promise to pass it unchanged into local law by the following year. The FFR essentially "introduces severe fiscal restrictions upon the local government" through the establishment of guidelines on "government spending and borrowing, bidding for public projects and rules for financial reporting" (Fuller 2012c). When the time to pass the framework into law arrived, the Caymanian legislature initially proposed first one amended version of the FFR and then another, only to be notified that the proposed law would not be accepted by the United Kingdom. In the end, the third amendment – which contained the entirety of the original FFR signed by the premier – was proposed and passed into law with UK approval. The Caymanian government's initial position of steadfast resistance to the impositions of colonial authority at the start of this ordeal quickly dissolved into one of disgruntled acquiescence to colonial rule (see Fuller 2012a, 2012b; Fuller and Connolly 2012). In Bush's own words, "I have fought against these positions, but I am now forced [to accept them] through the dictate of the UK government" (Fuller 2012a). In the aftermath, the Cayman Islands government remains plagued by a cash flow shortage which it finds itself unable to resolve in the short term given the restrictions on borrowing imposed by the FFR. The start of 2013 found the Cayman Islands in a period of austerity, in which the solution to the budget crisis is seen to lie in the slashing of civil service positions, benefits and salaries (Fuller 2013). As communicated by UK-appointed Cayman Islands governor Duncan Taylor in late 2012, the British Overseas Territories minister will continue to "have a [substantial] say in the setting of the [Cayman Islands] budget" until government finances are in a state of full compliance with the FFR (Fuller 2012c).

Considering the precarious nature of the Cayman Islands' position vis-à-vis the global economy and the colonial authority, it makes sense that the state and its officials have in law and in media discourse turned to an emphasis on drastic immigration regulations as the supposed key to securing the autonomy and prosperity of those classified as "Caymanian". However, in the aftermath of both the global economic and Caymanian budget crises, it is clear that the agency of the state to navigate such treacherous waters and steer "the good ship Cayman" (Bush 2010a) towards a clear horizon and sunny skies remains fundamentally constrained. As such, political life in the Cayman Islands is caught in a contradiction, within which a condition seen as necessary for socio-economic prosperity (the perpetuation of the colonial relationship with the United Kingdom) necessarily undermines the capacity of the state to effectively articulate the sense of autonomy so central to Caymanian discourses on national identity. And in the balancing act between the demands of these two phenomena, "foreign" workers (and Jamaicans in particular) suffer the brunt of the discourses of difference which inform the hierarchical organization of Caymanian society.

Acknowledgements

I would like to acknowledge that this paper was written with the support of a Social Sciences and Humanities Research Council Doctoral Award. Parts of a previous version of this paper have appeared in Gill 2013.

Notes

1. A larger body of literature on relations of governance between British Overseas Territories and the UK government does exist – see Clegg 2006, Clegg and Gold 2011, Davies 1995, Drower 1992, Hintjens 1997, Hintjens and Hodge 2012, Killingray and Taylor 2005, McElroy and de Albuquerque 1995, Ramos and Rivera 2001, Skelton 2000, Skinner 2002, Sutton and Payne 1994, Taylor 2000 and Thorndike 1989.
2. A search conducted in May 2012 for the names of these nations in combination with variants of "nation", "migration" or "citizen" in the following databases yielded no relevant results: Social Sciences Abstracts, Social Sciences Index, JSTOR, Expanded Academic ASAP, Academic OneFile, ProQuest, Sociological Abstracts, Anthropology Plus and Anthrosource.
3. The *Cayman Compass* is one of the two largest local newspapers and the only electronically available source of news which has online archives; these date back to 2004.
4. However, just a few pages earlier Craton notes the complete lack of action on the part of the government to address the underlying socio-economic issues which pushed "black immigrants" into slums perceived by Caymanians as "breeding grounds for disease and crime" (Craton 2003, 373).

5. The irony of all this should not be lost on the reader. Amit-Talai (1997) informs us that a number of the founders and key organizers of the national institutions whose mandate is to preserve and promote Caymanian identity are themselves North American, European and Caribbean expatriates, not Caymanians. Furthermore, the majority of the staff that keep these institutions in operation are also foreigners (Amit-Talai 1997, 57, 61). In addition, Craton, the historian of the Caribbean chosen by the Caymanian government to pen the comprehensive history of the nation and its people, is described on the inside flap of the back cover of his text as a British national who has been living in Canada since 1970.
6. Regarding Craton's reference to "Caymanian Brackers": Cayman Brac is one of the three Cayman Islands; Grand Cayman and Little Cayman are the other two.
7. Thus, from the outset, of anxieties over migration and belonging in the Cayman Islands we encounter the imbrication of concerns over economic prosperity with fears of racial degeneration. This is a theme that will be taken up in relation to the contemporary discourses of migration and belonging later in the chapter.
8. The reports from the Economics and Statistics Office do not include percentages. These I calculated from the data provided.
9. However, the Caymanian status of even someone who possesses Caymanian citizenship (that is, BOTC associated with the Cayman Islands) can be revoked by the state if that person leaves the Cayman Islands for more than five years (see IL 2009, sec. 22 [1], [2], [9], [10]; sec. 23; sec. 24; sec. 27).
10. The Bill of Rights is the first attempt to enshrine human rights in the Caymanian constitution and became effective in November 2012.
11. The fact that this discussion took place in 2006 rather than when the law was passed in 2003 requires some explanation. Because the first "rollovers", as they are referred to locally, did not take place until 2006, the real impact of the new immigration law was not felt until 2006; as such, it garnered much greater public attention that year.
12. In other words, business enterprises are not bound by cumbersome legal commitments to their expatriate workforce and can essentially hire and fire as they see fit.

References

Amit-Talai, Vered. 1997. "In Pursuit of Authenticity: Globalization and Nation Building in the Cayman Islands". *Anthropologica* 39 (1): 53–63.

———. 2001. "A Clash of Vulnerabilities: Citizenship, Labor, and Expatriacy in the Cayman Islands". *American Ethnologist* 28 (3): 574–94.

BNA (British Nationality Act). 1981. http://www.legislation.gov.uk/ukpga/1981/61/contents.

Bush, McKeeva. 2010a. "Statement of the Premier of the Cayman Islands, the Honourable McKeeva Bush on 16th September 2010". *Cayman Compass*, 16 September. http://www.compasscayman.com/caycompass/2010/09/16/Statement-of-the-Premier-of-the-Cayman-Islands,-The-Honourable-McKeeva-Bush-on-16th-September-2010/.

———. 2010b. "Premier Bush's Address to the Country". *Cayman Compass*, 9 December. http://www.compasscayman.com/caycompass/2010/12/09/Premier-Bush-s-address-to-the-country/.

CICO (Cayman Islands Constitution Order). 2009. http://www.constitution.gov.ky/pls/portal/url/item/781CB30D809315B9E0406F0A6F1F3DF5.

Clegg, Peter. 2006. "The UK Caribbean Overseas Territories, New Labour, and the Strengthening of Metropolitan Control". *Caribbean Studies* 34 (1): 131–61.

Clegg, Peter, and Peter Gold. 2011. "The UK Overseas Territories: A Decade of Progress and Prosperity?" *Commonwealth and Comparative Politics* 49 (1): 115–35.

Cohen, Colleen Ballerino. 1998. " 'This Is de Test': Festival and the Cultural Politics of Nation Building in the British Virgin Islands". *American Ethnologist* 25 (2): 189–214.

———. 2010. *Take Me to My Paradise: Tourism and Nationalism in the British Virgin Islands*. New Brunswick, NJ: Rutgers University Press.

Connell, John. 2001. "Eternal Empire: Britain's Caribbean Colonies in the Global Arena". In *Islands at the Crossroads: Politics in the Non-Independent Caribbean*, edited by Aarón Gamaliel Ramos and Ángel Israel Rivera, 115–35. Kingston: Ian Randle.

Craton, Michael. 2003. *Founded upon the Seas: A History of the Cayman Islands and Their People*. Kingston: Ian Randle.

Davies, Elizabeth. 1995. *The Legal Status of British Dependent Territories: The West Indies and North Atlantic Region*. Cambridge: Cambridge University Press.

Drower, George. 1992. *Britain's Dependent Territories: A Fistful of Islands*. Aldershot, UK: Dartmouth.

ESO (Economics and Statistics Office: Government of the Cayman Islands). 2007. "Immigration: 10 Year Work Permit Profile (Including Renewals Pending) by Nationality".

———. 2008. "Immigration Work Permit (Including Renewals Pending) by Nationality".

Fuller, Brent. 2008. "Key Employees at Issue". *Cayman Compass*, 29 December. http://www.compasscayman.com/caycompass/2008/12/30/Key-employees-at-issue/.

———. 2009a. "1,800 Hold Permanent Residency Status". *Cayman Compass*, 5 February. http://www.compasscayman.com/caycompass/2009/02/06/1,800-hold-Permanent-Residency-status/.

———. 2009b. "Work Permits Down 12.4 per cent". *Cayman Compass*, 18 November. http://www.compasscayman.com/caycompass/2009/11/18/Work-permits-down-12-4-per-cent/.

———. 2011. "Adviser Says Nine-Month Rollover Is Minimum". *Cayman Compass*, 21 February. http://www.compasscayman.com/caycompass/2011/02/21/Adviser-says-nine-month-rollover-is-minimum/.

———. 2012a. "Premier Backs Down". *Cayman Compass*, 8 November. http://www.compasscayman.com/caycompass/2012/11/08/Premier-backs-down/.

———. 2012b. " 'This Is What They Wanted': Third Version of Fiscal Framework Bill Proposed". *Cayman Compass*, 15 November. http://www.compasscayman.com/caycompass/2012/11/15/-This-is-what-they-wanted-/.

———. 2012c. "UK Fiscal Framework May Stay in Law". *Cayman Compass*, 29 November. http://www.compasscayman.com/caycompass/2012/11/29/UK-fiscal-framework-may-stay-in-law/.

———. 2013. "Top Stories of 2012: Government Budget Woes Worsen". *Cayman Compass*, 2 January. http://www.compasscayman.com/caycompass/2013/01/02/Top-stories-of-2012--Government-budget-woes-worsen/.

Fuller, Brent, and Norma Connolly. 2012. "Premier: Cayman Islands 'Difficult to Push'". *Cayman Compass*, 3 November. http://www.compasscayman.com/caycompass/2012/11/02/Premier--Cayman-Islands-'difficult-to-push'.

Gill, Sean. 2013. "The Dilemma of Nationalism: Migrant Labour, Economic Crisis, and the Politics of Belonging in the Cayman Islands". *Canadian Journal of Latin American and Caribbean Studies* 38 (2): 238–53.

Hintjens, Helen. 1997. "Governance Options in Europe's Caribbean Dependencies". *The Round Table: The Commonwealth Journal of International Affairs* 86 (344): 533–47.

Hintjens, Helen, and Dorothea Hodge. 2012. "The UK Caribbean Overseas Territories: Governing Unruliness Amidst the Extra-Territorial EU". *Commonwealth and Comparative Politics* 50 (2): 190–225.

Hobsbawm, Eric. 2007. *The Invention of Tradition*. Cambridge: Cambridge University Press.

ID (Immigration Department of the Cayman Islands). 2008. "Permanent Residence Points System". 7 January. http://www.immigration.gov.ky/portal/page?_pageid=1608,2524669&_dad=portal&_schema=PORTAL .

———. 2010. "Work Permits". 17 March. http://www.immigration.gov.ky/portal/page?_pageid=1608,2524798&_dad=portal&_schema=PORTAL.

IL (Immigration Law, 2009 Revision). 2009. 16 June. http://www.immigration.gov.ky/pls/portal/url/item/455C741C66B51D84E0408D030B0AB366.

Killingray, David, and David Taylor, eds. 2005. *The United Kingdom Overseas Territories: Past, Present, Future*. London: Institute of Commonwealth Studies.

Markoff, Alan. 2006a. "Jamaican Dilemma Detailed". *Cayman Compass*, 8 October. http://www.compasscayman.com/caycompass/2006/10/09/Jamaican-dilemma-detailed/.

———. 2006b. "Jamaican Consul Responds to Ritch". *Cayman Compass*, 16 October. http://www.compasscayman.com/caycompass/2006/10/16/Jamaican-consul-responds-to-Ritch/.

———. 2006c. "Clifford: All Immigrants Welcome". *Cayman Compass*, 20 December. http://www.compasscayman.com/caycompass/2006/12/20/Clifford--All-immigrants-welcome/.

———. 2010. "Bush Supports 30-Day Rollover Break". *Cayman Compass*, 20 September. http://www.compasscayman.com/caycompass/2010/09/20/Bush-supports-30-day-rollover-break/.

Maurer, Bill. 1995. "Writing Law, Making a 'Nation': History, Modernity, and Paradoxes of Self-Rule in the British Virgin Islands". *Law and Society Review* 29 (2): 255–86.

———. 1997. *Recharting the Caribbean: Land, Law, and Citizenship in the British Virgin Islands*. Ann Arbor: University of Michigan Press.

———. 2000. "A Fish Story: Rethinking Globalization on Virgin Gorda, British Virgin Islands". *American Ethnologist* 27 (3): 670–701.

McElroy, Jerome, and Klaus de Albuquerque. 1995. "The Social and Economic Propensity for Political Dependence in the Insular Caribbean". *Social and Economic Studies* 44 (2/3): 167–93.

Oakes, Betsy. 1992. "Workers in the British Virgin Islands: The Complexities of Residence and Migration". *Social and Economic Studies* 41 (1): 67–87.

Ramos, Aarón Gamaliel. 2001. "Introduction: Caribbean Territories at the Crossroads". In *Islands at the Crossroads: Politics in the Non-Independent Caribbean*, edited by Aarón Gamaliel Ramos and Ángel Israel Rivera, xii–xxi. Kingston: Ian Randle.

Ramos, Aarón Gamaliel, and Ángel Israel Rivera, eds. 2001. *Islands at the Crossroads: Politics in the Non-Independent Caribbean*. Kingston: Ian Randle.

Skelton, Tracey. 2000. "Political Uncertainties and Natural Disasters: Montserratian Identity and Colonial Status". *Interventions: International Journal of Postcolonial Studies* 2 (1): 103–17.

Skinner, Jonathan. 2002. "British Constructions with Constitutions: The Formal and Informal Nature of 'Island' Relations on Montserrat and Gibraltar". *Social Identities: Journal for the Study of Race, Nation and Culture* 8 (2): 301–20.

Sutton, Paul, and Anthony Payne. 1994. "The Off-Limits Caribbean: The United States and the European Dependent Territories". *Annals of the American Academy of Political and Social Science* 533: 87–99.

Taylor, David. 2000. "British Colonial Policy in the Caribbean: The Insoluble Dilemma – the Case of Montserrat". *The Round Table: The Commonwealth Journal of International Affairs* 89 (355): 337–44.

Thobani, Sunera. 2007. *Exalted Subjects: Studies in the Making of Race and Nation in Canada*. Toronto: University of Toronto Press.

Thorndike, Tony. 1989. "The Future of the British Caribbean Dependencies". *Journal of Interamerican Studies and World Affairs* 31 (3): 117–40.

Conclusion

Hilbourne A. Watson

The contributors to this volume variously connect issues of sovereignty, citizenship, belonging, freedom and justice to globalization, consistent with their particular research interests. Employing a non-traditional critical perspective on globalization enriches theoretical analysis by redirecting scholarly attention away from nationalist-oriented (state-centric) interpretations of the state, sovereignty, power, citizenship and belonging. In most of the chapters in this volume the national state and territoriality remain the unit of analysis, intentionally or by default. The contributions on the non-independent territories of Puerto Rico and the Dutch Caribbean (by Aarón Ramos), the French overseas departments (by Justin Daniel) and the non-self-governing territory of the Cayman Islands (by Sean Gill) show by default that sovereignty and citizenship provide the context for formal (juridical) equality without offering a way to transcend class inequality and the racialization of social relations under capitalism, which has implications for national belonging. This is clearly the case for Caribbean people residing in the "metropolitan" countries. Broadly speaking, contributors tended to be critical of the social and economic inequalities that shape social life for Caribbean people residing in the "metropole". For example, Sean Gill shows that the British Nationality Act makes it very difficult for many workers (particularly from Jamaica), whose labour power contributes to capital accumulation in the Cayman Islands, to achieve permanent residence or British citizenship, confirming that the interest of capital in labour revolves primarily around the worker's ability to produce exchange value.

The United States and the European Union have redefined trade, investment, financial services and tourism in line with the logic of the US-instigated post-9/11 global security strategy. The adoption of austerity measures to address fallout from the global economic and financial crisis is part of a strategy for waging class struggle from above, by shifting the adjustment burden onto the shoulders of the working classes. No matter the degree of conflict, tension or other problems that surface in the relationship between the non-independent territories and the "metropolitan" powers, there seems to be little direct support for the independence (sovereignty) option as the three contributors (Ramos, Daniel and Gill) point out. In the French Caribbean the response to the impact of the 2008 global economic and financial crisis and its reverberations assumed the form of highly publicized political struggles against deteriorating economic and social conditions, coupled with demands for reform within the French republican system rather than a call for sovereignty as an end in itself.

The leaders of Commonwealth Caribbean states are comfortable operating under the US-led hegemonic security regime, which extends to the global multilateral and regional institutions. In global affairs, Caribbean Community and Common Market (CARICOM) states have a high visibility for their size; however, they lack the capacity to exercise "effective sovereignty". In chapter 1 Hilbourne Watson does not deny that independent states in the Caribbean are sovereign; rather, he insists that those states do not exercise "effective sovereignty" in the conditions of relentless global capitalist integration, which accelerates the decoupling of sovereignty from territory and exposes the theoretical and empirical limitations of territorially fixed concepts of sovereignty, power, democracy, citizenship and national belonging. His explanation in chapter 2 of how Barbados achieved sovereignty and how the Cuban Revolution continues to test US hegemony supports the argument that sovereignty is historical rather than organic and is therefore subject to contestation and negotiation – even for the United States, which has an unmistakable capacity to exercise for "high political sovereignty" within a hegemonic framework.

Alex Dupuy argues otherwise, suggesting that "modern capitalism gave rise to an inclusive liberal democracy that universalized the concept of citizenship but disempowered the citizenry" (1996, 567). The French Revolution defined universality within the context of the eighteenth-century bourgeois democratic trajectory. Dupuy concludes that the exploitation of labour that is built into capitalism compromises both the labour and citizenship rights of the Haitian working class, throngs of which have been largely reduced to a reserve army of labour. Thus droves of working-class Haitians are forced to rely on transnational capital to intensify the exploitation of their labour power at home and abroad, hoping to raise their material standard of living. Their predicament, however, is that their labour power is still generally cheaper than the machines they use to produce commodities for the global market, which traps most of them in unskilled, low-wage, labour-intensive employment. In chapter 3, Dupuy shows that the Haitian Revolution remains incomplete, considering that the great mass of the population is forced to reimagine a future pregnant with the possibilities of what the "government of 1800 had done for the slaves who overthrew colonialism and racial slavery".

In contemporary Haiti "the system of forced child labour known as 'restavec' encourages impoverished families to send their children to wealthier families with more resources, which often results in children being exploited" or otherwise greatly subjected to abuse (*Jamaica Observer*, "Three Caricom Countries Linked to Modern Day Slavery", 17 October 2013). Two other sovereign states in the "Caribbean Community . . . listed on the global index on modern slavery are Suriname at 68th and Guyana 77th" (ibid.). Modern-day slavery envelops masses of Haitian children and sizeable numbers of other individuals in other sovereign Caribbean states, indicating that the struggle to anchor the moral imperative of personhood comes up against constraints arising from the primacy attached to the right to exploit. The inclusiveness, which liberal democracy is assumed to represent, amounts to a form of exclusion for many that mirrors the tension between the bourgeois state, capital and the nation against the struggle for self-determination, which transcends sovereignty and nationality. The point here is that liberal notion of "essential rights . . . as the inalienable heritage of all human beings and as the specific language of specific nations" (Arendt 1973, 231) is subject to the laws of the state, yet the state's first requirement is to defend and protect the right of capital to exploit, by subsuming labour under capital. This is necessary because labour is forced to produce capital – its opposite – as the precondition of its own social reproduction. Thus the universal rights of man assume concrete form and therefore make sense only within concrete historical conditions of inequality under capitalism.

Linden Lewis concludes that struggles for freedom are connected with broader social justice struggles, arguing that the denial of each or both makes it impossible to exercise citizenship effectively. In chapter 4 of this volume, he emphasizes that "[s]ocial justice is at the heart of an embrace of citizenship, insofar as it addresses the issue of human dignity" which has to do with "ensuring equal worth of persons". Lewis emphasizes that historically constituted citizenship is realized through struggle and resistance geared to expanding space for achieving democratic rights. The fact that the sovereign state is founded on domination, violence and exclusion also shows that democracy in Caribbean and other societies is already constructed on the economic and political foundation of the right to exploit. Struggles around citizenship and belonging might force the state and capital to make certain concessions that might alleviate gender and other forms of oppression under the banner of democracy; however, those struggles cannot abolish exploitation without which capitalism ceases to exist. Thus, the state (political coercion) and the market (economic compulsion) provide the context in which societies wage struggles for democracy that lack social content.

In chapter 5 Anton Allahar concludes that the capitalist democracies in the Caribbean face "ethno-racial" contradictions that highlight the lack of "social and class equality", and increase the fraught nature of the experience of different groups living as citizens. Allahar argues that the concept of global citizen and citizenship implies a "bottom up" way of looking at citizenship beyond territorial borders, opening up space to rethink the paradigm beyond state-centric conceptions of space. He thereby implies that citizenship is part of the contradictory process of producing national persons via the cultural institution of the nation state, which is rooted in forms of separation and difference that are characteristics of modernity. The issues Allahar addresses around belonging suggest that, for many, acquiring legal citizenship is easier than exercising it and that democracy, which privileges difference at the expense of commensurability, is not well equipped to resolve contradictions it purports to address.

In chapter 6, Aarón Ramos notes that the statehood party in Puerto Rico has become the most organized, having gained the upper hand in fighting for material, economic and social benefits from the mainland to temper the impact of the persistent economic crisis that is in line with pragmatic neo-liberal priorities. In the Dutch Caribbean, the absence of strong organized support for independence contrasts with a convergence of views that local culture and political priorities should be respected by The Hague – a situation that also has very strong resonance across the Puerto Rican political landscape.

According to Justin Daniel in chapter 7, French citizenship has remained elusive for citizens of the French Antilles, a situation that reflects the contradictory relationship between the principle of cosmopolitanism that fails to overcome the exclusions built into liberalism and suggests that French citizenship remains a work in progress for French citizens as a whole. Daniel draws attention to recent efforts made by the French Republic to embrace multiculturalism when dealing with demands arising from citizens from the overseas department. In these efforts, multiculturalism is part of a larger neo-liberal strategy that works to reinforce exclusion and mask substantive inequality and privilege established through the racialization of social relations. The right to be different, which is associated with the discourse of multiculturalism, characterized the post-war "Liberal Hour" when, as Kenan Malik (1996) observes, measures were adopted in the West to use culture as a default for race, with the intention of preserving racial ordering and white supremacy, while claiming to leave behind the legacies of the fascist and racist terror that enveloped Europe during World War II. The focus on "culture and culturology in . . . postwar liberalism" reinforced "racial essentialism", which "helped reify struggles against . . . segregation, racial discrimination, inequality, and poverty . . . by separating discussion of injustice from capitalism's logic of reproduction" (Reed 2013, 52). The reality is that all working-class citizens and residents living in France face class and other obstacles to exercising citizenship rights, consistent with how liberal democracy mediates class and related contradictions of gender and ethnicity under capitalism.

Sean Gill concludes, in chapter 8, that it would be very difficult to understand the concept of "prosperity" that people living in the Cayman Islands embrace without accounting for the role played by the inflows of transnational capital and a ready supply of exploitable foreign labour. Gill recognizes that, procedurally, certain categories of persons meeting the legal residency requirement of five years in the Cayman Islands are eligible to apply for naturalization as a British Overseas Territories citizen, under provisions of the British Nationality Act. The impact of the global capitalist crisis in the Cayman Islands complicates how the territory deals with working-class migrant workers, especially from Jamaica, versus persons who are eligible to apply for certificates of direct investment or certificates for persons with independent means. This strategy categorizes residents in ways that make some eligible to belong while certain others are forced to exist in an unstable and uncertain status. The power of private capital becomes paramount in shaping the contours of public policy on immigration and residency in the Cayman Islands. The Cayman Islands colonial state acts deliberately to prevent Caymanians from becoming a numerical minority in the territory, by limiting and regulating access to employment and legal residence by other nationalities. Legal and extra-legal (including economic and financial) provisions feature heavily in determining who is eligible to become Caymanian, with economics, class and race affecting how belonging is constructed under the British Nationality Act. The Caymanian reserve army of labour is mainly foreign, with Jamaican nationals bearing the brunt of resentment, marginalization and insecurity.

All Commonwealth Caribbean states reached sovereign statehood as constitutional monarchies within the British Commonwealth of Nations. The postcolonial state and civil society in the Commonwealth Caribbean inherited and preserved the authoritarian infrastructure from British imperialism, confirming that continuity rather than discontinuity shaped the postcolonial political dispensation. Today, the republics – Guyana and Trinidad and Tobago, both with strategic natural resources: bauxite and oil – are mired in a vortex of violence and material insecurity that plagues masses of working-class African- and Asian-descended people. Commonwealth Caribbean states and societies have not broken with patriarchy, hierarchy, authoritarianism or national chauvinism – institutional forms that are bound up with sovereignty and complicate one's ability to process contradictions arising from the exercise of citizenship, identity formation and the sense of membership in a nation state. The nation state is not an end in itself. Rather it is a means to an end, as can be seen from the weakening of its cultural moorings under pressure from contradictions surfacing in our deterritorializing world: international migration and global integration have contributed to terms like "nations unbound" and to dual citizenship, diasporic transnational families and global identities. Sovereignty is historical and exclusionary, and imposes constraints on belonging and social life, making it more difficult to live as full humans. Contradictions arising from globalization show that national sovereignty is not our human destiny.

The leaders of CARICOM states exploit the political links to the United Kingdom, opportunistically asserting legacies of democracy tied to an outdated and static notion of Westminster politics the British left behind. This logic is tied to the myth of exceptionalism regarding those West Indian regions with British roots, which helps to explain why the CARICOM states are prone to emphasize difference at the expense of commensurability in dealing with the Caribbean region at large (see Lora 2013). CARICOM governments also behave as though the economy operates at the behest of the state and society, where politicians have their political base; in fact economic power is heavily concentrated in the hands of transnational capital with the dominant local business stratum as secondary.

Democracy myths, which intersect with globalization myths and sovereignty myths, include at least the following: (1) politics and economics exist as two separate spaces in which the sovereign state holds a monopoly of political power and upholds democracy, while capital (which owns the means of production) manages the economy on the basis of self-interestedness and purported equality between capital and labour based on buying and selling labour power; (2) capital and labour enter into a market-determined relationship as free equals to negotiate the labour contract in conditions where power is fixed and resides in the "sovereign" people and (3) the exercise of democratic rights, such as voting, translates into more power and more democracy for the people and less for the state and capital. Myths are produced when we treat the institutions humans create for the purpose of social reproduction as extensions of natural law, in the process emptying history of any social content.

The undeniable reality is that capitalist market democracy cradles nationalism, which stimulates xenophobic impulses towards exclusion and insecurity in ways that reinforce the prejudices of territorial sovereignty, while capital stakes its right to exploit beyond national territory and nationalist ideology, which ensnares masses of working-class people and reinforces ideological divisions along lines of nationality, ethnicity and gender. The sovereign state remains part of the problem rather than the solution to the problem of world order, complicating the fields of individual and collective existence. It is difficult to make sense of the forms of state and non-state violence across the Caribbean without considering the crisis that inheres in the social relations of capitalism. The current crisis in the Caribbean finds the state moving increasingly in the direction of depoliticizing and criminalizing politics (especially working-class politics) – in the process exploiting the artificial separation of politics from economics – and treating social relations between people as technical relations between things. This tendency flows partly from the relentless process of global capitalist integration that narrows the space for representative government at the national level and makes political contestation to limit the predations of transnational capital seem suspect. Globalization in exposing sovereignty myths also demands the reconfiguration of sovereignty to reflect the reality of a world that is being spatially reconfigured, a shift that reflects neither an attack on nor mortal threat to sovereignty, without which globalization as we know it would not be possible.

Caribbean international relations scholars would do well to bury the ghost of 1648 – the Peace of Westphalia – which did not bring about modern sovereignty or national states. There is no empirical evidence for claims that sovereign statehood is a direct result of the Thirty Years' War (1618–48). The Peace of Westphalia was silent on sovereignty and it certainly did not give the world modern sovereign states or the nation state as a cultural institution, as Andreas Osiander and Benno Teschke have shown (see chapters 1 and 2 of this volume). Interstate anarchy has its ideological roots in the state of nature fiction and it engenders the false inside-outside dichotomy axiomatic in much of international relations discourses. Anarchy is an ideological assumption about the world that lacks global ruling power; it is not a statement of fact about the fixed nature of a territorially divided world dominated by sovereign states.

To argue that sovereignty is not the antidote to disorder or anarchy requires an acknowledgement that anarchy is the "characteristic social form of capitalist modernity" (Rosenberg 1994). By this logic, anarchy is not the "antithesis of sovereignty", which means that sovereignty and its supposed antidote – anarchy – are not "mutually exclusive and mutually exhaustive" (see Devetak 2005, 170). In the real world the two spaces – inside (state) and outside (international system) – are mutually constitutive: the plausibility of anarchy depends on denying its sovereign other, a move that signals a "double exclusion" (170–71). Terms such as "anarchy" and "sovereignty" that are conveniently tethered to territory demand that we embrace the idea of an unobtainable reality with pre-social origins. We need a theory grounded in a transformative concept of the relationship between humans and nature that breaks free of the static logic that derives our subjectivity from a notion of alientated self-interested men and self-interested states constituting an anarchical world. Such a transformative concept has the potential to free us from the untenable position of assuming that we must first exhaust territorial sovereignty (Joseph 2012) in order to advance to a new Caribbean federation. Such ideological reasoning is incapable of directing our imagination or political practice beyond those forms of exclusion that are part of the legacies of the alienating and alienated sovereign state.

All sovereign states and non-independent territories in the Caribbean are by now forced to confront the fact that their sovereign or non-sovereign existence does not flow from anything that inheres in sovereign or non-sovereign statehood, given that their social existence is conditioned by the politically determined, uneven distribution of power that is produced in the relations between ruling forces that dominate national states on the one hand and the broader struggle for our universal humanity on the other. By this measure, political status such as sovereignty is a means to an end. The reality is that global capitalist integration reflects attempts by owners of wealth that dominate national and global politics to integrate the world in order to reproduce themselves more effectively on a global scale. It is this contradictory process of global integration that opens up possibilities for charting paths towards worthwhile post-sovereign futures. The effective starting point for studying modern political ontology in the contemporary world is not the territorial state but, rather, the global context and social forces of which states and their populations are agents and products.

The crisis of the sovereign state can be seen to be a part of the larger crisis of global capitalism, if we bear in mind that crisis inheres in the capital relation itself. The notion that capitalism is human destiny fosters the misconception that the real option open to the working classes is to fight to strengthen democracy – a notion that misses the point that modern democracy is a bourgeois-class project.

Such a misconception draws on the nineteenth-century idea of progress, according to which a form of enlightened liberal capitalist equilibrium awaited us as the end point of human history. The reality, however, is that historical systems are by definition limited and limiting, such that any attempt to view liberal democracy and its social democratic variants as the end point of political evolution amounts to imposing a closure on history – a neo-Hegelian move designed to totalize the non-totalizable.

David Harvey advances seventeen "ideas for political praxis" in which he asks what the "contradictions of capital tell us about anti-capitalist political praxis" (2014, 294). With global implications stemming from his analysis in mind, he argues that his "X-ray into the contradictions of capital . . . does help frame an overall direction to anti-capitalist struggle even as it makes and strengthens the case for anti-capitalist politics" (294).

His first idea is to support struggles aimed at achieving the "direct provision of adequate use values for all (housing, education, food, security, etc.)" (Harvey 2014, 294) to take precedence over market-determined, "profit-maximizing" provisions that concentrate wealth in the hands of a few at the expense of the majority. Second, he calls for the creation of a "means of exchange . . . that facilitates . . . but limits or excludes" the private accumulation of "money as a form of social power" (294). Third, he suggests the establishment of "common rights regimes . . . the creation, management and protection of which lie in the hands of popular assemblies and associations" (294). Fourth, he calls for setting up "economic and social barriers" to guard against the "appropriation of social power by private persons" and against class exploitation, which must be "universally frowned upon as a pathological deviancy" (294–95). Fifth, Harvey supports reorganizing production to meet social needs and overcoming the law of value, by creating "associated producers freely deciding on" socially determined priorities and needs as the most realistic way to dissolve the class opposition between capital and labour (295). Sixth, he suggests that transcending commodity production necessitates creating social conditions to "maximize time for free activities conducted in a stable and well-maintained environment protected from dramatic episodes of creative destruction" (295). Seventh, he proposes defining social needs based on mutually arrived at criteria and designing ways to satisfy those needs that are not only beneficial but also rewarding.

Eighth, he says we need to produce technologies for getting rid of drudgery and the alienation of social labour by dissolving "unnecessary distinctions in technical divisions of labour, liberate time for free individual and collective activities, and diminish the ecological footprint of human activities" (Harvey 2014, 295). Ninth, Harvey favours harnessing "automation, robotization and artificial intelligence" to reduce the "technical divisions of labour", and "dissociate essential residual technical divisions of labour" from "social divisions of labour" (295). The idea is to free society from the "rule of experts" and requires rotating "[a]dministrative, leadership and police function . . . among individuals within the population at large" (295). Tenth, it is necessary to form "popular associations" based on "decentralized competitive capacities of individuals and social groups to control monopoly and centralized power over the means of production" with the goal of securing "differentiation in technical, social, cultural, and lifestyles innovations" (295).

The eleventh step is to promote the highest possible diversification for living and being socially, including "relations to nature" territorially and in larger collectivities, allowing free, orderly "uninhibited . . . movement of individuals" within and across borders, with provisions for representatives in different spaces to assemble regularly to "assess, plan, and undertake common tasks and deal with common problems at different scales: bioregional, continental, and global" (Harvey 2014, 296). Twelfth, Harvey calls for the abolition of all "inequalities in material provision . . . other than those" associated with the idea of "from each according to his, her, or their capacities" and distribution according to "his, her, or their need" (296). The thirteenth step involves the gradual erasure of the "distinction between necessary labour done for distant others and work" for one's own reproduction. This would mean that the household and commune would have to be institutionalized to ensure that "social labour" becomes socially grounded in the household and that communal work becomes the primary form of "unalienated and non-monetized social labour" (296). Fourteenth, it is important to ensure that social provisions such as "education, health care, housing, food security, basic goods, and open access to transportation" are readily accessible to all, in order to "ensure the material basis for freedom from want and for freedom of action and movement" (296).

Fifteenth, allowing for differences arising from "uneven geographical development", it is necessary to set up economic "convergence around zero growth", to promote and achieve the "greatest possible development of individual and collective human capacities and powers and the perpetual search for novelty . . . to displace the mania for perpetual compound growth" (Harvey 2014, 296). Sixteenth, mindful of the organic link between humans and nature, it is incumbent on us to use natural resources for our mutual needs with due diligence to protect "ecosystems . . . [and allow for the] recycling of nutrients, energy and physical matter to the sites" of origin, and promote conscious "re-enchantment with the beauty of the natural world, of which we are a part" and to which we have a necessary obligation to "contribute through our works" (297). Seventeenth, Harvey concludes by calling for disalienation at the human and creative levels to arm ourselves individually and collectively with self-confidence, advancing boldly to construct a new world informed by the "experience of freely contracted intimate social relations and empathy for different modes of living and producing", in which "everyone is considered equally worthy of dignity and respect, even as conflict rages over the appropriate definition of the good life" (297).

Working towards the "political praxis" thus outlined necessitates waging a relentless war against all prevailing forms of "discrimination, oppression and violent repression within capitalism as a whole" (Harvey 2014, 297). Territorial sovereignty and perpetual capitalist crises reproduce domination, suspicion, insecurity, marginalization, unemployment, poverty, hunger, alienation and other forms of dehumanization that make it difficult to imagine the possibility of universal (world) citizenship and a genuine sense of belonging to humanity. With the ongoing "struggle against capital and its contradictions" in view, it is possible to evolve a social world "through permanent and ongoing revolutions in human capacities and powers" (297). Harvey's point is that it is difficult if not impossible to prescribe solutions for any problem if we do not understand the nature and cause of the problem. To deny that another world is possible is to impose closure on history.

The secular utopianism that informs Harvey's proposals is radically different than the millenarian utopianism associated with religious prescriptions about the future. Dialectically, global capitalism lays the foundation for transcending the very forms of sovereignty, citizenship and belonging it engenders.

References

Arendt, Hannah. 1973. *The Origins of Totaliarianism*. New York: Harcourt.

Devetak, Richard. 2005. "Postmodernism". In *Theories of International Relations*, edited by Scott Burchill, Andrew Linklater, Richard Devetak, Jack Donnelly, Matthew Paterson, Christian Reus-Smit and Jackqui True, 161–87. 3rd ed. New York: Palgrave Macmillan.

Dupuy, Alex. 1996. A review of *Democracy against Capitalism: Renewing Historical Materialism,* Ellen Meiksins Wood. *Contemporary Sociology: A Journal of Reviews* 25 (4): 567–69.

Harvey, David. 2014. *Seventeen Contradictions and the End of Capitalism*. New York: Oxford University Press.

Joseph, Tennyson. 2012. "Towards a New Democracy and a New Independence: A Program for the Second Independence Revolution". Paper presented to a Common Sense Convois at the Lloyd Best Institute of the West Indies, Scarborough, Tobago, 24 March.

Lora, Ivan Ogando. 2013. "Dominican Republic – CARICOM: Unfinished Business". *Great Insights* 2 (7): 13–14.

Malik, Kenan. 1996. *The Meaning of Race: Race, History and Culture in Western Society*. New York: New York University Press.

Reed, Adolph, Jr. 2013. "Marx, Race, and Neoliberalism". *New Labor Forum* 22 (1): 49–57.

Rosenberg, Justin. 1994. *The Empire of Civil Society: A Critique of the Realist Theory of Inter-ational Relations*. London: Verso.

Contributors

Hilbourne A. Watson is Professor Emeritus, Department of International Relations, Bucknell University, Lewisburg, Pennsylvania. His publications include *The Caribbean in the Global Political Economy.*

Anton L. Allahar is Professor, Department of Sociology, University of Western Ontario, London, Ontario. His publications include *Caribbean Charisma: Reflections on Leadership, Legitimacy and Populist Politics*, *Sociology and the Periphery: Theories and Issues* and *Class, Politics and Sugar in Colonial Cuba.*

Justin Daniel is Professor of Political Science, University of the French Antilles and French Guiana. His publications include *Les outre-mer à l'épreuve du changement: Réalités et perspectives des réformes territoriales.*

Alex Dupuy is the John E. Andrus Professor of Sociology, Wesleyan University, Middletown, Connecticut. His recent publications include *Haiti: From Revolutionary Slaves to Powerless Citizens: Essays on the Politics and Economics of Underdevelopment 1804–2013* and *The Prophet and Power: Jean-Bertrand Aristide, the International Community, and Haiti.*

Sean Gill is a PhD candidate, Social and Political Thought, York University, Toronto, Ontario.

Linden Lewis is Professor of Sociology, Department of Sociology and Anthropology, Bucknell University, Lewisburg, Pennsylvania. His publications include *The Culture of Gender and Sexuality in the Caribbean* and *Caribbean Sovereignty, Development and Democracy in an Age of Globalization.*

Aarón Gamaliel Ramos is Professor of Social Sciences, University of Puerto Rico. His publications include *Las ideas anexionistas en Puerto Rico bajo la dominación norteamericana* and (co-edited with Ángel Israel Rivera Ortiz) *Islands at the Crossroads: Politics in the Non-Independent Caribbean.*

Index

www.ingramcontent.com/pod-product-compliance
Lightning Source LLC
Chambersburg PA
CBHW022354280326
41935CB00007B/186

* 9 7 8 9 7 6 6 4 0 5 5 0 2 *